T0215188

EMERGING DIGITAL TECHNOLOGIES AND INDIA'S SECURITY SECTOR

This book is an introductory account for policy makers, academia, and interested readers on the digital technologies on Indian Military. It covers three technologies – AI, Blockchain, and Quantum communications – and provides a detailed account on the military use cases. It evaluates the readiness of Indian Military in these technologies. A foundational text, it not only provides key policy analysis but also identifies the gray areas for the future research in the security studies.

The volume will be essential reading for scholars and researchers of military and strategic studies, especially future warfare, AI and Blockchain, and South Asian studies. It will be of interest to general readers as well.

Pankaj K Jha is Professor with JSIA, O.P. Jindal Global University, and Director of Centre for Security Studies (CSS). He is also Executive Director of CESCUBE, a think tank.

Arun Teja Polcumpally is Technology Policy Analyst at Wadhwani Institute of Technology Policy, Delhi.

Vedant Saigal is Assistant General Manager (University Administrative Services) at the Office of International Affairs and Global Initiatives, O.P. Jindal Global University.

EMERGING DIGITAL TECHNOLOGIES AND INDIA'S SECURITY SECTOR

AI, Blockchain, and Quantum Communications

Edited by Pankaj K Jha, Arun Teja Polcumpally, and Vedant Saigal

Routledge
Taylor & Francis Group

LONDON AND NEW YORK

Designed cover image: © KanawatTH / Getty Images

First published 2024
by Routledge
4 Park Square, Milton Park, Abingdon, Oxon OX14 4RN

and by Routledge
605 Third Avenue, New York, NY 10158

Routledge is an imprint of the Taylor & Francis Group, an informa business

© 2024 Center for Security Studies, Jindal School of International Affairs

British Library Cataloguing-in-Publication Data
A catalogue record for this book is available from the British Library

ISBN: 978-1-032-43358-5 (hbk)
ISBN: 978-1-032-77370-4 (pbk)
ISBN: 978-1-003-48270-3 (ebk)

DOI: 10.4324/9781003482703

Typeset in Sabon
by Apex CoVantage, LLC

CONTENTS

TABLES

CONTRIBUTORS

Editors

Dr. Pankaj K Jha – B.A. (Hons.) (University of Delhi); M.A., M.Phil., Ph.D. (Jawaharlal Nehru University, New Delhi)

Pankaj K Jha is Professor with JSIA, O.P. Jindal Global University, and Director of Centre for Security Studies (CSS). He is Executive Director of a research-oriented think tank, known as CESCUBE. Dr. Pankaj K Jha was Director (Research) with Indian Council of World Affairs for more than two and a half years (2014–2017). He had worked as Deputy Director with National Security Council Secretariat (2012–2013). He has been the visiting fellow with Centre for International Security Studies, Sydney University (2009) and Institute for South Asian Studies, Singapore (2006).

He has authored three books on *India and China in Southeast Asia: Competition or Cooperation* (2013) and *India and the Oceania: Exploring Vistas for Cooperation* (2016). His latest book is on *India, Vietnam and the Indo-Pacific: Expanding Horizons* (2020).

Dr. Arun Teja Polcumpally – B. Tech (Electrical), M.A., Ph.D. International Affairs (O.P. Jindal Global University)

Dr. Arun Teja Polcumpally is Technology Policy Analyst at Wadhwani Institute of Technology Policy, Delhi. He was Research Associate at the Centre for Security Studies and Visiting Fellow at the Center for Excellence for AI in Human Security. He formerly had a brief stint as Editor at Jindal Centre for the Global South and an associate at Center of Excellence (CoE) for AI in Human Security, Hyderabad, India. His area of research is the impact of emerging digital technologies like AI and Blockchain on the global power structure. He also works on the International Relations' theoretical analysis of the technological impacts.

Vedant Saigal – B.A. (Hons.) Global Affairs, M.A. Diplomacy, Law, and Business (Jindal School of International Affairs, O.P. Jindal Global University)

Vedant Saigal is Assistant General Manager (University Administrative Services) at the Office of International Affairs and Global Initiatives, O.P. Jindal Global University. He has a Master's degree in Diplomacy, Law and Business from the Jindal School of International Affairs (JSIA) and a keen interest in Artificial Intelligence and International Security. With a commitment to academic excellence and an unyielding curiosity, he looks forward to contributing to the ever-evolving landscape of Defense and National Security.

Contributors

Sonchita Debnath

Ms. Sonchita Debnath is Doctoral Fellow at Jindal School of Government and Public Policy. Her research tries to understand the community-level factors that determine clean technology's adoption and usage. She has prior research experience with the Government of Maharashtra on mapping food habits among tribals and several other nongovernmental organizations (NGOs) working on impact assessment and designing surveys. She has been invited to various guest lectures within Jindal and outside colleges. She also has experience in teaching at the graduate level.

Rushil Khosla

Rushil is Research Assistant at the Centre for Security Studies.

Poornima Vijaya

Ms. Poornima Vijaya is presently enrolled as Research Fellow at Nehghinpao Kipgen's Centre for Southeast Asian Studies and Ph.D. Scholar at Jindal School of International Affairs in O.P. Jindal Global University. Her research focuses on the changing geopolitical dynamics in the Asia-Pacific region, International Relations theories, middle power politics, and great power rivalry. She tweets @PoornimaVijaya.

INTRODUCTION

Arun Teja Polcumpally

Who wouldn't be interested in the stories of the military and in the events portraying a soldier's valour and bravery? It is expected that to those readers who love to watch movies like *Border, LOC Kargil, Lakshya, URI* and so on, this book will strike a chord. This book is an analytical account of the future of the Indian military. It is divided into two parts. The first part delves into a conceptual understanding of the technological impact on military affairs. It also provides a detailed account on the global competition among digital technologies, emphasising on Russia, China and the US. The second part delves into data-influenced geopolitics and the importance of Artificial Intelligence (AI), blockchain technology and quantum communications in military affairs. Finally, the book explores whether India is ready for such advanced technologies.

The book stresses emerging strategic environments and operational challenges anchored to information technologies. This book builds up an analysis keeping in mind that digitalisation is imperative to improve operational readiness and combat efficiency of the military. In order to provide the Indian Armed Forces with the requisite capacity in the field, it is vital for the organisations involved in the defence sector to run along with the digital curve and make their turns accordingly. For them, to maintain such pace, this book acts as a guide and is also helpful for scholars, defence officials and others contributing to the nation's security. It helps them understand the possible options for India to consider, to become a better digitalized force altogether.

Current Developments Regarding This Research

A search using the keywords "emerging technology" + "national security" + "India" in Microsoft Academic resulted in 1032 search results, and a search

DOI: 10.4324/9781003482703-1

in Google Scholar resulted in 1740 results. Both searches are done between January 1, 2017, and September 7, 2022.

The first 10 pages of the results in Microsoft Academia did not produce any paper on military and digital technologies. Only one paper was found relevant that focused on drone detection, which has an application in the military (Carrio et al., 2018).

Screening of 10 Google Scholar search pages provided a better result than Microsoft Academia. It is found that the research is conducted on public engagements in nano-technology (Barpujar, 2011), exploratory study on Indian space strategy (Chandrashekar, 2016), general implications of AI (Vempati, 2016; Bommakanti, 2020) and Information Technology–based governance and business (Chaturvedi et al., 2011; Ranjan, 2020; Sarkar, 2014). Within the 10 search result pages, there was no research paper on the mapping of revolutionary change in warfare and emerging digital technologies with India as a vantage point. From the search results, it can be established that a potential secondary search is possible on this topic.

This book is divided into two parts. Part I provides a conceptual understanding of technology-induced changes in military affairs. The conceptual explanation will follow the current geopolitical scape of frontier technologies and India's position on adopting digital technology in its military. Part II deals with AI, blockchain and quantum communication technology. Along with this, the cyber security apparatus of India is analysed.

Part I

The first chapter brings in the context for the entire book and describes the difficulties in integrating the frontier digital technologies into the military. While examining the frontier digital technologies and their impact, the chapter argues that the state is still the main agency in conducting international relations. The digital technologies are opined to aid the state to increase its coercive power over the public. This argument has been explained by mapping the digital technologies and the agencies that use them. The chapter maintains that the frontier digital technologies unquestionably change the military affairs and asserts that India should proactively work towards adopting those technologies.

The second chapter introduces the reader to the concepts of Revolution in Military Affairs (RMA). The explanation is provided with information technology as a vantage point and is built on the societal impact of emerging technologies. Taking the discussion to the military, the concepts of revolution, warfare and the changes occurring in how war is/will be waged in the future are explored. An extensive dependence on RAND organisations shows that the chapter is very precise in its analysis. AI technology has been taken as an example to showcase the possibility of RMA in military. After establishing that the frontier digital technologies can bring an RMA, the second chapter espouses conditions of hybrid warfare. The amalgamation of the traditional military, the usage of local proxy militia, exertion of economic pressure, disinformation campaigns and exploitation of the existing social divisions is called hybrid warfare. Employing coercive information warfare leading to psychological control of the societies has been given a greater importance in the hybrid warfare. The chapter opines that every entity that has control over information technology can wage psychological war on any nation or a specific society. Further, it is asserted that new-generation warfare is won with psychological control over people (Wither, 2016). In such a scenario, using digital technologies to improve national security becomes a desideratum. With the aggregation of emerging digital technologies into the defence, there is an emerging view of having separate cyber and space forces (Winkler et al., 2019). These changes make it evident that the old hard power usage in the war is no longer a viable strategy. It looks like militaries have to use hybrid strategies to achieve a victory and sustain it. Substantiating the argument that frontier digital technologies would bring an RMA, an impressive list of historical revolutions in military has been documented. It is interesting to see that the chapter carefully treads its argument by separating the revolution in military affairs and the revolution in war.

The third chapter argues with the premise that in the anarchical world with rapidly growing technologies, a state has to invest on the research and development of the digital technologies. Those states that do not focus on the innovations of digital technologies, such as AI, blockchain and quantum technology, would forever import the technologies. The main discussion that this chapter brings is the geopolitical competition between the major powers including Russia, the US and China. During the Trump presidency, the aggressive stance of the US against the growing Chinese technology acquisition shows that China is challenging the US supremacy in the knowledge-building domain.

The chapter argues that Chinese Communist Party (CCP) is the major investor in the defence technology research and development in China. Though a surge in private investments is observed, the state has a representation and influence in the decision-making board of private companies. Similarly, the defence industry of Russia is also dominated by the state. It has been observed that Russia is taking steps to encourage research in the technologies like AI through its Advanced Research Foundation (ARF). The US is advanced in terms of research and development, as it allows private industry and pushes huge state funds into the defence research. With a capitalistic orientation of defence industries, the US emerged as a sole superpower after 1991. The emergence of China as a global economic power challenged the US supremacy over the geopolitics. With the current pace of advancements in the digital technologies, the chapter opines that the global rivalry would be between Russia, China and the US.

In the fourth and final chapter of Part I, the strategic implications and the readiness of Indian military are assessed within the context of the advanced digital technologies. The author quickly and precisely traces the Indian military approach and their strategic ploys. The author notes that India consistently changes its strategic stance. It is observed from the period of having a single belligerent in the early 1950s to the state becoming a regional power in the 21st century. As of the year 2022, the chapter asserts that India's greatest military challenge is China's informatisation and intelligentisation. In this context, the fourth chapter discusses the recent developments in the Indian military arsenal and its road map to the military digitisation. It identifies that there are a significant number of projects that are mentioned in the compendium reports of the Army which are not solved and implemented. It is also noted that problems that appear in an annual compendium of reports will reappear in the next year's report. Such tracing helps the reader in understanding the vital areas where digital technologies are required. Finally, this chapter provides a method to observe India's readiness to the changing technologies.

Part II

Part II of the book builds up on the foundations laid by Part I. The introductory chapter of Part II, that is the fifth chapter, provides an analytical description of how digital technologies impact a society. Rather than treading the path of traditional security involving military, this chapter emphasises the threat to the democracy. Before explaining the threat to the democracy, this chapter highlights the importance of data securitisation and its legislation. Perspectives of Yuval Noah Harari and Jamie Susskind are used to strengthen the conceptual and philosophical understanding of the data-based technologies and their impact on the society. This conceptual description is followed by the examination of the phenomenon of perception control. The question whether data becomes a new weapon for the authoritarianism in the democracies is discussed upon in this chapter. This chapter confirms that data-led digital technologies are not only making unprecedented changes in the traditional security institutions but also impact the non-traditional security.

The sixth chapter explores the usage of AI in the Indian Armed Forces and how the military technologies make use of AI for defensive or offensive purposes. The chapter explains the role of AI in the three branches of the Indian Armed Forces, that is, Army, Navy and the Air Force. The challenges faced by Indian defence establishment are explained with an emphasis on additional capital requirement, AI bias. The future warfare is opined more to be hybrid warfare coated with information tactics. In addition, cyber capacities are opined to be an alternative to the nuclear deterrence. The chapter concludes asserting that to achieve battlefield dominance, the military forces are continuously seeking greater combat effectiveness, and they can do so by establishing more research and development in the field of AI (Pant, 2018).

With the profound understanding of AI and its uses in the Indian Armed Forces, the seventh chapter looks at the other domain known as quantum communications. Similar to the previous chapter, this section of the book will highlight the use of technology in the military. With an international lens, emphasis is laid on the development of the technology in China, India, the US and Europe, and a comparative analysis is provided. The importance of quantum communications and the unparalleled security it offers through the quantum key distribution (QKD) method is explained in detail. Will India be able to become the major cyber power in this century? Will the investments made by India in the field of quantum communications contribute to it becoming the cyber-technology powerhouse? How different is India's position in terms of digital infrastructure from that of the US and China? These questions definitely pose a great scope of relevance in today's highly advancing world. This chapter provides a direction to analyse what these questions demand for and provide an understanding of what the future perhaps brings.

The eighth chapter is about the usage of blockchain technology in the military. The chapter is organized into three different sub-sections that provide an elaborated understanding on history and the whole working of the blockchain technology. The chronological order is that provides a systematic analysis of the whole evolution of the blockchain technology. This chapter explains how this type of technology is being seen as a panacea for all the issues and difficulties that are currently being faced by the system. As the challenges are intertwined with new developments, the chapter throws light on issues that perhaps would help the implementation of technology in the hierarchical system of the military.

The ninth chapter of the book revolves around the social-technical iterations that eventually create a new social. This new social further creates a security threat known as cyber security. This stands as one of the most important chapters of the book as it involves a direct civilian threat through the mode of computers' illegal use of the cyberspace altogether. The significance of this particular chapter is important not only for the officials working in the defence sector but also for the ordinary citizens of a country. Hence, observing the events that cause the cybercrime and lead to various devastating consequences becomes equally important. This chapter does not really look at the comparative analysis of different countries with India but brings them into a common space that is created by threats emerging in the cyber world. As the word suggests, where comes security come threats and challenges; therefore, this chapter emphasises on the cyber security structure of India and espouses on how the country is responding to the upcoming challenges. The development of an ecosystem which is underway in recent years will be discussed upon. In a nutshell, this chapter aims to provide an initial reading on the cyber security issues and the way in which India dealt with it.

The concluding chapter comments on the aspect of RMA in the digital world. In addition to its comment on the earlier chapters, it asserts that the RMA-level innovations should be carried out to increase the deterrence and non-lethal weaponry. Further, the chapter concludes that the countries that are close to the US would benefit more from the latest digital innovations. While reiterating the RMA, this chapter asserts that the revolution brought by the frontier digital technologies shall bring a complete change in the way command centres operate. With tactical internet, and AI imbibed with data from nano sensors, every minute detail will be considered in taking decisions on the battlefield. Further, all those details will be monitored in the real time by the unit command located away from the field. While detailing the challenges, the chapter focuses on the ethical and operational challenges in implementing the frontier technologies into the military. Closing the book, the concluding chapter opined that India should have a robust cyber security strategy designed on the blueprints of the future laden with frontier digital technologies.

This book is expected to serve all the interested readers with a detailed conceptual note on the revolution in military affairs that is hoped with the frontier digital technologies. With a detailed analysis of the AI, blockchain and quantum communication technologies, this book serves the purpose of providing a foundational reading for all those who work practically on these technologies in the military domain. It helps the readers to identify the problem areas and the potential business areas to capture anchored on these three technologies. Further, the cyber security lacuna and the possible bridging of that lacuna are also analysed. It warps the long discussion of the nine chapters by reiterating the importance of securitisation of the frontier digital technologies.

References

Barpujari, I. (2011). Public Engagement in Emerging Technologies: Issues for India. *Quantum Engagements: Social Reflections of Nanoscience and Emerging Technologies*, 123–137.

Bommakanti, K. (2020). AI in the Chinese Military: Current Initiatives and the Implications for India. ORF Occasional Paper No. 234.

Carrio, A., Vemprala, S., Ripoll, A., Saripalli, S., and Campoy, P. (2018, October). Drone Detection Using Depth Maps. 2018 IEEE/RSJ International Conference on Intelligent Robots and Systems (IROS) (pp. 1034–1037). IEEE.

Chandrashekar, S. (2016). Space, War, and Deterrence: A Strategy for India. *Astropolitics*, 14(2–3), 135–157.

Chaturvedi, M., Gupta, M. P., and Bhattachrya, J. (2011). Information Security Issues With Emerging Next Generation Networks in Indian Context. *Proceedings of 8th International Conference on E-Governance* (pp. 78–90). Emerald Group Publishing Limited.

Pant, A. (2018). Future Warfare and Artificial Intelligence: Visible Path. IDSA Occasional Paper 4–50.

Ranjan, P. (2020). Industry 4.0 and Industrial Information Services in India: A Proposal. National Seminar on Industry 4.0: A Roadmap for Indian Business, 2018

Sarkar, S. (2014). The Unique Identity (UID) Project, Biometrics and Re-Imagining Governance in India. *Oxford Development Studies*, 42(4), 516–533.

Vempati, S. S. (2016). *India and the Artificial Intelligence Revolution* (Vol. 1). Washington, DC: Carnegie Endowment for International Peace.

Winkler, J., Marler, T., Posard, M., & Cohen, R. (2019). Reflections on the Future of Warfare and Implications for Personnel Policies of the U.S. Department of Defense. *RAND Cooperation, 43*.

Wither, J. (2016). Making Sense of Hybrid Warfare. *Connections: The Quarterly Journal*, 73–87.

PART I

1

FRONTIER TECHNOLOGIES WILL ENHANCE THE 'POWER' OF THE STATE

Arun Teja Polcumpally

In general, there are plenty of books written and re-written on military strategies. Even regarding the Indian military, there is good literature on its history (Raghavan, 2016), achievements (Rawat, 2019a, 2019b), and biographies (Punia and Damini, 2021). Some books explain India's nuclear strategy (Sethi, 2009) and India's cold war-based developmental politics (Engerman, 2018). However, there is not much work done on the impact of digital technologies on Indian military affairs. Though some books detail the cyber-attacks (Dilipraj, 2017) and try to explain the overall implications of cyberspace on Indian security (Sharma, 2018), there is less work specific to AI, Blockchain, and quantum communication. At the onset, this book details how the advanced technologies of the 21st century impact Indian military affairs. It deals in detail with the impact of AI, Blockchain, and quantum communication technologies on the Indian military. This chapter provides a foundation for the rest of the chapters by building a context for the complexities of integrating frontier technologies into the military.

Advanced Digital Technologies and Their Impact

In the 21st century, all businesses and even societies are connected through virtual platforms. In terms of Schumpeter's innovation theory, current developments in information technologies are considered to bring a third technology-induced societal revolution (Hilbert, 2020). The first and second are material transformation and the industrial revolution, respectively.

It was never in the history of mankind that people across the globe were connected without psychically interacting. This interconnection is not empowered by the state but by the internet-based social platforms

DOI: 10.4324/9781003482703-3

floated by big multinational companies. With the information flowing freely across borders, nongovernmental organizations and corporates are gaining the upper hand over the states. Though this narrative has become normalized, from a historic point of view, it is very short-lived. The current information technology–led societal revolution also started in 2002 (Hilbert, 2020). If calculated, it has been just two decades.

The very technologies that strengthen globalization, such as the internet and other Information and Communication Technologies (ICT), have quickly given a counter-narrative. There is an increase in state initiatives worldwide to control the internet. Data legislation, social media regulations, regulation of Artificial Intelligence (AI) by design, and usage of lethal autonomous weapons are all controlled by the state. If not yet, they are the only ones with the legitimate authority to do it. States are again becoming all-powerful. Further, the fact that the globalization process is anchored to the trade agreements between the states reiterates the point that the states are still important political entities. Substantiating this point, a German research think tank has published a research paper concluding that even in the internet age, the public still feels that it is the government's responsibility to maintain stable country-to-country relations (Stanzel, 2018). It cannot be blindly said that the state is all-powerful in the internet age. It can only retain its past status if it adapts to the change happening due to the ICT and bring institutional changes. By this, it can be argued that the state is still the main party in maintaining international relations.

Military Used to Be the Innovation Base, but That's No Longer the Case

The state's rise and fall of power is anchored mostly to the development and production of knowledge. One outcome of knowledge is technology. States, since their formal establishment in 1689, ushered their dominance using technology to their advantage (Lele, 2019). Earlier, most technological advancements were often found on the military front, providing the state with an edge to be superior to other states. There were no private establishments that would undertake research from the state or conduct their own research with a bigger budget than the state and use them for their own purposes. This is not the case in the world where liberal economic thought prevails. Facebook (or Meta), Alphabet, and Microsoft have their own research centres with their own funding. Their innovations cannot find a place in many of the state's budget allocations. Virtual reality, AI, Blockchain technology, and quantum technology are some of such technologies.

All such emerging digital technologies are claimed to disrupt the social fabric across the world (Polcumpally, 2021). Warren Chin, while exploring the relationship between *war* and the sustained relevance of *state*, concludes that the distributed nature of digital technologies, their research, and their development will make states secure their monopoly on violence (Chin, 2019). With little difference between the civil and the military technology development, weak and violent non-state actors can easily have their hands on the new technologies and wage war against the states whose laws and organizational setups are not equipped to deal with those new technologies (Chin, 2019).

The major powers of the 21st century have taken note of the importance of digital technologies in securing their power. In the United States, research and development of such disruptive technologies as nanotechnology and AI is directly funded by the Defense Advanced Research Projects Agency (DARPA). China has a similar story. This shows the importance of defence investments in emerging technologies by two technology giants today. From this brief, it is evident that research and innovation are no longer with the state or military but with private companies. However, this chapter argues that even though the latter is the current situation, the state still holds the reins of power.

Importance of the Advanced Digital Technologies and the Power They Provide to the State

The narrative that Alan Turing was the critical factor in shifting the tide of the Second World War (Hilton, 1989) onto the Axis powers is seldom heard. It was his electro-mechanical machine that decrypted the daily codes of German messages that, in turn, helped the Allies to take advantage. In one way, it is not wrong to say that the start of the *International Relations* discipline has ICT as one of its fundamental structures, which has been neglected unfortunately. During the cold war, the KGB of the Soviet Union had developed a computing machine VRYAN, which was used to make sense of US and the North Atlantic Treaty Organization's (NATO) economic and security data to determine the nuclear warfare risk (Kiggins, 2018). The Soviet Union's strategic decisions were dependent on the latter. Both the communist state structure and the democratic west strengthened their blocs using digital technologies.

Alvin Toffler in his book *Powershift*, released in 1991, predicted that in the digital communications age, power would be anchored to the knowledge created by the electronics infrastructure (Toffler, 1991). Here is an excerpt from Toffler's book, which reiterates that information tactics become the fundamental tool for the emergence of a new hegemony:

> In the incoming political crisis that face the high-tech democracies, all sides – politicians and bureaucrats, as well as the military, the corporate lobbies, and the swelling tide of citizens groups, – will use "info-tactics." . . . [W]ith knowledge in all its forms becoming more central to the power,

with data, information, and knowledge piling up and pouring out of computers, info-tactics will become ever more significant in political life.

(Toffler, 1991)

Heuristic observation is enough to tentatively conclude that information technologies help the state to increase its strength domestically and internationally. However, information technologies are making states authoritative irrespective of their political cultures. The fading of democracy and liberal values is specially tagged to ICT (Polcumpally, 2022). Authoritarian regimes are getting strengthened because of their capacity to monitor and control public behaviour using AI technology.

One example is the manipulations of the US elections by a private company, Cambridge Analytica (Wylie, 2019). Manipulation of elections and voters' behaviour with perks is the inevitable political game played in democracies. From the start of the democracy, the election contestants wooed the public in good or bad ways. However, the extent to which these AI algorithms are used to manipulate public opinion and even reality is exorbitant. Because of this, advanced digital technologies become culprits here. AI algorithms used by Cambridge Analytica are seen to gain the most dangerous attribute of power – perception control (Susskind, 2018). This allows the people and entities operating or having the ownership of AI to control the behaviour and thinking of the public. Some opine that the public in the digital world is just being considered as data providers who are ready to be exploited (Calzada, 2018). With people becoming data providers from every aspect of their life – taste, likes, dislikes, political inclination, financial status, interests – AI is ready to be trained under the cloud data of the world, ignoring the borders and existing international laws. A country that controls the data and has the algorithms to extensively and innovatively analyse it would get control over the people worldwide (Bartoletti, 2020). Arguments such as AI being considered as the harbinger of the new cold war between the US and the People's Republic of China (PRC) are also looming over the IR scholarship (Susskind, 2018). Without a doubt, AI and its convergence with other technologies will invent a new society altogether (Anderson and Lee, 2018). Now, it also seems that a new technology race has been started among the states across the world.

To understand the importance of the rapid change that digital technologies bring, an example is elaborated here. During the early days of transistor development, people thought that the technology was just an additional component or, maximum, it would do is to replace the vacuum tubes. The rest of the functioning would be the same. In no time, the machines developed using transistors became known as personal computers. A computer that was only a privilege of the rich is now a basic tool of society. It replaced bookkeepers, manual calculations, record keepers, and so forth. Another example of such technological innovation in the past is cell phones and the internet. Internet was initially developed by the US agency DARPA for internal communications. When such a system was made available for the civilian world, it changed the basic functioning of the world. Today, there are numerous technological Innovations that even internet developers couldn't have imagined. Some such groundbreaking innovations are GPS, e-commerce, digital supply chain management, and social media. With these innovations, the US is the country that gained the most. Today, the software developed in Silicon Valley is used almost across the world.

The Case of AI and Its Role in Strengthening the State

AI singularity engulfs the general public with fear of replacing human agency and encouraging authoritarian control. A paper from Harvard Kennedy School's Belfer Center for Science and International Affairs reiterates that the technologies like AI make radical governments (Allen and Chan, 2017). An article published in *Nature* asserts that AI is used to provide better governance and economies (Savage, 2020). Indian government think tank, NITI Aayog, in its discussion paper on AI, highlights the usage of AI in improving education, healthcare, agriculture, and manufacturing (NITI Aayog, 2018). Prime Minister Narendra Modi says that "AI is a tribute to human intellectual power" (DD News, 2020). AI is one such technology that can become both radical and non-radical, depending on how it shapes itself and also on how it is shaped.

Currently, AI, with its machine learning and deep learning algorithms, can recognize patterns from any dataset. It can be images, heat signatures, radar data, satellite images, language, and the like. Anything that can be displayed on a screen can be an input to AI. These characteristics will make it revolutionary. Thus, when the Belfer Center's report said that technologies like AI would produce authoritarian governments, it is more about the inherent repressive nature of the existing governments.

In another instance, the Global Technology Summit of 2019, organized by Carnegie – India, was themed on the *future of data*. Sessions during the summit focused on unheard-of topics such as taxation of data usage, cross-continental digital pipelines, hyper-personalization of medicine, free trade agreements on data, cloud act, and AI governance (Carnegie India, 2019). This annual conference was completely dedicated to emerging digital technologies and their unknown impact on the present political, economic, and social structures. Until recently, AI was thought of as creating disruptions in business and industries. Now its impact is felt in every sector.

It is time to accept and understand that the latter *disruptions* have entered global politics, especially in democracies where the usage of such digital tools is unregulated. The lack of an institutional system at the national, regional, and world levels incessantly calls for a new repertoire of global governance and a new understanding techno-politics of international relations.

Understanding Technology-Induced Geopolitics

To understand the upcoming technology-induced societal and political changes globally, devolving the agency status to anthropomorphic systems (human-technology interactions) and providing sufficient ontological and epistemological weight to such systems become necessary (Kiggins, 2018). This is similar to what Latour says about the object being the agencies (Latour, 2005). Performing social science research is also evolving with the evolved data analysis techniques. Lingren suggests that social science scholars should adopt computational social science to efficiently understand society (Lingren, 2020). All of these developments show that digital technologies are becoming ubiquitous. In the coming years, it will no longer be about what technology can do for us; rather, it will be what we should allow it to do (Stansberry et al., 2019). Maybe it's time for the world to accept that technology has made a huge change to society (both its ontological reality and epistemological understanding). The states' power and military strength cannot be sustained without digital technologies being incorporated.

Without a doubt, today's emerging and promising technologies including ledger technologies, AI, and ubiquitous 5G connectivity have the potential to change the nature of warfare. The latter appears to be a sweeping statement, but there is no way one would brush away this argument. Within this premise, this book aims to explore whether the emerging technologies would bring a revolution in warfare between the nation-states and the Indian military. It significantly looks at where India is situated in the global technology competition and if these technologies really do bring a revolutionary change to the Indian military.

India Should Be Proactive and Anticipate Future Security Issues

Figure 1.1 represents the percentage of population using internet in India. The increasing trend shows the increasing numbers of internet users per country. With the internet users, the data generators also increase. The data includes economic behaviours, social interactions, travel data, personal information, and so forth. Analysing the meta data, browsing trends, and heat maps will also tell the social behaviour of a country. India is increasingly generating such data, and it is being stored in offshore servers, giving access to companies that further share their access with the countries where they are located. Because of this critical information about the public, the information will be given away to foreign countries, providing them with an undue advantage.

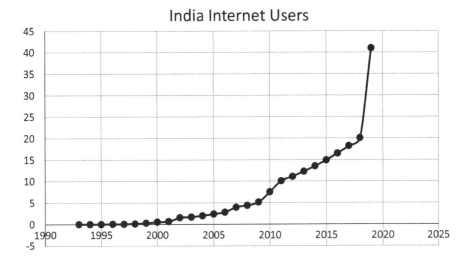

FIGURE 1.1   India Internet Users (graph derived from the data set of International Telecommunication Union (ITU) World Telecommunication/ICT Indicators Database)

Advanced technologies will have data as its core component. The cross-border exchange of big data will lead to unknown security issues.

> Just over the horizon are newly emerging technologies, including robotics, artificial intelligence, genetics, synthetic biology, nanotechnology, 3-D manufacturing, brain science, and virtual reality, that will make today's cybercrime seen like child's play. These innovations will play essential roles in our daily lives in just few years, yet no in-depth, broad based study has been completed to help understand the unintended attendant risks they pose.
>
> *(Sood, 2016)*

This is an excerpt from Research and Analysis Wing's (R&AW) former secretary Vikram Sood's book, *The Future of Intelligence*. In the year 2022, when this book was initiated, this excerpt seemed to be relevant, and even in the near future, it stays relevant. Technology is ever growing, and as the future becomes present, the unknown future still looms, and the policymakers would be in a constant loop of lagging behind the technological advancements.

In order to tackle such unknown issues, security establishments are changing their operations. An example to show the change in operations of security establishments is the collaboration of Amazon Web Services (AWS) and Central Intelligence Agency (CIA) of America. As per the deal made by

AWS and America's CIA in 2014, AWS will operate behind the intelligence community's firewall and will share its information with 17 American intelligence agencies (Sood, 2016).

Before the advent of internet and social media, human intelligence (HUMINT) was given higher priority. The information gathered from HUMINT was used to make decisions. Now such information is in the hands of private companies. The state has to ask for their cooperation, or else, they have to build another ecosystem altogether for the public.

Given the disruptive capacities of the advanced digital technologies in the daily lives of people and the militaries, it is worth taking a look at the readiness of Indian military establishment regarding these technologies. Since independence, the Indian government has neglected the area of strategic studies (Singh, 2015). All the academia and its rigour have been put aloof from the strategic decision-making of the defence and external affairs ministry (Sen, 2019). It is considered that only post-2014, the Indian universities are increasingly investing in defence and strategic studies, and foreign universities are collaborating with Indian private universities and think tanks on the issues of strategic studies (Sen, 2019). The fall of the Soviet Union and the increase in the security dilemma have forced states across the world to take a realist stance and put the national interest ahead (Sen, 2016).

The growing importance of India's own perspective on security has also been emphasized by India's external affairs minister, S. Jaishankar (Jaishankar, 2020). With the growing applications of big data and increasing requirements for new approaches to digital security, India is left with no choice but to investigate into the potential use cases of the advanced digital technologies and make a clear road map to integrate them into the armed forces. It might as well need to change the existing organizational structures, but the work has to be started. The next section assesses the current cyber security projects in India.

Cyber Security Projects in India

The cyber security organizational structure of India and their functions show that India knows that cyber capabilities are necessary to maintain its military power. Operations such as tapping phone calls, getting access to social media conversations, and text messages are some notable cyber capacities of India. Lieutenant General Davinder Kumar's work provides the cyber security apparatus of the Indian security establishment (Table 1.1). Other media sources are referred to provide their operational status.

The Geopolitical Tussle on Technology Urges India to Ramp Up Its Military Capabilities

The current tussle between the existing dominant power, the United States, and the emerging great power, China, is on acquiring the leadership of

TABLE 1.1 Cyber Security Apparatus of India (Kumar, 2016)

Sl no	Organization	Operation	Establishment/ Project Started	Budget Allocated Approximation (crores)
1	National Cyber Coordination Centre (NCCC)	Cybercrime prevention strategy, cybercrime investigation training, review of legislations, cyber intelligence sharing	2014 (not fully operational as of 2021)	770
2	Botnet Cleaning and Malware Analysis Centre	Detects botnets that trigger cybercrimes and suggests the device owner to remove it	2019	90.5
3	Central Monitoring Systems (CMS)	Unhindered access to phone calls, text messages, social media conversations	2011	590
4	National Critical Information Infrastructure Protection Centre (NCIIPC)	Protects India's critical information infrastructure (CII)	2014	NA
5	Network Traffic Analysis System (NeTRA)	Mass surveillance project	2008 (project design completed)	NA

the frontier technologies. It is no surprise that China's Belt and Road Initiative (BRI), since 2015, is focused to make Digital Silk Road (DSR) the priority (Eder et al., 2019). The United States started to counter China's rise in exporting its technology influence using initiatives like anti-Huawei campaigns. Such developments urge India to consider these developments seriously and evaluate the potential use cases of these emerging technologies in the Indian security establishment.

From the purview of technology and innovation in the military, Indian defence forces try to tackle the visible external threat. Investments in multi-role combat aircraft, UAVs, and futuristic soldiers are an old game. The recent Indian defence budget reiterates the modernization of the armed forces, but there is no mention of the research and development of emerging technologies. No matter how much modern weapons are procured, India remains a reactionary power. It can be changed if its approach towards defence research changes. It must anticipate future warfare and take such modern war to the adversary.

References

Allen, G., and Chan, T. (2017, July). Artificial Intelligence and National Security. *Belfer Center*. Retrieved from www.belfercenter.org/publication/artificial-intelligence-and-national-security

Anderson, J., and Lee, R. (2018). Artificial Intelligence and the Future of Humans. *Pew Research*. Retrieved from www.pewresearch.org/internet/2018/12/10/artificial-intelligence-and-the-future-of-humans/

Bartoletti, I. (2020). *An Artificial Revolution: On Power, Politics and AI*. London: The Indigo Press.

Calzada, I. (2018). (Smart) Citizens from Data Providers to Decision-Makers? The Case Study of Barcelona. *Sustainability*, 10(9). https://doi.org/10.3390/su10093252

Carnegie India. (2019). Global Technology Summit 2019. *Carnegieinida.org*. Retrieved from https://ceipfiles.s3.amazonaws.com/pdf/GTS+Report+2019.pdf

Chin, W. (2019). Technology, War and the State: Past, Present and Future. *International Affairs*, 95(a), 766–783. Retrieved from https://watermark.silverchair.com/iiz106.pdf?token=AQECAHi208BE49Ooan9kkhW_Ercy7Dm3ZL_9Cf3q-fKAc485ysgAAAtcwggLTBgkqhkiG9w0BBwagggLEMIICwAIBADCCArkGCS qGSIb3DQEHATAeBglghkgBZQMEAS4wEQQMWIEITddIZXlnfjyWAgEQgII CisuurOVsTfUkIK414r401U8RhP6fVuQpLgHTRJeqjNV1vefB

DD News. (2020, October 5). PM Narendra Modi Addresses Artificial Intelligence #RAISE2020 Summit. *YouTube*. Retrieved from www.youtube.com/watch?v= nkdqYNFDaCI

Dilipraj, E. (2017). *Cyber Enigma: Unraveling the Terror in the Cyber World*. New Delhi: KW Publishers.

Eder, T. S., Arcesati, R., and Mardell, J. (2019, August 28). Networking the "Belt and Road" – The Future Is Digital. *Mercator Institute for China Studies*. Retrieved from https://merics.org/en/tracker/networking-belt-and-road-future-digital

Engerman, C. D. (2018). *The Price of Aid*. New Delhi: Harvard University Press.

Hilbert, M. (2020). Digital Technology and Social Change: The Digital Transformation of Society from a Historical Perspective. *Dialogues Clin Neurosci*, 189–194. https://doi.org/10.31887%2FDCNS.2020.22.2%2Fmhilbert

Hilton, P. (1989). Reminiscences of Bletchley Park, 1942–1945. *A Century of Mathematics in America*, 1, 291–301.

Jaishankar, S. (2020). *The India Way: Strategies for an Uncertain World*. New Delhi: Harper Collins.

Kiggins, R. (2018). *The Political Economy of Robots: Prospects for Prosperity and Peace in the Automated 21st Century*. London: Palgrave Macmillan.

Kumar, D. (2016). Cyber Security: Status and Imperatives. In G. Kanwal (Ed.), *The New Arthashastra: A Security Strategy for India* (pp. 268–286). New Delhi: Harper Collins.

Latour, B. (2005). *Reassembling the Social: An Introduction to Actor Network Theory*. New York: Oxford University Press.

Lele, A. (2019). *Disruptive Technologies for the Militaries and Security*. Singapore: Springer.

Lingren, S. (2020). *Data Theory*. Polity. https://doi.org/978-1-509-53927-7

NITI Aayog. (2018). *National Strategy for Artificial Intelligence*. New Delhi: NITI Aayog.

Polcumpally, A. T. (2021). Artificial Intelligence and Global Power Structure: Understanding through Luhmann's Systems Theory. *AI & Society*, Volume 37, 1487–1503. https://doi.org/10.1007/s00146-021-01219-8

Polcumpally, A. T. (2022). The Relation Between Digital Technology and Democracy. Global Dimensions of Democracy and Human Rights: Problems and Perspectives (pp. 202–213). IGI Global.

Punia, R., and Damini, P. (2021). *Operation Khukri: The True Story Behind the Indian Army's Most Successful Mission as Part of the United Nations.* New Delhi: Penguin eBury Press.

Raghavan, S. (2016). *India's War: The Making of Modern South Asia, 1939–1945.* New Delhi: Penguin.

Rawat, R. B. (2019a). *Kargil: Untold Stories from the War.* New Delhi: Penguin.

Rawat, R. B. (2019b). *Guns, Guts, and Glory.* New Delhi: Penguin eBury Press.

Savage, N. (2020). The Race to the Top Among the World's Leaders in Artificial Intelligence. *Nature, 588,* 102–108. https://doi.org/10.1038/d41586-020-03409-8

Sen, G. (2016). The Conceptual Underpinnings of National Security. In G. Kanwal, *The New Arthashstra* (pp. 1–10). New Delhi: Harper Collins Publisher India.

Sen, G. (2019). Conceptualising Security and Security Studies. In G. Kanwal, National Security Perspectives (pp. 1-17). Center for Land Warfare Studies.

Sethi, M. (2009). *Nuclear Strategy: India's March towards Credible Deterrence.* New Delhi: KW Publishers.

Sharma, M. K. (2018). *Cyber Warfare: The Power of the Unseen.* New Delhi: KW Publishers.

Singh, S. (2015). The State of Security Studies in India: Limitations and Potential. *Millennial Asia,* 6(2), 191–204. https://doi.org/10.1177/0976399615590520

Sood, V. (2016). The Future of Intelligence. In G. Kunwal (Ed.), *The New Arthashastra* (pp. 108–126). New Delhi: Harper Collins publisher India.

Stansberry, K., Anderson, J., and Rainie, L. (2019, October 28). Experts Optimistic about the Next 50 Years of Digital Life. *PEW Research Center.* Retrieved from www.pewresearch.org/internet/2019/10/28/experts-optimistic-about-the-next-50-years-of-digital-life/

Stanzel, V. (2018). Introduction. In V. Stanzel (Ed.), *New Realities in Foreign Affairs: Diplomacy in the 21st Century.* German Institute for International and Security Affairs. Retrieved from www.swp-berlin.org/publications/products/research_papers/2018RP11_sze.pdf

Susskind, J. (2018). *Future Politics.* Oxford: Oxford University Press.

Toffler, A. (1991). *The Power Shift.* New York: Batnam Books.

Wylie, C. (2019). *Mind Fu*k: Inside Cambridge Analytica's Plot to Break the World.* London: Hachette India.

2

WAR, HYBRID WAR, AND REVOLUTION IN THE MILITARY

Arun Teja Polcumpally

Introduction

Let this chapter start with an assertion that the Industrial Revolution and technological progress have changed the nature of war (Khatte, 2018), and in the 21st century, it is the turn of digital technologies. This is true because the Industrial Revolution brought new technologies in warfare, and its grandeur is showcased in the two world wars (1914–1919 and 1934–1945). Centuries earlier, militaries used weapons such as swords, spikes, bows, and arrows. In addition, information dissipation and propaganda is also an ancient tool used to manipulate the enemy or say for psychological coercion but had a limited scope. However, a combination of technological weapons and psychological coercion always made grand strategies. As initially asserted, industrialization and associated technologies brought new tools to warfare. They brought tanks, guns, and all munition-based weapons to the military's disposal. With such heavy weaponry, coercive techniques took a back seat. With the internet and allied technologies, coercive techniques are again at the front seat (if I may say!). By the time this book is out, readers might be aware of the usage of autonomous weapon systems that are used in the Ukraine war. That means advanced digital technologies have already gained their usage in the conventional military. However, psychological warfare is more pervasive and is being used subtly. Here, the coercive techniques are used on the general population. These coercive techniques leading to psychological warfare are visible as people are increasingly using the internet and other technologies for all socio-economic activities. This chapter delves more into the combination of the coercive techniques anchored to the frontier digital technologies and conventional weapons and thus describes the concept of hybrid warfare and Revolution in Military Affairs (RMA).

DOI: 10.4324/9781003482703-4

Today, across societies, technologies including Artificial Intelligence (AI), ledger technologies, nanotechnology, and quantum technologies are being anxiously discussed. AI is becoming an unquestionable human assistant; ledger technologies revolutionize document storage and verification; nano-technologies reduce the physical size of material and uphold Moore's law in semiconductor devices; quantum technologies provide unprecedented speed and security of communications. These technologies impact all sectors of society invariably. From the previous chapter, it is clear that frontier technologies in the information and communication sector will enhance the strength of the state. A person who has read George Orwell's *1984* or Aldous Huxley's *Brave New World* would easily understand the kind of revolution these technologies can bring. Heuristics are enough to hypothesize that there is a high probability that the current developments in information technologies may hand over complete authoritarian control of society to a single entity. It might create what Foucault and Bentham called a *Panopticon* society. The world of Orwell, Huxley, or even Margaret Atwood might no longer be dystopian fiction. However, this is biased thinking arising from the fear of the unknown impacts of digital technology (Polcumpally, 2021). Though this type of thinking is biased, because of the existence of uncertainty, it is reasonable to pose the question: Will these technologies also bring a revolutionary change in the militaries across the world?

A technical report of the RAND organization argues that it is already time to have a fundamental shift in the entire military intelligence structure because of information technologies (Ish et al., 2021). These anticipations align themselves with the uncertainties caused by the new digital technologies. With the advent of the internet and smartphones, it is easy to think that the need for human intelligence in military affairs will become obsolete. The world has already seen a great shift in military affairs after the two mass destruction weapons – nuclear and biological – were invented. The shift brought by them changed the military structures (Barger, 2005). A similar change in global security is anticipated because of the increased information technology capacities (O'Hanlon, 2018). This information technology is considered to be an equal danger alongside the latter because it super-empowers an individual and not just states (Barger, 2005).

In the world of growing internet-operated devices and AI-assisted systems, the capacities of states, non-state actors, and even individuals will be enhanced exponentially. With the correct technology, one could inflict substantial damage on any region. For example, anyone with enough capital and resources can combine AI with biotechnology and create a mass destruction weapon. Hypothetically, think how difficult it would be for some scientific personnel to start the SARS Covid-19 pandemic. It is not! A small code that remotely triggers the virus burst is sufficient for the virus leakage to happen. This shows that security issues are not expected from known organizations or nation-states. Any entity, be it private or even individuals, can gain the capacity to inflict irrevocable damage to international society. With these advanced technologies, the idea of securitization itself has to be changed.

At the Beijing–Xiangshan forum held in 2018, People's Liberation Army (PLA) Major General Ding Xinagrong, Deputy Director of the General Office of China's Central Military Commission, emphasized that to be on par with the global advanced military, they have to focus on the ongoing military revolution comprising digital technologies (Allen and Chan, 2017). In the same conference, a private military equipment company executive, Zeng Yi, opined that the future of warfare would be loaded with AI systems, including the command structure (Allen and Chan, 2017). This incident of the conference is highlighted here because China is one of the major powers to undertake research and development in large-scale digital technology, and it is the only one that publicly emphasizes on the nature of dual use. Another research shows significant investment by the Defense Advanced Research Projects Agency (DARPA) in emerging technology projects, where most of them involve AI and other information technologies (Polcumpally, 2021). This shows that the usage of digital technologies is definitely going to change the existing arsenal of the military.

It is clear that the scope of warfare is not limited to the battlefields. It has expanded to the entire population. Conventional military attacks will be (or potentially can be) combined with psychological warfare, which can impact the entire country's population. Recognizing the latter, this chapter is expected to serve as a primer to the military personnel, defense analysts, military strategists, bureaucracy, and general public who want to understand the reality of the impact of digital technologies on Indian military. This work will focus on a single question: Will digital technologies bring a change in Indian military affairs?

In order to effectively provide an answer to the latter question, it is necessary to understand and define the concept of RMA.

> [I]f you can't define something, you can't measure it, and if you can't measure it, you can't know if you are changing it.
>
> *(Wylie, 2019)*

What Is Revolution in Military Affairs?

RMA is an academic concept explaining the way a sudden change occurs in the military. This academic conception is opined to bridge the gap between scholars and military practitioners (Mets, 2001). RMA is not some objective reality to be captured or achieved. It is an explanation to the change that happened in the military. Not all the technologies are capable to bring an RMA. Many mistake RMA as an addition of a new weapon that completely replaces the old one. When an RMA is supposed to happen, it can either render the existing techniques obsolete and bring new ones or establish new competencies by creating a completely new dimension of warfare (Hundley, 1999). It can also be both.

RMA cannot occur solely on the advancement of technology. For example, in the digital era, if AI is advanced and every repetitive action is automated, it does not automatically mean that there is an irrevocable change in the military. There might still be the same command structure and military techniques used, but the work might catch speed and improve its efficiency. The only change would be the addition of AI. In order to call it an RMA, such breakthroughs should be accompanied by new structural and organizational changes. The military personnel also should be able to comprehend the change and use the new technology. Here are three points to be noted to call any change to be a revolution:

1. Unmet security challenges by the traditional or status quo military.
2. Linking already-existing technological breakthroughs to the new security challenge.
3. Organizational change to accommodate the new technology.

In the 21st century, where digital technologies are nearly impossible to be detached from the lives of the public, RMA is to be expected in the same digital direction. It is predicted that RMA is highly probable when the military completely adopts advanced computer hardware and software (O'Hanlon, 2018). A comprehensive list of characteristics of RMA has been compiled by Deborah Barger in her RAND technical report (Barger, 2005). A similar list has also been made by a RAND report of 1999 (Hundley, 1999). However, this research will consider those conditions that are sufficient to look at the possibility of RMA with the amalgamation of digital technological advancements.

Among the two RAND lists, one feature from the 2005 report stands out. It espouses that the country that develops the technology will have a first-mover advantage. There is also another feature saying that the technology is always used by the country other than the one that invented it. When digital technologies are considered like AI, first-mover advantage definitely stands tall as a feature of RMA. The characteristics that define the RMA are listed in Table 2.1.

Given these as features for RMA, the advanced digital technologies surely have a chance to bring a revolution. Especially, AI has already established that it will bring a horizontal change in all the sectors of the society (Polcumpally, 2021). Further, AI is not a stand-alone technology. It has to be combined with other technologies to make it useful. Table 2.2 charts the possible changes that AI in combination with different sectors can bring. This chart showcases the possibility of an RMA when only AI technology is

TABLE 2.1 Characteristics of Revolution in Military Affairs

Sl No	Characteristics of Revolution in Military Affairs (RMA)
1	Are rarely brought about by dominant players
2	Bestow an enormous and immediate military advantage on the first nation to exploit them in combat
3	Are often adopted and fully exploited first by someone other than the nation inventing the technology
4	Are not always technology-driven
5	Technology-driven RMAs are usually brought about by combinations of technologies rather than individual technologies
6	Do not necessarily involve new weapons
7	Appear to have three components: technology, doctrine, and organization
8	As many fail as are successful
9	Often take a long time to come to fruition
10	The military utility is frequently controversial and is in doubt up until the moment it is proven in battle
11	Also occur in the business world
12	Are the result of multiple innovations

TABLE 2.2 AI Mapping with Various Sectors to Bring Unprecedented Changes

Other Technologies		Resultant Change
Advertisement		Precision targeting
Drugs		Quick vaccine development
Genomics		Personalized medicine
Policing	Artificial Intelligence	Hyper-surveillance
Democracy		Manufactured consent
Weapons		Lethal Autonomous Weapon Systems (LAWS)
Social media + Search engines		Filter bubbles and psychological control

considered. RMA can be brought more quickly and with an expanded scope if blockchain and quantum communications are considered.

A more surrealist picture of the amount of change AI can bring when combined with other technologies can be seen from Meta's development of the metaverse. For those who watch science fiction TV shows and Japanese anime that adopt virtual reality (VR) into their story lines, it becomes much easier to picture this. Recently, on 28 October 2021, Facebook Inc. has rebranded itself into Meta Platforms Inc.; however, rebranding is not the takeaway news here. This rebranding exercise is anchored to its vision of creating a metaverse VR social platform. To describe it in short, a metaverse user can build a second life where the user can experience happiness, sense of achievement, money, and social bonds. Virtual homes, currency, food, clothes, travel, and so forth can be made in such an alternative world. What more! These creations can also be monetized to be used in the real world. For those who love playing computer games and watching science fiction TV shows, Facebook's roadmap to the metaverse will be a path to their dream reality. This surely will be a dream come true for Sheldon Cooper, Leonard Hofstadter, Howard Wolowitz, and Rajesh Koothrappali (popular TV show – *The Big Bang Theory*). Though the VR project of Facebook has been under development for years, the world took note of it when it rebranded itself to Meta. Now, it is beyond doubt that human-machine interaction technologies are the future. The capacities of advanced digital technologies are clear with AI as an example.

Any nation in control of these technologies will hold the power to dictate the behavioral terms to the public within the country and also outside the political boundaries. As per the understanding of the RMA, frontier technologies including AI, blockchain, and quantum communications have the potential to bring changes in the military organization and tactics and brings solutions to unmet security challenges. If RMA is the future prediction, the current phenomenon is the mixture of traditional warfare and digital technologies. The next section delves into the combination of the pervasive ability of digital technologies and conventional military capacities.

Hybrid Warfare

The employment of coercive information tactics is the most distinguishing feature of the recent descriptions of hybrid warfare. Generally, information is always used to get an advantage over an enemy by corrupting their thoughts using counter-narratives. Recently, such techniques are used in Islamic State's (IS) campaigns in the Middle East (UNICRI and UNCCT, 2021) and also by Russia in its Ukraine operations (Scott, 2022). From the 2014 event of Crimea Peninsula annexation by Russia, hybrid warfare has become quite a buzzword. In addition to the traditional military, the Russians used local proxy militia, exerted economic pressure, utilized disinformation campaigns, and exploited the existing social divisions. Such usage of widespread techniques to cripple a nation holistically is what is understood and described as a hybrid warfare (Monaghan, 2015). An aggregation of conventional and non-conventional methods in the warfare is generally thought of as hybrid warfare.

As discussed earlier, with the emergence of digital technologies, state and non-state actors have gained the capacity to widen their scope of influence (Wither, 2003). Both can wage psychological war on any nation. There is an opinion that new-generation warfare is won with the psychological advantage (Wither, 2003). With the integration of emerging digital technologies into the defense, there is an emerging view to have a separate cyber and space forces (Winkler et al., 2019). These changes make it evident that the old hard power usage in the war is no longer a viable strategy. It looks like militaries have to use hybrid strategies for their success.

The hybrid warfare is also compared to the term that is coined by two Chinese colonels – *unrestricted warfare* (Wither, 2003). It says that there are no restrictions in this new type of warfare, and such an unrestricted area provides a wide range of cyber-attacks. A computer virus can cripple the entire national economy if the country is digitally modernized. A perfect example of this incident is the denial-of-service (DoS) attacks on Estonia in 2007 (McGuinness, 2017). Banking services, media, government online services, and communications were halted. This halt was assisted by massive misinformation drives. Today, countries are increasingly using the internet and computers to deliver public services. Thus, all the critical infrastructures such as electricity power plants, heavy machinery, internet, digital govern-ance systems, and e-commerce can be shut down in an instant, halting the entire economy.

As discussed in the earlier section, the pervasive nature of advanced digital technologies is capable of dictating behavioral terms to the public. Directly or indirectly, a country can have a grip on the political thought, market, and deci-sions of the public in another country. This is an example of a psychological warfare. In terms of traditional attacks, Estonia's distributed denial-of-service (dDoS) attack of 2007 is a good example. A country can initiate DoS attacks by sending malware into the computer systems of another country's digital infrastructure. Critical infrastructures such as electricity supply, power plants, and healthcare services are impacted. This is the capacity of the existing digital technologies. However, with advanced technologies such as blockchain, quan-tum communications, and AI, the scope can be expanded to such a level that a company can have a world monopoly over knowledge production.

For example, in India, any general query is raised in the Google search, and the answers provided are generally accepted. None of the users will ques-tion the authenticity and bias of the search engine. Such queries will be asked by students, academicians, and policymakers. The answers provided by the search engine dictate the knowledge of the query makers. That means stu-dents learn from the select material, academicians conduct research from biased materials, and policymakers anchor to the biased narratives and re-search in formulating national policies.

What Is War?

RMA and hybrid warfare have already been discussed. This section brings the core concept – war – and questions its definitional significance. In the socially constructed world, war has been attributed to the *means to achieve ends* by the states (Howard, 2012). Of course, on a philosophical level discussion, war cannot be confined to states. It can be attributed to any entity, even individuals. On a practical note, the term *war* is used when the warring entities are sovereign states. Else, they are termed *skirmishes, terror attacks, revolts, insurgencies*, and so on. Clausewitz defines war as "an act of violence intended to compel our opponents to fulfil our will" and also as "War is nothing but a continuation of political intercourse, with a mixture of other means" (Dennen, 1980). After analyzing the short literature review (Howard, 2012), (Sagan, 2017) on the conceptual understanding of *war*, it is concluded that the term *war* is generally used to denote the military acts of states against other states in achieving some fixed political ends. Generally, the narratives that carry the term *war* are associated with mass violence, which is legally supported by a recognized group against another recognized group.

The analysis of whether digital technologies like AI and blockchain would bring a revolution in the warfare is a food for a long philosophical debate. This is because it first triggers debate on the conceptual understanding of the term *war* and then the term *revolution* and on the technology's impact on the conceptualized terms – *war* and *revolution*. An example of the debate is, one might say the term *war* is never attributed to a weapon or a clash between the sovereign states. Further, there are terms like *civil war, economic warfare*, and *cyber warfare* that fall outside the constructs of organized violent clashes between the sovereigns. Leaving out the unnecessary debates, which is as good as an academic exercise, we shall take the definition provided by the *Oxford Dictionary of Politics*:

> War is an armed conflict between two or more parties, usually fought for their political ends . . . most numerous sources of theories . . . argue that war is caused by the political construction of states and ideologies they express.
>
> *(Iain, 2009)*

An armed conflict between two parties usually fought for their political ends using hard and soft power together is hybrid warfare, as understood in the previous section. If the technology brings an RMA, it should have occurred in the history already. As of the development of the book and, hopefully, when the book hits the market, RMA would still be a long dream for the militaries worldwide. The next section gives a gift on the history of technology-induced change in the nature of warfare helping to provide more clarity on the technology-induced RMA.

Technology-Induced Change in the Nature of Warfare

As discussed in the earlier section, the core aspect of RMA is that it must change the paradigm of the warfare or the way the military operates. The old ways of conducting battle should be rendered obsolete. One simple example from the history of warfare is mechanized projectiles of munitions powered by gunpowder rendered archers obsolete.

The technologies mentioned in Table 2.3 have created a revolution in the way the attacks are conducted within the war dimension. Here the dimension means the operational space of the military – land, water, and air. With the advent of digital technologies and the internet, cyber dimension has become a new space for conducting the war.

Initial RMA technology can be attributed to the usage of bronze weapons and armor. Then came the chariot technology with composite bows. With the discovery of iron, metal weapons and armors were supplied to the whole of the armies. Earlier, bronze was expensive and was used only by elite soldiers. The invention of gunpowder brought a major revolution in the medieval and modern military history. Soldiers were no longer carrying swords and other metal weapons and charged straight against the enemy.

Rather than the chariot, and other primitive military technologies, the invention and usage of gunpowder can be regarded as the true RMA. It changed the way the military organized itself. The munitions powered by

TABLE 2.3 A List of Technological Advancements That Generated RMA

RMA	Nature of Paradigm Shift	Core Competency	Dominant Player
Carrier Warfare	Created a new operational and tactical-level model for naval warfare	Accurate naval gunfire of battleship fleets (rendered obsolete)	Battleship fleets (US and British)
Blitzkrieg	Created a new operational and tactical model for land warfare	Static defense of prepared positions by infantry and artillery (rendered irrelevant)	French Army
ICBM	Created a new dimension of warfare (intercontinental strategic warfare)	Long-range, accurate delivery of high-yield nuclear weapons (a new core competency)	
Machine Gun	Created a new tactical model for land warfare	Ability to maneuver massed infantry forces in the open (rendered obsolete)	All armies employing massed infantry forces in the open
Longbow	Created a new tactical model for land warfare	Man-to-m combat capability of knights on horseback (rendered obsolete)	French Armoured Cavalry

the firepower of phosphorous needed a machine that can be made and repaired by a few people. It opened a new defense manufacturing industry that never existed. Old strategies became obsolete. A similar major revolution was brought by the introduction of aircrafts during World War I. In the 20th century, in addition to the aircraft technology, electronic equipment like Radar, Sonar, and Radio have changed the battle strategies significantly. However, rather than ringing an RMA, these electronic technologies of the 20th century have increased the military efficiency. It has not changed the way war is waged and did not bring an overwhelming change in the structure and organization of the military.

In the middle of the 20th century, with the historic military (mis) event of Hiroshima and Nagasaki, a new structure, doctrines, and ideas of warfare developed. Nuclear deterrence triggered an arms race but never trigged an all-out war. Any skirmishes between the nuclear powers were short-lived, which was not the case earlier. Nuclear technology ushered in the age of technological dominance. Militaries that have the latest technology on their side and their forces are dynamically adopting newest techniques and technologies become the strongest ones.

In a strict sense of RMA, considering the entirety of armed forces, there are only two events (Inamdar, 2008). One is when human societies adopted settled agriculture and organized forces to safeguard their resources. The second is during the Industrial Revolution, which brought a profound change in the complete way of living and warring material, strategy, and organization. The current RMA is expected to be anchored on emerging digital technologies (Inamdar, 2008) (Kirkpatrick, 2001). It is opined to be seen in two stages:

> The present stage is based on stand-off platforms, stealth, precision, information dominance, improved communications, computers, GPS, digitization, smart weapons and jointness. The second stage, somewhat in the future, may be based on robotics, non-lethality, psycho-technology, cyber-defence, nanotechnology, brilliant weapon systems, hyper-flexible organizations and fire-ant warfare.
>
> *(Inamdar, 2008)*

Another point to be noted from history is that the dominant military powers seldom come up with an RMA. It might be because they will be occupied with making a profit from the existing technology both on a monetary basis and on a warfare basis. However, for India, if the technology is proven and the organization required is viable, will the status quo military establishment accept it? Do they have the required expertise to operate the new technology? Indian Military Academy (IMA) and National Defence Academy (NDA) are not particularly IITs and IISc to bring an elite technical and scientific regiment. They impart quick decision-making skills and a lot of discipline. Of course, the cadets passing out of IMA have a working knowledge of their corps and units. For example, a Composite Technical Regiment will have a requisite engineering skill but not a scientific enquiry into the concepts and theories.

A country that develops technological breakthroughs is not necessarily the recipient of the first-mover advantage. History shows that the founding country seldom has the advantage (Hundley, 1999). A successful adaptation of the new revolutionary technology into the military should have three categorical reorganizations: technology, doctrine, and institution (Hundley, 1999). These technologies are not developed out of thin air. It takes decades of research and another decade into successful implementation.

Securitizing Information Technology: A Buzan Perspective

In this chapter, we have explored the evolving landscape of military affairs in the context of information technology and its potential to usher in revolutionary changes. We have delved into the concept of RMA, the emergence of hybrid warfare, and the profound influence of advanced digital technologies on the military. Now, let us conclude by applying Barry Buzan's theory of securitization to the field of information technology.

Buzan's theory of securitization provides a valuable lens through which we can analyze the evolving role of information technology in the realm of security. According to Buzan, securitization is the process by which an issue is framed as an existential security threat, justifying extraordinary measures and responses. We can observe this process unfolding in the information technology domain.

In recent years, information technology-related issues such as cyber-attacks, data breaches, and digital espionage have been increasingly framed as security threats at the national and international levels. Governments and organizations now recognize that the misuse of digital technologies can have severe consequences for national security, economic stability, and public safety. This recognition has led to the securitization of information technology. The securitization of information technology has resulted in the allocation of significant resources, both in terms of funding and human capital, to address cybersecurity challenges. Governments have developed national cybersecurity strategies, established specialized agencies, and formed international partnerships to combat cyber threats. This policy response is a direct outcome of securitization. It is a no-brainer that states have already securitized the IT.

In addition to the concept of securitization of IT, Buzan's theory also emphasizes the role of the audience in the securitization process. In the case of IT, the audience includes policymakers, military leaders, businesses, and the general public. As these stakeholders perceive the growing importance of IT security, they exert pressure on governments and institutions to securitize the issue further. As discussed earlier in the chapter, the scope of the threats have increased with the adoption of advanced digital technologies.

Implications of New Securitization

The securitization of information technology has significant implications for military affairs. Though it might not have brought an RMA, it has prompted a shift in military intelligence structures and the development of new doctrines and strategies. The rise of swarming drone technology, cyber espionage, and psychological warfare exemplifies this shift.

Securing swarming drone operations requires not only safeguarding communication networks but also countering adversarial drone swarms. Nations must invest in AI-driven counter-drone systems to protect against this emerging threat. The criticality of securing digital technologies is evident in cyber-espionage incidents where nation-states attempted to infiltrate the AI systems guiding missile defense or autonomous drones. These attacks underline the need for robust cybersecurity measures to protect not only the hardware but also the algorithms powering these technologies. The ongoing conflict in Eastern Europe highlights (Russia–Ukraine conflict, Armenia–Azerbaijan conflict) the importance of securitizing hybrid warfare. The nations involved must continuously monitor and counter disinformation campaigns, cyberattacks on critical infrastructure, and conventional military movements. This real-time challenge underscores the need for adaptive strategies.

These analytical insights demonstrate the multifaceted nature of securitization in the context of digital technologies and military affairs. The evolving threat landscape necessitates adaptive and forward-looking strategies to protect national interests.

Conclusion

In conclusion, Buzan's theory of securitization provides one of the many available frameworks for understanding how information technology has become securitized in the context of military affairs. As information technology continues to advance and permeate every aspect of society, the process of securitization is likely to intensify. The fusion of digital technologies with conventional military capabilities raises new questions about the nature of warfare, security, and the role of states and non-state actors in shaping global affairs.

As we move forward, it is essential for scholars, national security decision-makers, and the broader public to remain vigilant and critically assess the securitization of IT. The ongoing evolution in military affairs, driven by digital technologies, demands a comprehensive understanding of the risks and opportunities they present. This chapter serves as a foundation for further research and analysis in this dynamic field, contributing to our ability to navigate the complex intersection of technology and security in the 21st century.

References

Allen, G., and Chan, T. (2017, July). Artificial Intelligence and National Security. *Belfer Center*. Retrieved from www.belfercenter.org/publication/artificial-intelligence-and-national-security

Barger, D. G. (2005). *Toward a Revolution in Intelligence Affairs*. Santa Monica, CA: RAND Corporation.

Dennen, J. (1980). On War: Concepts, Definitions, Research Data a Short Literature Review and Bibliography. *Core.ac.uk*. Retrieved from https://core.ac.uk/download/pdf/12857871.pdf

Howard, M. (2012). Military History and the History of War. In R. H. Williamson Murray (Ed.), *The Past as Prologue: Importance of History to the Military Profession* (pp. 12–20). Cambridge: Cambridge University Press. https://doi.org/10.1017/CBO9780511818943.002

Hundley, R. O. (1999). *Past Revolutions, Future Transformations*. Santa Monica, CA: RAND Corporation.

Iain, A. M. (2009). *Oxfords Consise Dictionary of Politics* (3rd ed.). Oxford: Oxford University Press.

Inamdar, S. G. (2008). RMA: A Selective Monographic Overview. *Journal of Defence Studies*, 2(2), 146–165.

Ish, D., Ettinger, J., and Ferris, C. (2021). *Evaluating the Effectiveness of Artificial Intelligence Systems in Intelligence Analysis*. Santa Monica: RAND Corporation. https://doi.org/10.7249/RR-A464-1

Khatte, A. (2018, August 16). Artificial Intelligence Is a Key to Future International Relations Dynamics. *Analytics India Magazine*. Retrieved from https://analyticsindiamag.com/artificial-intelligence-is-a-key-to-future-international-relations-dynamics/

Kirkpatrick, P. D. (2001). Revolutions in Military Technology, and Their Consequences. *The RUSI Journal*, 146(4), 67–73.

McGuinness, D. (2017, April 27). How a Cyber Attack Transformed Estonia. *bbcnews*. Retrieved from www.bbc.com/news/39655415

Mets, D. R. (2001). What Is a Revolution in Military Affairs (RMA)? In *The Long Search for a Surgical Strike*. Air University Press. Retrieved from www.jstor.com/stable/resrep13887.8

Monaghan, A. (2015). The War in Russia's Hybrid Warfare. *The US Army War College Quarterly: Parameters*, 45(4), 8.

O'Hanlon, M. (2018). A Retrospective on the so-Called Revolution in Military Affairs, 2000–2020. *Brookings*. Retrieved from www.brookings.edu/wp-content/uploads/2018/09/FP_20181217_defense_advances_pt1.pdf

Polcumpally, A. T. (2021). Artificial Intelligence and Global Power Structure: Understanding through Luhmann's Systems Theory. *AI & Society*. https://doi.org/10.1007/s00146-021-01219-8

Sagan, S. D. (2017). The Changing Rules of War. *Daedalus*, 146(1), 6–10.

Scott, M. (2022, March 10). As War in Ukraine Evolves, So Do Disinformation Tactics. *Politico.eu*. Retrieved from www.politico.eu/article/ukraine-russia-disinformation-propaganda/

UNICRI and UNCCT. (2021). Algorithms and Terrorism: The Malicious Use of Artificial Intelligence for Terrorist Purposes. A Joint Report by UNICRI and UNCCT. *United Nations*. Retrieved from www.un.org/counterterrorism/sites/www.un.org.counterterrorism/files/countering-terrorism-online-with-ai-uncct-unicri-report-web.pdf

Winkler, J. D., Marler, T., Posard, M. N., Cohen, R. S., and Smith, M. L. (2019). *Reflections on the Future of Warfare and Implications for Personnel Policies of the U.S. Department of Defence.* Santa Monica, CA: RAND Corporation.

Wither, J. K. (2003). British Bulldog or Bush's Poodle? Anglo-American Relations and the Iraq War. *Parameters*, 67–82.

Wylie, C. (2019). *Mind Fu*k: Inside Cambridge Analytica's Plot to Break the World.* London: Hachette India.

3

QUEST FOR MILITARY SUPREMACY – THE UNITED STATES VS. CHINA VS. RUSSIA

Poornima Vijaya

Introduction

In contemporary geopolitics, the vital issue is the probability of an era with mounting strategic competition in several spheres, such as political, economic, military-technological, and space, which causes significant alterations in the international security milieu (Mazarr, 2018). The forefront of growing rivalries is the contest for primacy over security, institutions, and economic and military innovations between the key powers: the United States, Russia, and China.

The Trump presidency espoused an unprecedented stance concerning China by describing China as a "revisionist power seeking to change the status quo and displace the United States in the Indo-Pacific Region" in the 2017 US National Security Strategy. Similarly, the 2018 National Defence Strategy labels China as a "strategic competitor engaging in rapacious economics and offensive military capabilities to coerce the states in the Indo-Pacific Region" (The White House, 2017). The emergence of the Biden era in 2021 evidenced no apparent shift in threat perceptions from China. The latest phone call in July 2022, lasting two hours between the two heads, dwindled the agenda discussing mainly Taiwan and Ukraine issues, among other matters. Despite the rhetoric of open communications in issues such as supply chains, macroeconomics, global energy, health, and food security, achievements on these fronts remain consistently limited due to political differences and public discourse.

In response to this, the White House report on 28 July 2022 read, "[T]he call was a part of the Biden Administration's efforts to maintain and deepen lines of communication between the United States and the PRC and responsibly

DOI: 10.4324/9781003482703-5

manage our differences and work together where our interests align" (The White House, 2022a, 2022b, 2022c; China Briefing, 2022). Trump's assertiveness will be reminisced in foreign policy circles for his confrontational persona. However, Biden's challenge comprises a rapidly growing China in many areas, including military production, technologies, innovation in cyber and space, and essentially the mounting sphere of influence.

Amidst such challenges, Biden and the senior officials in his administration are perceptively at odds between advocating "competition" and "engagement" simultaneously (Mishra, 2022). The shift in the United States' stance on China has led to mounting insights into a two-part strategy: Engagement and Strategic Balancing towards China. This narrative shift in the United States' policy towards China changed when China became a rising power unwilling to accept establishments, institutional frameworks, divisions, and bifurcations of borders (Work, 2015). It would be naïve to presuppose that China does not possess long-term strategic goals that will ensure that China is not just a mere theatre actor but also an intimidating Asian power that holds the capacity to deter the United States (Lee, 2016). Strategic competitions are not new, of course. Repeatedly, such competitions have been deep-seated in antiquity – from the Spartan and Athenian Grand Strategies in the 5th century BCE to the ideological dissections between the Soviet Union and the United States during the Cold War era.

Today, the United States sustains an array of long-term security tests in several areas worldwide and endures a mounting, complicated relationship, especially with China and Russia, that is deep-rooted in cooperation, conflict, and competition, simultaneously. In August 2021, China took military intelligence across the globe by surprise when China tested its nuclear-capable hypersonic missile, which circumnavigated the globe before hitting its apparent test target (Sevastopulo and Hille, 2021). As advancements come to the fore, new threats arise for nations to mitigate. The US Justice Department in 2020 released data on two Chinese hackers actively working with the state officials in China charged with hacking into computer systems of several hundred people, including government, companies, and nongovernmental organizations (NGOs), and targeting confidential information and intellectual property (DoJ, 2020). Scilicet, the future of Russian warfare is vested in asymmetrical advantages, as Putin's *superoruzhie* (super weapons) as new and advanced weapons systems, unveiled in 2018, signalled Russian intent to "counter the perceived conventional military superiority of great power competitors such as the U.S. and its NATO allies" (Bendett et al., 2021). Chinese and Russian astounding progress in military technology and innovations in warfare are reality checks as US officials realize the gravitas in the threats emanating from the East.

As new geopolitical theatres, such as the Indo-Pacific, rise as a sphere for power competition, hot conflicts, and strategic partnerships, the emergence of the New Cold War between the United States and China adds complexities to regional security and international cooperation. Furthermore, a revisionist power such as Beijing, challenging the post-1945 US-led world order, combined with an increasing proliferation of hybrid warfare and the perceptive value of grey-zone tactics, adds more complexities in a hyper-connected world (Doyle and Rumley, 2019). In this regard, American policymakers have highlighted several concerns on Chinese revisionism, thereby making Indo-Pacific cooperation on emerging technologies crucial to the region.

> This intensifying American focus is due in part to the fact that the Indo-Pacific faces mounting challenges, particularly from the [People's Republic of China] PRC. The PRC is combining its economic, diplomatic, military, and technological might as it pursues a sphere of influence in the Indo-Pacific and seeks to become the world's most influential power. The PRC's coercion and aggression spans the globe, but it is most acute in the Indo-Pacific.
>
> *(The White House, 2022b)*

The Chinese government has been taking advantages of its geography, resources, and political structures, wherein their initiatives on the Belt and Road Initiative, wolf warrior diplomacy, resource concentration in the pursuit of the "great rejuvenation of the Chinese nation" (DoD, 2020). Although accumulating increasing military, economic, and nuclear capabilities, China has additionally resorted to using information and emerging technologies to sharpen its strategic abilities (Rim, 2023).

The Chinese Communist Party perceives "perpetual competition" in their relations with other great powers. PRC believes to "exist in a world where the most-vigilant great powers endure prosperity and security" (Christensen, 1996). Thus, Chinese official documents routinely evidence such perceptions in their reference to hegemonic politics and "cold war mind-set"[1] – explicitly referring to hegemons in Asia and, broadly, around the world. Chinese economic and demographic might has played a crucial role in strengthening modernization across all domains of its warfare (DoD, 2020). As their perspectives on strategic competition enduring the Cold War ethos is brought to the fore, China is persistently outspoken on the global nature of the competition, thus implicitly expressing that the nature of the threat is beyond the geographical confines of the Indo-Pacific (Zhao, 2019). Under the assertive leadership of Xi Jinping, China has averred a vision of a world order that accommodates Chinese interests in the global power systems. History is witness to systemic vulnerabilities in hegemonic contestations. Hence, Chinese leaders and scholars maintain optimism in their prospects of managing the strategic competition and restoring a new equilibrium between the greater powers in the world (Zhao, 2019).

In addition, Chinese informatization and intelligentization efforts are not without an emphasis on military might, thereby considering emerging technologies such as quantum information, Artificial Intelligence (AI), cloud computing, and unmanned weapons systems to push a change towards intelligentized warfare (US Department of Defense, 2022). To counter these new forms of threat, the United States is formulizing long-term strategies to secure advantages over China. In this regard, the Biden administration has shown renewed interest and recommitment to Science, Technology, Engineering, and Mathematics (STEM) fields (The White House, 2022c).

Russia, however, formerly Soviet Union, has been engulfed in a strategic rivalry for several decades. During the times of the Cold War, the ensuing competition spanned several spheres, from society, ideology, and political ambitions to promulgating ideas on military issues and evolving threat perceptions. The all-encompassing rivalry led to several proxy wars/conflicts across the globe, from the Korean War to the emergence of West Asia as a hotbed of such proxy conflicts. The strategic objectives for Russia in this military rivalry is to preserve its security, forms of government, and economic prosperity. Looking further closely, such goals set to realize one's larger strategic ambitions is Russia in a stable sphere of influence in the immediate post-Soviet neighbourhood (Mazarr, 2020). Efforts to stop the enlargement of the North Atlantic Trade Organization (NATO) and limit the expansion of the European Union can be analysed as Russian endeavours towards the creation of its own sphere of influence (Pezard and Rhoades, 2020). These strategies are, however, not well articulated to string in unison for a cogent strategy. However, Russian flexibility, seldom, their reactiveness, and practice of several forms of aggressive warfare keeps Russian options open, accommodating contingencies in tactical planning to realize their larger strategic ambitions of military and technological innovations.

In short, the patterns of strategic competitions are now much more complex, diverse, and capricious, with numerous competitions overlapping under different rules. Significant innovations in Chinese and Russian capabilities intensify the strategic completion between the three nations. This led to diminished power differentials between the three nations. Therefore, the means to engage in such competitions lie in varying pursuits of security and economic prosperity through institutionalized frameworks and strident military-technological-political rivalry to further one's power. The latter emphasizes the long-term strategies for competition intended to attain a relative gain over peer rivals across geopolitical, economic, technological, and military scopes (Mahnken, 2017).

Rapid advancements in "disruptive technologies" are altering the nature of military capability and strategy. Modern battlefields – including conventional, sub-conventional, and nuclear ones – are being decided by emerging technologies such as autonomous weapons, cyber weapons, weaponization of space, and AI, either alone or in combination with conventional modes of warfare (Tanwar, 2020). Prime Minister Narendra Modi stated that India, a latecomer to indigenous capacity production in contemporary military hardware, faces the urgent task of fusing the third and fourth industrial revolutions in military capabilities (Poonawalla, 2023). However, this transformation goes beyond simply integrating these cutting-edge technologies into India's military readiness. War is rarely won by technology alone; military strategy and tactics must incorporate it.

In India, however, thinkers and policymakers are realizing the intensity of mounting weaponizing information against India, as the country is witnessing a sharp increase in disinformation campaigns. Paul Antonopoulos (2021) in his analysis of Disinformation Lab Report reveals a possibility of international players such as Pakistan and Turkey in such image building. Perception is key to global branding, and perception management is a continuous work in progress. India has recently started to battle disinformation operations against it on international diplomatic forums by making prompt rebuttals and using information technology to its advantage. India is aware of these campaigns. In addition, the Ministry of Information and Broadcasting has decided to block YouTube channels and other websites that are proven to be disseminating false news and anti-Indian propaganda in conjunction with intelligence services. Twenty YouTube.com channels, two websites, and a misinformation network based in Pakistan had their content removed in December 2021 for promoting divisive material about the Indian Army, Ram Mandir, minority communities in India, General Bipin Rawat, Kashmir, and other topics (Ministry of Information and Broadcast, 2021). India has so far reacted to these defamation attempts mainly in order to protect itself. However, a comprehensive strategy is desperately needed to reduce the adverse effects of semination of such information to global branding and internal social harmony.

Disinformation narratives should be on surveillance for, if anything, they should be expected in the modern era of advanced information technology. Narratives are like an unending water stream. Ad hoc and episodic modes of confrontation are chosen over persistent efforts to challenge such narratives. It is important to monitor the information flow and, if necessary, limit it in its early phases. In this manner, arguments on national and international venues would not be fuelled by disinformation narratives. Other times, it is best to take a "wait and watch" approach until the plot fully develops. This would aid in creating the necessary countermeasure. It would be beneficial to track the source of information, especially for delicate Indian issues like Kashmir, the Northeast, human rights, and religious minorities, just to mention a few. Indian think tanks should also do field research in delicate areas, and the resulting papers should be widely disseminated. As a result, the material being produced assumes utmost significance. This additionally reveals the need for cohesion and cooperation between several departments of the government and the need for independent think tanks to produce credible and result-oriented research on such information warfare tactics (Barthwal, 2022).

The core element of this strategic rivalry is to examine whether Russia and China have the necessary capabilities for power projectile on a similar stance as the United States and how they, along with their allies, respond to such incremental changes in the status quo. The objective of this chapter is to describe briefly how China, Russia, and the United States have extended their margins of military-technology superiority in the strategic race for advanced and emerging technologies such as AI, cyber, quantum technology, blockchain, robotics, and other disruptive technologies.

Technologies and the Military Competition

Emergent technologies such as AI are extensively observed as a vital component of military efficiency and are advantageous for future innovations (Boulanin et al., 2020). Both in theory and practice, possessing such innovating, cutting-edge technologies equates to operative weapons systems, which translates to greater military power, further resulting in greater geopolitical control.

In tandem with the intensifying strategic competition between the United States, China, and Russia, the race to manipulate and assimilate emerging technologies into their militaries, national defence systems, and policies is also gaining momentum. Their mounting digital networking, data-fication, and connectivity characterize the age of the information revolution. Furthermore, the rise of intelligent machinery, AI, robotics, big data, analytics, quantum computing technology, science, information, and other cutting-edge innovations changes the course, nature, and characters of war in modern times (Kavanagh, 2019). In a constantly changing technological milieu, military organizations have to adapt quickly to become competitive in long-term strategic pursuits. Mitigating short-term challenges while adapting to an ever-changing security landscape remains a challenge. Extensive debates in Russia arose in the 1980s among the top government officials and political elites, underscoring "Military Technical Revolution". These deliberations were a response to the US reconnaissance strike capability using precision-guided weapons (Azrael and Payin, 1996). However, this debate was revised by the US foreign policy and defence officials along with policymakers, experts, and academics when they extended the scope to study both the impact of technology and also the ideational and organizational elements that enable the effective use of technology in the military domain, thus formalizing the debate to be known as Revolution in Military Affairs (RMA) (O'Hanlon, 2022). Because of the RMA debates, one of the most crucial conclusions was that every military organization expands its competence through new technologies, especially when weaponized to be eventually used by a command and control panel and by a professional organization.

As part of defence innovation, systematic efforts have been made to attain strategic defence outcomes. States that fail to pursue and invest in defence technological innovations, particularly when emerging technologies alter the strategic landscape of regions, will see their military balance of power shift in their favour, favouring those who boost innovation, which will throw the existing military balance of forces into disarray. Missile attacks in March 2022 and drone attacks in May 2022 were targeted at the US bases in Iraq in retaliation to the US killing of Soleimani, which is a recent example that exposes American strategic vulnerabilities as Washington blames Iran-backed militia for these attacks (Ismail and Davison, 2022; Iraq Security and Humanitarian Monitor, 2022). If armed, violent confrontations occur between a great power and a developing one, this imbalance will become even more pronounced. In other words, the success of encouraging defence innovation in one country will have far-reaching consequences for other countries, particularly incrementalistic big powers engaged in strategic competition. To become a technologically advanced superpower, the United States has pushed defence innovation. China and Russia are also investing extensively in defence research in order to compete with the United States, which accounted $801 billion as its military expenditure in 2021 (Statista Report, 2022). Chinese military expenditure amounted to $293 billion and Russia expensed at $66 billion in the same year (Maizland, 2022).

Disruptive technologies and their capabilities, however, are not uniformly distributed across the geopolitical lines. The diffusion of new and strong military technologies, as well as the capacity to use military capabilities, differs greatly between China, Russia, and the United States. In RMA, any revolutionary, creative technology is a time-consuming procedure. However, the changing nature of warfare with modern technologies has created a need for a level-playing field, fuelling deeper pursuit for innovation in the three states: China, Russia, and the United States.

Chinese Quest in Developing Dual-Use Technology

In its pursuit to become a global tech giant, China has strengthened its military, which would inevitably win them wars. In achieving so, China has embarked on a mission towards *civil-military integration* (CMI) to proliferate cutting-edge dual-use technologies. China uses several methods to encourage native technological innovations and access to foreign technology and proficiency to leapfrog in the technological innovations against the United States, Russia, and Europe. This catapulting assertiveness of China will severely impact the civilians and military in intersections of cyber and human rights, bringing to the fore the complexities of individual rights, and privacy in Chinese surveillance technologies. These surveillance technologies serve as key enablers for domestic control; however, they carry dangers in exporting such tools resounding of Chinese political and economics aspirations abroad (Binnendijk and Kirchberger, 2021).

While many countries, including the European Union (EU), neither have any coordinated strategies for promoting the advancement of indigenous technologies nor have any mechanisms to protect its indigenous innovation, China is catching up and, to some extent, even surpassing the European capabilities (Nouwens and Legarda, 2018).

In civil and military domains, technological advancements and innovations have become focal points for all the governments in advanced countries. The scale, scope, and capabilities of such innovations and modern technology continue to expand to date. The number of devices with the Internet of Things (IoT) reached 24 billion in 2020, and the estimated cost flow for the same was approximately US$6 billion (Biggs et al., 2016). The global market for AI that is utilized in robotics and systems was anticipated to reached US$153 billion in 2020 (Meola, 2018).

Xi Jinping's leadership tends to focus on policies that promote technological innovation and development (Xinhua News, 2021). In the efforts to drive China towards the 2049 centenary goal of becoming a prosperous modern socialist state and to build a highly advanced top-tier military with the capacity to win China many wars, Xi has relied on two-branched strategies that promote military modernization: by making the government-owned defence enterprises globally competitive and more efficient and by thriving on innovation and, at the same time, also seeking inspiration and increasing the innovation potentials of commercial and civil sectors. Precisely, China has been financing and investing in its determined quest to integrate emergent technologies for dual use (E.U. Council Regulation, 2009). The goal is to ensure that the People's Liberation Army (PLA) surpasses conventional military technology to accomplish its dominance across several domains. Technologies and innovations in AI, cyber domains, software, automation, and blockchain are primarily civilian in their nature and applications. However, the relevance of these innovations is proliferating in the defence sector, which will eventually determine how the wars will be fought.

Chinese Technological Innovation Toolkit

In the recent past, the Chinese government has encouraged several industrial reforms and formalized plans that emphasized indigenous development of technologies and innovations to eventually produce high-end products with emerging technologies (Schoff and Ito, 2019). Simultaneously, China has invested in its national research centres, such as the PLA Academy of Military Sciences (Aryan, 2021). The military sphere of innovations in China is at a crucial phase, considering that PLA has been undergoing a series of modernization and innovation reforms in the conventional capabilities. China has been seeking to leverage innovative, new, and emergent technologies to help China play leapfrog in its strategic competition with the United States (DoD, 2020).

The Chinese government has planned a whole-of-government slant that will enable them to close the technological gaps with the Western countries in domains such as robotics, unmanned automation, AI, quantum computing and software, space technologies, supersonics, and hypersonic weapons. It remains heavily centred at the top levels of leadership within the CCP, thus warranting an effective, systematized top-down model with the central government playing a central role in boosting innovation. The Chinese plans are centred on specific sectors at local and national levels with incentives to promote localization, productivity, and market creation. Technological innovators are thus created with the help of government funding, selective foreign investments, protectionist policies at the domestic markets, imports of talent and technology, and through acquisitions and mergers with western firms. Industrial espionage is another effective tool in the Chinese innovation toolkit (Munoz, 2015).

CMI strategies (referred to as Civil-Military Fusion; 军民融合 in China) have expanded remarkable responsiveness from the government under Xi Jinping's governance. It stimulated the ease of entry for private sector businesses into the Defence Technological Industrial Base (DTIB).

State-owned enterprises presently dominate the Chinese defence sector. With the reduction of barriers, the proliferation of the private sector in the DTIB framework is thus on an upsurge. CCP technological innovation committees are integral in more than thirty-five tech giants in China to ensure that the firm's objectives do not stray from those of the party (Feng, 2017). Nevertheless, bridging the gap between private- and public-owned enterprises remains an ongoing challenge.

In the last decade, Chinese digital technologies have become a reckoning force for the world and especially the United States. Xi Jinping, focusing on all party efforts and state achievements, has spent considerable resources in strengthening and transforming the Chinese digital architecture under a comprehensive strategy – Building Digital China (建设数字中国) (Dorman, 2022). At its initial conception, the strategy concerted most efforts in using digital technologies to improve economic efficiency, digital governance, and e-commerce. Xi's digital Fujian evolved to refurbish their visions of Digital China and also to include efforts and resources spent on digital smart weapons especially using cyber to principally improve their national competitiveness and operating efficiency and achieve national rejuvenation of a modern, socialist great power (People's Daily Online, 2020). New Type Infrastructure, a digital China mission, motioned to accelerate the new type of infrastructure in the digital and energy sectors (NDRC Political Research Office, 2021). "National informatization", as part of the overarching goals of the strategy, preliminarily gathers cyber talents. Cyber great power ambitions are one of the cornerstone strategies of Digital China. As tech war between China and US perils, leading American scholars unify in identifying China as a leading threat to their security. The CrowdStrike 2021 report highlights that a 67 percent of cyber-attacks on America emerging from China consisted of elements of state-sponsorship (CCP) intrusions, when compared to the Russian government, considered responsible for 1 percent of cyber-attacks from mid-2020 to mid-2021 (Alspach, 2022).

Russia's Strategic Technological Advancements

Russia has been carefully monitoring the technological developments in China and the United States and assessing the long-term implications while actively finding means to counter them. In this setting, Russia has been focused on aligning itself with the First Offset Strategy to counter the Pentagon's Third Offset Strategy.[2] This focus on the implementation of the First Offset Strategy implies a greater prioritization in the development of tactical and strategic nuclear weapons. It essentially means that Russia prioritizes military developments using both tactical and strategic nuclear weapons. In the strategic thought of Russia, control of sophisticated nuclear weapons will destabilize any advantages that the United States, NATO, or China has in the regions (Boston and Massicot, 2017). The basis of the Russian Defence Strategy is laid upon the strategy to ensure Russia is a nuclear superpower. Historically, Russia has never terminated its nuclear, strategic, and tactical weapons development programmes, even during its dark days in 1991 to its economic boom in the 2000s.

Russia emphasizes nuclear development as it is an inexpensive means to ensure strategic deterrence. The service wing that controls the on-ground intercontinental ballistic missiles (ICBMs) is a critical element of the Russian nuclear triad that accounts for 5 percent of their defence spending (Lenta Ru, 2015). Despite economic downturns, their nuclear projects continued to expand and grow. For instance, Russia has been innovating and deploying new ICBMs – R.S. 24 Yars and Borei standard Ship, Submarine, Ballistic Nuclear (SSBNs) missiles armed with AI technology. In addition, Russia has been developing two new categories of nuclear missiles to deter the US defence shields in Europe. Rail-based ICBM missile systems have begun in Russia and developments, advancements, and innovations in hypersonic vehicles for the ICBMs (Lenta Ru, 2016). Russia has taken strategic and non-strategic threats seriously and has always believed in preparedness through effective countermeasures to mitigate the threats, mainly from major powers such as the United States and China.

Of many extensive programmes in Russia towards military modernization, another programme emphasizes the development of an advanced version of the Tu-160 Blackjack, a strategic bomber whose production is based in Kazan. Russia has earnestly taken measures to mitigate any threat to Russia and the efficacy of the Russian Nuclear Programs by deploying and embarking on its strategic countermeasures. The Russian state-run television in 2015 reported a policy that took place in the Kremlin. This meeting discussed the advancements and presence of strategic weapons under Status 6 – a project designed to create and advance 10,000 kilometres+ ranged nuclear torpedoes that can travel great depths up to 1000 metres at an increased speed. The stated goal of this project was aimed at the destruction of coastal cities and nuclear installations (Ru, 2015). Today, Russia pays immense attention to developing, deploying, and advancing a wide array of nuclear and tactical weapons, including nuclear bombs, nuclear-powered cruise missiles, torpedoes, short-range nuclear missiles, and nuclear-powered long-range missiles.

The significant advantage for Russia in its comparative advantage over the United States is its variety and the improved quality of weapons delivery systems that can strategically warrant the effectiveness of nuclear weapons and forces for the near future in Russia.

The second element in Russian strategic technological advancements is a bit more ambitious. Russia has been countering the United States and the Chinese weapons initiatives using indigenous projects similar to one another while emphasizing a narrowed and a small-scale focus. The Advanced Research Foundation (ARF) was established in October 2012 as the Russian counterpart for the United States Defence Advanced Research Projects Agency (DARPA). The ARF aims to lay importance on research and development of high pay-off and high-risk technologies that include AI, unmanned underwater weapons and vehicles, cognitive technologies, hypersonic and supersonics, additive technologies, and energy weapons. Russia has been advancing in essential areas such as energy weapons, hypersonic weapons, and crewless underwater vehicles. These projects have received heavy financing for many years and continue to the present under ARF (Advanced Research Foundation of the Russian Federation Website).

Several Russian technological innovations are still in their infancy. The Russian military faces an insurmountable challenge in converting disruptive technologies into actual technological capabilities (Raska and Kashin, 2017). Due to the limited capacities of and strained political relations with Western countries, Russia will likely aim to forge industrial partnerships with major non-Western countries, such as China and India, to ensure stable financing and cooperation on technological projects. India-Russia relations were at a high when India and Russia jointly ventured into producing BrahMos cruise missiles. In addition, Russia and the PLA have begun joint development programmes to develop wide-body passenger aircraft and advanced heavy helicopters. The intention behind establishing and commencing two joint venture programmes with the Chinese is firm in the space industry. Chinese microchip technology will be used in liquid fuel rockets to be purchased by Russia. The negotiations surrounding the purchase are ongoing, and it is said to be the beginning of Sino-Russian friendship and cooperation.

Over the past two decades, Russian developments in the digital and the cyber domains gained momentum alongside its military modernization. As Kremlin weaponized internet, powerful cyber tools are used in pursuit of its larger strategic and political ambitions. The Soviet's "active measures" are known as "hybrid warfare" today despite carrying similar characteristics. Russian hybrid warfare phenomena are disinformation and manipulation (Soviet's strategy of active measures) to also now include broader information operations, counterfeiting, suppression of political movements, opposition, and support for insurgents (Llyod, 2021). Chief of the General Staff of Armed Forces Valery Gerasimov, centrally facilitating in including cyber as a crucial aspect of Russian Grand Strategy, in 2013 writes,

> In the 21st century, we have seen a tendency towards the blurring the lines between the states of war and peace. Wars are no longer declared, and having begun, proceed according to an unfamiliar template, thus emphasizing on the non-military vs. military ratio as 4:1, in this process, underscoring the political, social, economic measures to mitigate threats through espionage, propaganda, subversion, concertedly with cyber-attack capabilities.

In March 2022, private companies and digital organizations were called to "lock their digital doors" by Biden, citing new intelligence on Russian cyber-attacks on the United States. While such warnings appear plausible, the West is often described to fear critical infrastructural attacks, especially energy and use of disruptive software, among other digital tactics (Tidy, 2022).

The United States Defense Advanced Research Projects Agency – Innovations and Challenges

The US defence industry has been discussing an array of defence capability requirements as a top priority to invest in. Such an investment is believed to shape the United States' tactics, strategy, and its use of force in today's world (Cordesman and Hwang, 2021). The Department of Defence (DoD) endeavours technologically unique projects, operations, and organizational paradigms to help the United States sustain its military advancements and superiority over its adversaries such as China and Russia. This superiority lies in the operational[3] and the advanced levels of war,[4] thus reinforcing its conventional deterrence capacity. One such element on which the DoD emphasizes largely is institutional agility, which aims to ameliorate the capability to innovate, out-think the adversaries, and re-think its technology sources and product delivery. In the recent past, the DoD has focused its goals on integrating and streamlining the science and technology (S&T) ventures to aid sustained, long-term research and development in the essential technologies and leveraging opportunities, including cyber, emergent from the commercial division (Cooley et al., 2020). In achieving so, the DoD has used all the available and potential bases of technological advantage from a conventional industrial base to suppliers and academic circles to help conceive a comparative advantage by rendering technological capabilities into solutions that can diminish any arising coercions.

Under the Obama administration, the efforts to ensure US strategic advantage were embedded in his Third Offset Strategy. This strategy came into the public eye when presented in the 2014 Defence Innovation Initiative (DII) strategy papers. This document presented the crucial efforts undertaken by the US defence sector in its quest for innovative ways to support them sustain the US military dominance in times when the US military dominance in fragile and failed states worldwide has been decreasing due to budget constraints and the US public opinion (Walton, 2016).

The DII then stressed the revamping of the defence industry towards institutional agility that would help the United States speed its military innovation and advancements in selective areas, which includes leadership, a diverse range of research and development projects, defence management and teams, long-term projects aimed at defence innovations, and on-field and off-field invention technologies, and invigorate war-gaming efforts to advance and assess alternate means to achieve its strategic objectives of novelty in operationalization. Scilicet, the Third Offset Strategy conducted various experiments and demonstrations on the advancement and capability of weapons systems while simultaneously designing novel concepts that will operationalize and shape the US military's superiority, advancements, innovation, and tactical strategies (Pellerin, 2016).

The Trump administration, when it came into effect, was quick to discard the term "The Third Offset". Nevertheless, the Trump administration is said to have continued its programmes, priorities, and efforts to exploit technologies used in the Fourth Industrial Revolution to prolong the US military's superiority to bring unparalleled defence capabilities (Pellerin, 2015). These measures include machine learning by blending AI with autonomy to respond to cyberattacks, attacks against infrastructure, and missile attacks instantaneously. Another element of Trump's military modernization strategy is to leverage human-machine collaborations by using supercomputers to help people become faster, more efficient, and better at making decisions. In addition, Trump improved human-assisted operations by creating manned and unmanned projects' innovations. Subsequently, Trump promoted network-enabled weapon-grade systems where weapons were plugged into comprehending commands, controlling communications routes, and building intelligence. Other confidential modernization areas are linked with emergent technologies in deterrence, particularly amalgamating cyber and nuclear deterrence (Gertz, 2016).

Comprehensively, the United States continues to be a leading innovator in military modernization affairs, thus pioneering in futuristic technologies, even with the slow rate of adoption and adaptation. However, the tactical effectiveness of the US military advancement depends upon the growth in institutional agility and adaptability and upon the financial investments and incrementalistic capital to promote military modernizations. Therefore, the United States has been leveraging human-assisted operations to counter the advancements promoted by its adversaries.

The nexus of military and technological innovation has steered the genesis of modern technologies amidst the re-emergence of power competitions. The dissemination and the confluence of new technologies – nanotechnology, quantum technologies, AI, space technology, electronic miniaturization, and unmanned weapons systems – alter the course of a conflict, as seen over time. New and hybrid approaches combined with cyber forces and others have are steadily replacing the conventional warfare tactics. Emerging trends in military innovation are transforming the nature and course of the battlefield in terms of lethality, connectivity, autonomy, and sustainability (StartUs Insights, 2022; Anonymous, 2021). The patterns in the challenge, tactical responses, and adaptability define the US strategic advantages in the milieu of long-term competitions and rivalries.

Implications of the Strategic Rivalry – the United States vs. China vs. Russia

In the contemporary world, the United States, China, and Russia have continued their pursuit of novel technologies, acquisition, development, and deployment to build advantage upon one another to influence programs and the strategic decisions of their adversaries (Mahnken, 2012). Thomas Mahnken's study, "Thinking About Competitive Strategies", in the book, *Competitive Strategies for the 21st Century*, has stated that there are four distinct yet complementing strategies employed by the three countries: 1) strategies of denial, 2) cost-imposing strategies, 3) attacking a competitor's strategy, and 4) attacking the political systems of the competitor (Mahnken, 2012).

The use of denial strategies emphasizes the importance of convincing adversaries to take necessary actions to prevent them from attaining their political objectives. To deter and dissuade the rival from taking aggressive actions, cost-imposing strategies convince the rival of the high cost of such proposed actions. Such strategies also seek to reroute the rival's resources into seemingly important but strategically unimportant areas, such as economic and political areas. Attacking a competitor's strategy purposes to slim the adversary's strategic choices.

During the 1970s and 1980s, the development of the US AirLand Battle maxim persuaded Russia to realize its ability to execute a similar strategy. At present, the Chinese anti-access/area-denial (A2/AD) strategy correspondingly aims at refuting and attacking the United States' power prognostication and its sphere of influence in East Asia. Lastly, the strategies confronting the adversary's political system expect to exploit the internal factions within the systems to one's comparative gain. For instance, during the Cold War era, the United States launched its Strategic Defence Initiative (SDI) that augmented the debates with the leadership of the Soviet Union on the direction, characterization, finance, and the strategic advantage gained in competing with the United States in its space development and exploration projects (Mahnken, 2012).

The features of the contemporary engagement between Washington, Moscow, and Beijing suggest all four competitive strategies discussed earlier. Nevertheless, there are many contested debates on the diverse strategic vistas regarding the goals, objectives, and strategic motivations that indulge the great powers in the race. Central to the challenged debates are the following questions:

1 To what gradation do the three adversaries aim to maximize their hard power to achieve security, great power status, and the ability to influence geopolitical outcomes?
2 Does economic interdependence ensure peace and stability compared to intensifying economic competition and rivalry, thus increasing insecurity to propel China and the United States to seize and control access to wealth?
3 Do territorial and maritime disputations, when combined with hypernationalism, have the potential to escalate disputes?
4 Do disseminating values, ideologies, visions, culture, heritage, and history create a shared sense of identity, thus leading towards cooperation or reflecting an apparition of economic, political, and perhaps ideological cohesion between the adversaries?
5 Lastly, do multilateral institutions, frameworks, and norms intersect regional and global security interests towards stability and peace, or do they propagate and propel one another to seek decision-making powers to control the multilateral institution's rules, agendas, and norms to shape the prevailing world order?

(Friedberg, 1996; Pempel, 2012; Allison, 2015; Mazarr, 2018)

Great power competition is revived and combined with intense arms modernization and innovating military technologies. It indicates that conflicts and wars are neither inexorable nor unthinkable. In any case, confrontations between great power rivals possessing nuclear arsenal with a precise strike system can be considered as escalatory risks. Contemporarily, great powers are engaged in aggressive strategies and avoid any scenario leading to catastrophic wars. Instead, the great powers are engaged in diplomatic, non-military, economic cooperation, information exchange, peacetime collaboration, and paramilitary operations to gain a comparative advantage of territory and influence without engaging in any significant wars or conflicts (Gunzinger et al., 2017).

Indirect actions between adversaries include information warfare, cyber-infrastructure, political systems attacks, electronic attacks, and military operations and drills in disputed territory. The complex nature of cyber and information operativeness is manifested in inter-domain and cross-domain exchanges between cyber and other information spheres in civil and military realms. Such confrontations include cyber-attacks on political systems, attacking critical infrastructures, cyberspace attacks, and cyber espionage. The United States, Russia, and China have been competitively expanding their cyber capabilities with offensive, defensive, and AI-driven measures to combat and mitigate this threat. These modern warfare instruments are considered enablers and force multipliers for kinetic operations in land, air, sea, and space.

The complexity in such operations, exchanges, interactions, and interdependency across various sectors presents a new set of challenges to the conventional notions of warfare. According to Michael Raska, the interlinkages in military and civil elements of combat through evolving technologies such as quantum, blockchain, AI, nanotechnology, and software present certain challenges: 1) cross-domain deterrence and compellence (CDD&C) and 2) unbalanced A2/AD challenges severely affect modern warfare characteristics in the world and, especially in the Asia-Pacific region (Raska, 2019).

CDD&C denotes the deterrence of an act in one sector with a threat mitigation measure from another sector. In short, it implies that threats on the conventional and the non-conventional domains such as land, sea, air, space, and cyber may often be combined with tools such as economic, political, and diplomatic sanctions. This helps the United States, Russia, and China in deterrence. The adversaries are dissuaded from taking any offensive action, and coercive sanction will influence the rival to stop an act of aggression. Therefore, coercive measures across multiple spheres help influence an adversary's strategic choices (King, 2018).

India, however, is yet to formulate a comprehensive cybersecurity strategy and doctrine despite increased regional instability and a greater knowledge of the variety of cyber dangers it faces. China and Pakistan have increased their cyber-attacks on India as strategic rivalry in South Asia and the Indo-Pacific region has grown. Critical infrastructure in India, including nuclear power plants, electricity grids, telecommunications systems, hospitals, and financial institutions, has been the subject of cyber-attacks by both state and non-state actors. A rising number of people believe that China and Pakistan are working together to coordinate cyber-attacks in order to harm and disrupt India's vital industries, most recently during the post-Galwan crisis when Indian security agencies were placed on high alert (Bommakanti et al., 2023).

The Indian tactics of using emerging technologies, which will be discussed further in this book, should be aware of how the changes in the nature of war brought about by evolving technology should facilitate the conduct of war rather than causing it to happen on its own. Therefore, technology needs to be more effectively integrated to provide capabilities and command and control systems. The key to making technology available for successful military campaigns, whether defensive or offensive, will be integration rather than simple capabilities.

Subsequently, when deliberating on how such emergent technologies and modern warfare can affect the Indo-Pacific security arrangements, militaries have to cognize the changing nature of the Sino-US strategic rivalry. US allies in the region, Japan, Australia, and Singapore, are planning the potential involvement of the United States in emerging conflicts in South China and the East China seas vis-à-vis China. The degree of the United States' involvement will depend on the intensity of the conflict and the capacity of US allies to deter China. The nature of future conflicts is said to be grey zones that have high risks of escalations. In this context, new challenges emerge when a conflict zone is crowded with combatants and non-combatants. Military advancements, revolutionizing of military affairs, and technological innovations will not be effectual without structural, strategic, and operational adaptability. Discovering new and emergent opportunities for military innovation is essential. However, the changing military stance is essential to instantaneously respond to military, technological, and geostrategic shifts to hotbeds such as Asia, and Eastern Europe particularly gaining momentum, and largely around the world (Davis, 2000).

Eventually, the propagation of emergent technologies shaping military advancements is studied in a comparative arrangement using the lens of indulgent competitive military strategies and their efforts to polish operative deterring responses and countermeasures. Emerging technologies, however, are only disruptive to the degree that they will alter the nature of war: they will quicken the pace at which it is carried out, increase the degree of distance between enemies, and open new channels for the escalation and de-escalation of conflict. However, the essence of war will continue to be one that simply puts political objectives ahead of how the conflict is fought.

With strategic ambiguity in the region and growing insecurities in the international system, the United States, China, and regional actors must re-evaluate their theories of victory. In conclusion, new and emerging technologies will increasingly mould conflict and deterrence's strategic choices in the 21st century, thus driving the need for operational and strategic innovations to prepare, fight, win, and deter emerging conflicts.

Notes

1 China repeatedly mentions the term "Cold War mindset" in their official documents and press statements. See also, Foreign Ministry Spokesperson Zhao Lijian's Press Conference on 30 June 2022 (www.fmprc.gov.cn/mfa_eng/xwfw_665399/s2510_665401/202206/t20220630_10713185.html).
2 The Third Offset Strategy of the United States implemented in 2016 aims at improving and bolstering next-generation technologies to strengthen conventional deterrence capabilities, thus ensuring wars don't happen, says the Deputy Secretary of Defense, Bob Work (www.defense.gov/News/News-Stories/Article/Article/991434/deputy-secretary-third-offset-strategy-bolsters-americas-military-deterrence/).
3 Operational level of war is understood as a blueprint consisting of setting of intent, mission-readiness, and heavy planning designed to achieve larger strategic goals.
4 Advanced levels of war comprise fourth-generation (political warfare) and fifth-generation warfare involving cyber-attacks, autonomous weapons systems, social engineering, bio-war, and AI.

References

Advanced Research Foundation of the Russian Federation Website (2012). *Areas of Work*. Retrieved from https://fpi.gov.ru/projects/

Allison, G. (2015). The Thucydides Trap: Are the U.S. and China Headed for War? *The Atlantic*. Retrieved from www.theatlantic.com/international/archive/2015/09/united-states-china-war-thucydides-trap/406756/

Alspach, K. (2022, August 8). Russian Hackers Get Headlines, But China Might Be the Bigger Threat. *Protocol*. Retrieved September 2, 2022, from www.protocol.com/enterprise/china-hacking-ip-russia-cybersecurity

Anonymous. (2021). The Longer Telegram-Toward a New American China Strategy. *Atlantic Council*. Retrieved from www.atlanticcouncil.org/content-series/atlantic-council-strategy-paper-series/the-longer-telegram/

Antonopoulos, P. (2021, February 27). Disinfo Lab Report Reveals How Pakistan and Turkey Use the U.S. for Information War against India. *Greek City Times*. Retrieved from https://greekcitytimes.com/2021/02/19/disinfo-lab-pakistan-turkey-india/

Aryan, J. (2021, August 18). How China Aims to Augment Its Military Strength Using A.I. *Observer Research Foundation*. Retrieved July 5, 2022, from www.orfonline.org/expert-speak/how-china-aims-to-augment-its-military-strength-using-ai/

Azrael, J. R., and Payin, E. (1996). U.S. and Russian Policymaking with Respect to the Use of Force. *RAND Corporation*. Retrieved July 7, 2019, from www.rand.org/pubs/conf_proceedings/CF129.html

Barthwal. (2022, February 11). Information Warfare and India's Level of Preparedness. *Centre for Land Warfare Studies*. Retrieved September 30, 2023, from www.claws.in/information-warfare-and-indias-level-of-preparedness/

Bendett, S., Boulegue, M., Connolly, R., Konaev, M., Podvig, P., and Zysk, K. (2021, September 21). Advanced Military Technology in Russia. *Chatham House*. Retrieved April 10, 2022, from www.chathamhouse.org/2021/09/advanced-military-technology-russia

Biggs, P., Garrity, J., LaSalle, C., and Polomska, A. (2016). Harnessing the Internet of Things for Global Development. *International Telecommunication Union*. Retrieved September 4, 2022, from www.itu.int/en/action/broadband/Documents/Harnessing-IoT-Global-Development.pdf

Binnendijk, H., and Kirchberger, S. (2021, March). The China Plan: A Transatlantic Blueprint for Strategic Competition. *Atlantic Council*. Retrieved November 16, 2021, from www.atlanticcouncil.org/wp-content/uploads/2021/03/The-China-Plan-A-Transatlantic-Blueprint.pdf

Bommakanti, K., Nachiappan, K., Joshi, Y., Mohan, S., and Vats, A. (2023, May 8). *Emerging Technologies and India's Defence Preparedness*. Observer Research Foundation. Retrieved September 30, 2023, from www.orfonline.org/research/emerging-technologies-and-indias-defence-preparedness/

Boston, S., and Massicot, D. (2017). *The Russian Way of Warfare- a Primer*. RAND Corporation. Retrieved August 21, 2020, from www.rand.org/pubs/perspectives/PE231.html

Boulanin, V., Brockmann, K., and Richards, L. (2020, November). Responsible Artificial Intelligence Research and Innovation for International Peace and Security. *Stockholm International Peace Research Institute (SIPRI)*. Retrieved March 3, 2021, from www.sipri.org/publications/2020/other-publications/responsible-artificial-intelligence-research-and-innovation-international-peace-and-security

China Briefing. (2022, August 29). *US-China Relations in the Biden-Era: A Timeline*. Retrieved September 2, 2022, from www.china-briefing.com/news/us-china-relations-in-the-biden-era-a-timeline/

Christensen, T. J. (1996). Chinese Realpolitik. *Foreign Affairs*, 75(5), 37. https://doi.org/10.2307/20047742

Cooley, W., Hahn, D., and George, J. (2020, February 7). *Adapting for Victory: DOD Laboratories for the 21st Century*. National Defense University Press. Retrieved June 9, 2021, from https://ndupress.ndu.edu/Media/News/News-Article-View/Article/2076025/adapting-for-victory-dod-laboratories-for-the-21st-century/

Cordesman, A., and Hwang, G. (2021, August 3). Updated Report: Chinese Strategy and Military Forces in 2021. *Centre for Strategic and International Studies*. Retrieved September 5, 2021, from www.csis.org/analysis/updated-report-chinese-strategy-and-military-forces-2021

Davis, P. (2000). Defence Planning in an Era of Uncertainty: East Asian Issues. In N. Crawford and C.-I. Moon (Eds.), *Emerging Threats, Force Structures, and the Role of Air Power in Korea* (pp. 25–47). Santa Monica, CA: RAND.

Department of Defense. (2020, September 1). Military and Security Developments Involving the People's Republic of China 2020 [Annual Report to Congress]. *Department of Defense*. Retrieved March 28, 2021, from https://media.defense.gov/2020/Sep/01/2002488689/-1/-1/1/2020-DOD-CHINA-MILITARY-POWER-REPORT-FINAL.PDF

Department of Justice. (2020, July 21). Two Chinese Hackers Working with the Ministry of State Security Charged with Global Computer Intrusion Campaign Targeting Intellectual Property and Confidential Business Information, Including COVID-19 Research. *Office of Public Affairs*. Retrieved January 6, 2021, from www.justice.gov/opa/pr/two-chinese-hackers-working-ministry-state-security-charged-global-computer-intrusion

Dorman, D. (2022, March 28). China's Plan for Digital Dominance. *War on the Rocks*. Retrieved September 13, 2022, from https://warontherocks.com/2022/03/chinas-plan-for-digital-dominance/

Doyle, T., and Rumley, D. (2019, December 13). The New "Multiplex" Cold War in the Indo-Pacific. In *The Rise and Return of the Indo-Pacific* (pp. 45–67). https://doi.org/10.1093/oso/9780198739524.003.0004

European Union. *Council Regulation (E.C.) No. 428/2009 of 5 May 2009 Setting Up a Community Regime for the Control of Exports, Transfer, Brokering and Transit of Dual-Use Items*. Retrieved from http://trade.ec.europa.eu/doclib/docs/2009/june/tradoc_143390.pdf

Feng, E. (2017). Chinese Tech Groups Display Closer Ties with Communist Party. *Financial Times*. Retrieved from www.ft.com/content/6bc839c0-ace6-11e7-aab9-abaa44b1e130

Foreign Ministry Spokesperson Zhao Lijian's Regular Press Conference on 30 June, 2022. (2022, June 30). *Ministry of Foreign Affairs of the People's Republic of*

China. Retrieved July 23, 2022, from www.fmprc.gov.cn/mfa_eng/xwfw_665399/s2510_665401/202206/t20220630_10713185.html

Friedberg, A. (1996). Warring States: Theoretical Models of Asia Pacific Security. *Harvard International Review*, *18*(2), 12–68.

Gerasimov, V. (2013, February 13). Ценность науки в предвидении | Еженедельник "Военно-промышленный курьер". *Russian Media*. Retrieved April 14, 2021, from https://vpk-news.ru/articles/14632

Gertz, B. (2016). Pentagon Developing Pre-Launch Cyber Attacks on Missiles. *The Washington Free Beacon*. Retrieved from https://freebeacon.com/national-security/pentagon-developing-pre-launch-cyber-attacks-missiles/

Gunzinger, M., Clark, B., Johnson, D., and Sloman, J. (2017, October 2). *Force Planning for the Era of Great Power Competition*. Center for Strategic and Budgetary Assessments (CSBA). Retrieved February 10, 2021, from https://csbaonline.org/research/publications/force-planning-for-the-era-of-great-power-competition

Iraq Security and Humanitarian Monitor: May 19–26, 2022. (2022, May 26). *OCHA Relief Web*. Retrieved July 11, 2022, from https://reliefweb.int/report/iraq/iraq-security-and-humanitarian-monitor-may-19-26-2022#:~:text=On%20May%20 24%2C%20air%20defense,U.S.%20and%20International%20Coalition%20nations

Ismail, A., and Davison, J. (2022, March 14). Iran Attacks Iraq's Erbil with Missiles in Warning to U.S., Allies. *Reuters*. Retrieved September 9, 2022, from www.reuters.com/world/middle-east/multiple-rockets-fall-erbil-northern-iraq-state-media-2022-03-12/

Kavanagh, C. (2019, August 28). New Tech, New Threats, and New Governance Challenges: An Opportunity to Craft Smarter Responses? *Carnegie Endowment of International Peace*. Retrieved September 28, 2020, from https://carnegieendowment.org/2019/08/28/new-tech-new-threats-and-new-governance-challenges-opportunity-to-craft-smarter-responses-pub-79736

King, M. (2018). New Challenges in Cross-Domain Deterrence. *RAND Perspective*, no. 259. Retrieved from www.rand.org/content/dam/rand/pubs/perspectives/PE200/PE259/RAND_PE259.pdf

Lee, C. M. (2016). *Fault Lines in a Rising Asia*. Washington, DC: Carnegie Endowment for International Peace, 190.

Lenta Ru (2016, April 21). В России испытали гиперзвуковой управляемый боевой блок для баллистических ракет (Russia Has Tested a Hypersonic Re-Entry Vehicle for Ballistic Missiles). *Lenta.Ru*. Retrieved from https://lenta.ru/news/2016/04/21/agbo/

Lenta Ru (2015, November 11). *В Кремле прокомментировали кадры телеканалов с засекреченной системой Статус-6 (Kremlin Comments on TV Channels Reports on the Secret)*. Retrieved from https://lenta.ru/news/2015/11/11/oops/

Llyod, G. (2021, October 10). Hybrid Warfare and Active Measures. *Small Wars Journal*. Retrieved September 10, 2022, from https://smallwarsjournal.com/jrnl/art/hybrid-warfare-and-active-measures

Mahnken, T. (2012). Thinking about Competitive Strategies. In T. Mahnken (Ed.), *Competitive Strategies for the 21st Century*. Stanford: Stanford University Press.

Mahnken, T. (2017). A Framework for Examining Long-Term Strategic Competition between Major Powers. *SITC Research Brief*. Retrieved from https://escholarship.org/uc/item/0754362r

Maizland, L. (2022, June 14). China and Russia: Exploring Ties between Two Authoritarian Powers. *Council on Foreign Relations*. Retrieved September 4, 2022, from www.cfr.org/backgrounder/china-russia-relationship-xi-putin-taiwan-ukraine

Mazarr, M. (2018). *Understanding the Emerging Era of International Competition: Theoretical and Historical Perspectives*. Santa Monica, CA: RAND Corporation, 33.

Mazarr, M. (2020, April 15). Toward a New Theory of Power Projection. *War on the Rocks*. Retrieved September 1, 2020, from https://warontherocks.com/2020/04/toward-a-new-theory-of-power-projection/

Meola, A. (2018). What Is the Internet of Things (IoT)? Meaning & Definition. *Business Insider*. Retrieved from http://uk.businessinsider.com/internet-of-things-definition

Ministry of Information and Broadcasting. (2021, December 21). India Dismantles Pakistani Coordinated Disinformation Operation. *Press Information Bureau*. Retrieved May 30, 2023, from https://pib.gov.in/PressReleasePage.aspx?PRID=1783804

Mishra, V. (2020, September). From Trump to Biden, Continuity and Change in the U.S.'s China Policy. *ORF Issue Brief*. Retrieved September 13, 2022, from www.orfonline.org/research/from-trump-to-biden-continuity-and-change-in-the-uss-china-policy/

Munoz, A. G. (2015). Review: Chinese Industrial Espionage: Technology Acquisition and Military Modernization. *Studies in Intelligence*, *59*(4). Retrieved from www.cia.gov/library/center-for-the-study-of-intelligence/csi-publications/csi-studies/studies/vol-59-no-4/chinese-industrial-espionage-technology.html

NDRC Political Research Office. (2021, November 17). 【一图读懂 ｜ 新型基础设施建设重点】–国家发展和改革委员会. *NDRC Political Research Office*. Retrieved November 27, 2017, from www.ndrc.gov.cn/xxgk/jd/zctj/202111/t20211117_1304251.html?code=&state=123

Nouwens, M., and Legarda, H. (2018, December 18). China's Pursuit of Advanced Dual-Use Technologies. *International Institute for Strategic Studies*. Retrieved June 17, 2020, from www.iiss.org/blogs/research-paper/2018/12/emerging-technology-dominance

O'Hanlon, M. E. (2022, March 9). A Retrospective on the So-Called Revolution in Military Affairs, 2000–2020. *Brookings*. Retrieved May 14, 2022, from www.brookings.edu/research/a-retrospective-on-the-so-called-revolution-in-military-affairs-2000-2020/

Pellerin, C. (2015). Work: Human-Machine Teaming Represents Defence Technology Future. *Department of Defence News*. Retrieved from www.defense.gov/News/News-Stories/Article/Article/628154/work-human-machine-teaming-represents-defense-technology-future/

Pellerin, C. (2016). Deputy Secretary Discusses Third Offset, First Organizational Construct. *Department of Defence News*. Retrieved from www.defense.gov/News/News-Stories/Article/Article/951689/

Pempel, T. J. (2012). Security Architecture in Northeast Asia: Projections from the Rearview Mirror. In *Security Cooperation in Northeast Asia: Architecture and Beyond* (pp. 212–232). New York, NY: Routledge.

People's Daily Online. Illustration: Construction of "Digital China" General Secretary Xi Jinping's Layout. (2020, October 13). *People's Daily Online- the Communist Party of China News*. Retrieved December 29, 2020, from http://cpc.people.com.cn/n1/2020/1013/c164113-31890179.html

Pezard, S., and Rhoades, A. (2020). What Provokes Putin's Russia? *RAND Corporation*. Retrieved September 13, 2021, from www.rand.org/pubs/perspectives/PE338.html

Poonawalla, S. (2023, January 26). How PM Modi's "DESI" Formula Will Ensure India Leads Industry 4.0. *Times of India Blog*. Retrieved from https://timesofindia.indiatimes.com/blogs/rebel-with-a-cause/how-pm-modis-desi-formula-will-ensure-india-leads-industry-4-0/

Raska, M. (2019). Strategic Competition for Emerging Military Technologies: Comparative Paths and Patterns. *PRISM*, *8*(3), 64–81. Retrieved from www.jstor.org/stable/26864277

Raska, M., and Kashin, V. (2017). Countering the U.S. Third Offset Strategy: Russian Perspectives, Responses and Challenges. *RSIS Policy Report*. Retrieved from www.rsis.edu.sg/rsis-publication/idss/countering-the-u-s-third-offset-strategy-russian-perspectives-responses-and-challenges/#.Ybi35L1Bzre

Rim, H. J. (2023, January). The US-China Strategic Competition and Emerging Technologies in the Indo-Pacific Region: Strategies for Building, Dominating, and Managing Networks. *Asian Perspective*, 47(1), 1–25. https://doi.org/10.1353/apr.2023.0000

Ru. (2015, November 11). "В Кремле прокомментировали кадры телеканалов с засекреченной системой Статус-6 (Kremilin Comments on TV Channels Reports on the Secret)," Lenta.Ru, November 11, 2015, https://lenta.ru/news/2015/11/11/oops/

Schoff, J., and Ito, A. (2019, October 10). Competing with China on Technology and Innovation. *Carnegie Endowment for International Peace*. Retrieved September 14, 2022, from https://carnegieendowment.org/2019/10/10/competing-with-china-on-technology-and-innovation-pub-80010

Sevastopulo, D., and Hille, K. (2021, October 16). China Tests New Space Capability with Hypersonic Missile. *Financial Times*. Retrieved November 13, 2021, from www.ft.com/content/ba0a3cde-719b-4040-93cb-a486e1f843fb

StartUs Insights. (2022, September 7). *Top 10 Military Technology Trends for 2022*. Retrieved September 14, 2022, from www.startus-insights.com/innovators-guide/top-10-military-technology-trends-2022/

Statista. (2022, August 5). *Countries with the Highest Military Spending 2021*. Retrieved September 8, 2022, from www.statista.com/statistics/262742/countries-with-the-highest-military-spending/#:%7E:text=The%20United%20States%20led%20the,dollars%20dedicated%20to%20the%20military

Tanwar, C. S. S. (2020, July 27). Disruptive Technologies: Impact on Warfare & Their Future in Conflicts of 21st Century. *Centre for Land Warfare Studies*. Retrieved June 4, 2022, from www.claws.in/disruptive-technologies-impact-on-warfare-their-future-in-conflicts-of-21st-century/

Tidy, B. J. (2022, March 22). The Three Russian Cyber-Attacks the West Most Fears. *BBC News*. Retrieved September 13, 2022, from www.bbc.com/news/technology-60841924

U.S. Department of Defense. (2022, November 29). *2022 Report on Military and Security Developments Involving the People*. Retrieved September 30, 2023, from www.defense.gov/News/Releases/Release/Article/3230516/2022-report-on-military-and-security-developments-involving-the-peoples-republi/

Walton, T. (2016). "Security the Third Offset Strategy – Priorities for the Next Secretary of Defence," Joint Forces Quarterly, 3rd Quarter, 6–15; Chuck Hagel, "Memorandum – The Defence Innovation Initiative," Office of the Secretary of Defence, Washington, DC. Retrieved from www.defense.gov/News/News-Stories/Article/Article/603658/

The White House. (2017). *The National Security Strategy 2017*. Washington, DC: The White House. Retrieved from https://trumpwhitehouse.archives.gov/wp-content/uploads/2017/12/NSS-Final-12-18-2017-0905.pdf

The White House. (2022a, January 21). Fact Sheet: Biden-Harris Administration Actions to Attract STEM Talent and Strengthen Our Economy and Competitiveness. *The White House*. Retrieved from www.whitehouse.gov/briefing-room/statements-releases/2022/01/21/fact-sheet-biden-harris-administration-actions-to-attract-stem-talent-and-strengthen-our-economy-and-competitiveness/

The White House. (2022b, February). *Indo-Pacific Strategy of the United States*. Retrieved September 30, 2023, from www.whitehouse.gov/wp-content/uploads/2022/02/U.S.-Indo-Pacific-Strategy.pdf

The White House. (2022c, July 30). Background Press Call on President Biden's Call with President Xi Jinping of the People's Republic of China. *The White House*. Retrieved September 13, 2022, from www.whitehouse.gov/briefing-room/press-briefings/2022/07/28/background-press-call-on-president-bidens-call-with-president-xi-jinping-of-the-peoples-republic-of-china/

Work, R. (2015). The Third U.S. Offset Strategy and Its Implications for Partners and Allies. *Department of Defence*. Retrieved from www.defense.gov/News/Speeches/Speech/Article/606641/the-third-us-offset-strategyand-its-implications-for-partners-and-allies/

Xinhua News. (2021, May 29). Xi Focus: Xi Stresses Sci-Tech Self-Strengthening at Higher Levels. *Xinhua Net*. Retrieved February 14, 2022, from www.xinhuanet.com/english/2021-05/29/c_139976311.htm

Zhao, M. (2019). Is a New Cold War Inevitable? Chinese Perspectives on U.S. – China Strategic Competition. *The Chinese Journal of International Politics*, *12*(3), 371–394. https://doi.org/10.1093/cjip/poz010

4

NON-TRADITIONAL SECURITY + DATA

The Road Not Taken

Arun Teja Polcumpally

Introduction

Phrases like 'data is the new oil' (Joris Toonders, 2014) and 'data is the new nuclear power' (Bridle, 2018) have become common in advocating the geopolitical analysis of data. These terms are often used by the public, scholars, and technocrats to reiterate the importance of data. It has become a general knowledge that data is a fundamental functionary of emerging digital technologies (Polcumpally, 2021).[1] There are thousands of articles and books available providing a detailed description of how data-related technologies impact modern society.

Without giving a repetitive description of digital technologies and their impact on society, this chapter will brief future impacts of data-related technologies on the power of the state. The chapter, in its initial section, explains how digital technologies would acquire the capacities of perception control. The explanation is derived from the works of Jamie Susskind and Yuval Noah Harari. The explanation of perception control will be sufficed with the work of Cambridge Analytica's whistleblower, Christopher Wylie, and describes how data will become a new weapon for the authoritarians within democracies. This chapter aims to provide a vivid understanding of how data-related digital technologies will impact the future of political stability, culture, and, in turn, how it will impact the emerging non-traditional security aspects.

Note that the data in this chapter refers to digital data, which is created, stored, extracted, and derived from various digital activities.

Importance of Data and the Threat to Democracies

Human knowledge is a result of tacit and explicit knowledge acquired by years of experiences. These experiences are nothing but data gathered during

DOI: 10.4324/9781003482703-6

the lifetime to understand the human environment. Humans have a limit to their lifetime, but robots do not. Robots, with the accumulation of centuries of data, can excel in explicit and tacit knowledge in their own way.[2] This throws us the question of whether machines will become superior to humans. If machines indeed become intelligent, will the future socio-political structures offer them an unprecedented agency? What kind of risks would the current socio-political structures face, and how to make decisions to lower the negative impact? These are the questions that governments worldwide are focusing on. Governments across the world are still in the initial phase of making regulatory policies regarding these digital technologies. All across the world, data legislations are being focused on as they will be the foundation on which other technology regulations would be built. In other words, 'data' has been securitized. More details on the aspect of securitization have been provided in Chapter 3. By securitizing the data, states, worldwide, assert that it has become one of the pillars of defining national power. Traditionally, nuclear weapons decided the ultimate weapon and power of a state. Perhaps, nuclear weapons have to share their position of importance with the data.

An anecdotal comparison brings more clarity on how important the data is in shaping national power. One day, Michael Faraday made a sales pitch to William Gladstone. He was explaining his recent research on electricity and trying to convince Gladstone that it would be the future. When Gladstone asked, what is the immediate business use of electricity, Faraday did not have a market plan on the existing economic models. Instead, he said that "there is every possibility that you will soon be able to tax it" (Susskind, 2018, p. 5). Decades from now, electricity has become a fundamental technology used in our daily lives. Similar to Susskind, Jeff Bezos, Amazon founder and CEO, compares digital platforms like Amazon Web Services and Google to electricity.

> Jeff Bezos, Amazon's chief executive officer, compares it to electricity provision: whereas early factories had each its own power generator, eventually electricity generation became centralised and rented out on an 'as needed' basis.
> *(Srnicek, 2017, p. 39)*

Similar to electricity, data is used in every emerging digital technology product. Digital platforms are used by every firm that aims for digital transformation. Data is a crucial fundamental in governance, politics, education, healthcare, and so on. Data will become as important as electricity in human lives. As mentioned earlier, data has become a fundamental functionary of the digital society. We see its ever-pervasive nature and its expanding usage. Yet, we do not yet know its complete impact on national security or socio-political structures. Even if it is known, it is not measured.

A research report published by Brookings has listed technologies under the categories – Moderate Impact, High Impact, and Revolutionary Impact. Table 4.1 shows a list of technologies and their subsequent impact on the military affairs.

TABLE 4.1 Technology Impact According to Brookings Report

Technology Segment	Moderate Impact	High Impact	Revolutionary Impact
Sensors			
Chemical sensors		X	
Biological sensors		X	
Optical, infrared, and UV sensors	X		
Radar and radio sensors	X		
Sound, sonar, and motion sensors	X		
Magnetic detection	X		
Particle beams (as sensors)	X		
Computers and communications			
Computer hardware			X
Computer software			X
Offensive cyber operations			X
System of systems/Internet of Things			X
Radio communications	X		
Laser communications		X	
Artificial Intelligence/Big data			X
Quantum computing		X	
Projectiles, propulsion, and platforms			
Robotics and autonomous systems			X
Missiles	X		
Explosives		X	
Fuels	X		
Jet engines	X		
Internal-combustion engines	X		
Battery-powered engines		X	
Rockets		X	
Ships	X		
Armor		X	
Stealth		X	
Satellites		X	
Other weapons and key technologies			
Radio-frequency weapons	X		
Non-lethal weapons		X	
Biological weapons		X	
Chemical weapons		X	
Other weapons of mass destruction	X		
Particle beams (as weapons)	X		
Electric guns, rail guns		X	
Lasers		X	

Source: Adapted from O'Hanlon (2019)

In Table 4.1, any innovation in the conventional areas of technology such as ships, armory, fuels, missiles, internal-combustion engines, and the like make less impact on the military affairs, while technologies like battery-powered engines, chemical and biological sensors, and quantum computing make high impact. Technologies such as Artificial Intelligence (AI), robotics, Internet of Things (IoT), computer hardware and software, and offensive cyber operations are considered to bring revolution in the military affairs. All the high impact and the revolutionary impact technologies are digital technologies. All of them have data (with varying precision) as their fundamental functionary.

As discussed earlier, these data-based technologies are pervasive in the society. Even the advanced researches from US and Chinese militaries are focusing on these data-based technologies. It is hoped that this chapter lays a foundation before asking the reader to think more on the new security issues that arise in the future and how military should become more flexible to expand its operations beyond the borders. Importantly, rather than traditional security, data-based technologies create non-traditional security threats.

The current sensors and IoT devices can extract granular behavioral data that includes how a user uses the internet, where they look at their screen while browsing, and their places of visit, what kind of news they read, hospital visits, financial restrictions, and so forth. All of these data points when analyzed using advanced AI systems will help to catalog individuals. If such data of one country is in the hands of another country, the entire population and its behavior will be in their hands. It can be interpreted and manipulated. For India, the Digital Personal Data Protection (DPDP) Act, 2023, provides an undue advantage to the central government of India to take personal data from the companies. The collection of the data does not pose any threat to the freedom of citizens. However, the blanket usage of the collected data does pose a threat. As per the V-Dem report of 2021 and 2022, India is sliding in the democracy rankings; in such a scenario, one would assume that the data collected by the government can be used for the political advantage of certain parties or businesses. These are the kinds of non-traditional security threats that the data-based technologies bring.

In order to delve more into a conceptual argument of how important data is, Harari's *Homo Deus* and Jamie Susskind's *Future Politics* will be referred to in the subsequent sections of this chapter. Susskind's work gives a descriptive account of how the future of politics intertwines with digital technologies. Harari, on the contrary, provides a conceptual and philosophical account of how anthropomorphism is taking over the lives of all individuals. The following section gives an account of both the works to describe how pervasive data-based technologies are and how important it is for the military to have cognizance of it.

Susskind and Harari on Data Technology

Inferences of Impact of Digital Technologies From the Work of Jamie Susskind

Susskind strongly opines that advanced digital technologies with AI algorithms will control the lives of every individual. He does not say that computers would rule the world. He rather opines that people or entities that control these technologies will effectively control the digital life world. Following is an excerpt from the work of Jamie Susskind showing the latter argument:

> [E]ven if no particular person or group can be said to be 'in charge' at a given time, humans will be constantly subject to power from many different directions, constraining and guiding their behavior. That's the essence of power in the future.
>
> *(Susskind, 2018, p. 99)*

The control of society by those who operate the technology that defines most of the socio-economic activities is not uncommon. Before the internet, the scope and extent of the control were always limited. In general, control over individuals or power over them can be exerted by force or coercion (Hart, 1976, p. 291). With the limited scope and control, both types of power exertion – force and coercion – will be limited to the political boundaries. With the advent of the internet, information and data have been available across the world. In such a scenario, data-based technologies gain the capacity to change the nature of power.

> [H]ow we gather, store, analyze and communicate the information, in essence how we organize it, is closely related to how we organize our life. Digital life . . . pose a pretty fundamental challenge to how we have historically thought about the use of force.
>
> *(Susskind, 2018, p. 121)*

> The final way to exert power over people, without subjecting them to force or scrutiny, is to control what they know, what they think, and what they prepared to say about the world. A good way to get someone to refrain from doing something is to prevent them from desiring it in the first place.
>
> *(Susskind, 2018, p. 142)*

The aspect of power mentioned in these excerpts is known as perception control. This perception control can be exerted without any political boundary constraints. Only those that have complete control over the digital platform can assert such cross-border control over perceptions. (Hrudka,

2020) opines that Facebook cloaks its data practices by projecting itself as a democratizing platform. Srnicek (2017) argues that digital companies aim to become monopolies in the global market by providing digital platforms to service providers. The arguments that Facebook discretely accesses personal data and these platforms aim to become monopolies support each other. Not only private companies but also with the control of data and information, militaries can launch psychological warfare. Hard power that is mostly consisting of military's arm power will no longer be the defining attribute of national power. Because psychological warfare does not need military equipment like tanks, guns, battleships, and fighter jets, all it needs is a firm grip on the nation's behavior and a medium to input narratives tactically, favoring the host country.[3] This psychological war is completely a soft power.

Such shift in the nature of war is possible because it is difficult for public to log out of their devices and live in a physical world devoid of any digital interference. The continuous digital footprint of an individual makes it easy for the data aggregator like Google to understand and influence the behavior. As people depend more on the digital applications, the results that those applications provide will shape the decision-making of public. This is how data aggregators control the public. All the search engine results will depend on the digital footprint left behind by the individual. All these developments reiterate Susskind's conclusion that the one who controls these technologies will dictate the world, which appears to be viable one.

While Susskind showed a dangerous picture of how data-based technologies can make our society a complete panopticon, Harari provided a conceptual and philosophical backing for these fears. His take on how democracy gets into shambles and how dictatorship can dominate the states across the world gives more food for the thought on the importance of data. If the state or even non-state actors control the information, narratives, and services offered to public, liberalism, the concept and theory on which Western countries base their development, might no longer be sensible. The following section delves into an analytical inference on Harari's work.

Inferences From the Work of Harari

Harari's account of how control over information results in the control of human behavior is a good example to understand the dangerous impact of data control. Unlike Susskind, Harari explains how the devolution of agency from humans to machines is being carried out. This agency devolution has to be a known decision for the stable socio-political conditions. The following discussion delves into the possibility that machines can become more intelligent than humans.

Data as the Fundamental Attribute in the Evolution of Highly Intelligent Animals

While explaining the origin of intellect, emotion, or any feelings, Harari convincingly establishes that these are the result of the million years of stored experiences (Harari, 2016, p. 101). For example, an emotion of feeling attracted, fear, and indifference is the result of biochemical reactions within the body (Harari, 2016, p. 97). The decision of fear or love is an amalgamation of experiences collected and transferred by the genes. According to Harari, these are nothing but a set of complex algorithms evolved from millions of years. If today's data can capture subjective interpretation of a living being possible, then the creation of an artificial superintelligence is also possible. The important fact to note here is that data is the fundamental aspect. Earlier, nature has coded the algorithms, and the results are visible only after thousands of years. Now that the data can be artificially infused, quantum computing speed-training and generating complex algorithms becomes easier. The resulting products might be unimaginable.

Another aspect where numerous arguments are found is the hyphenation of consciousness and intelligence. For replacing many of the human-related actions, consciousness is not necessary. Describing this organized life, Harari espouses that with the super computing power, intelligence and consciousness are getting separated (Harari, 2016, p. 361). When intelligence is not same as consciousness, and can be achieved externally, even machines can be made intelligent. Playing chess, driving cars, teaching, and policing of public needed high intelligence when compared to other living beings on the earth. Well, now these tasks are being done by machines. Harari opines that the thinking of humans always having a unique ability that machines cannot reach is a wishful thinking.

Now we understand that data analysis, when coupled with ever-growing technologies, can even overtake all intelligent work. They can perform stock market analysis, manage wealth, prescribe medicine, construct houses, and be drivers, educational aids, and baking mechanisms. These are the areas where the world has already seen some development. The combination of Susskind's perception control and Harari's extreme analysis of AI systems poses an uncertain future in the conduct of national security.

Building on this context of data and its ability to create intelligent systems, the disturbance data and its related technologies in democracy are discussed. This is one of the most pressing issues to national security worldwide. The data that we talk about in the subsequent section is not a superficially generated one. It is a given by all the individuals using digital services across the world. The analysis performed on this data will lead to thought manipulation, misinformation propaganda, and so forth. If the earlier discussed possibilities of AI-led perception control becomes reality, there is a risk of democracy becoming a façade. The revealed work of Cambridge Analytica in 2018 shows the disruptions caused to the democratic political system by the existing data analysis algorithms. The revealing of Cambridge Analytica's data porting from Facebook and its machine learning algorithms profiling groups and manipulating the public behavior shook democracies worldwide. Cambridge Analytica has made it clear that in the data-based society, democracy no longer works well in the traditional sense.

The Case of Cambridge Analytica

Political campaigning in democracies is always about how the electoral candidates win the hearts of the public. Candidates undertake campaigns to push forward their agenda and election manifesto. Incidents like manipulation of public opinion, biased propaganda, and wooing public on the sentiment of religion, race, and ethnicity are generally observed. All of these tactics were overtaken by machines in the Cambridge Analytica's line of work.

In 2016 US presidential elections, Cambridge Analytica attempted to influence public behavior using their personal data. It used data of American citizens without their knowledge and consent. According to a whistleblower, the data is used to tap their behavior and mold according to the Republican Party's electoral gains (Wylie, 2019). Before the 2016 presidential elections, Steve Bannon, who was later appointed as National Security Advisor to President Donald Trump, was the principal investor in this company. After launching Cambridge Analytica's application on M-Turk of Amazon, Steve Bannon was awestruck to know that they can literally pull out life details of any individual residing in the US (Wylie, 2019, p. 110). Each of the board member has taken turns to call a random individual to verify the correctness of the data pulled by their application. All of them were successful and thus started the psychological war against the freedom to choose their elected representatives.

This data was not only used by Cambridge Analytica but was shared with Palantir technologies, as well. Palantir serves US federal and state governments providing them big data analysis (Wylie, 2019, p. 113). That means that what Cambridge Analytica had, the same was with the US government and most probably their intelligence agencies.

During the 2016 US presidential elections, Donald Trump and Ted Cruz were alleged to spend nearly $5 million each to Cambridge Analytica (Wylie, 2019, p. 140). The whistleblower Christopher Wylie also alleged that John Bolton, who is National Security Advisor for the term of 2018–2019, has paid Cambridge Analytica $1 million to explore the ways to encourage militarism in American youth (Wylie, 2019, p. 141). Not just the Americans but also Russians used this firm to reiterate how strong Vladimir Putin is. As per the account of Christopher Wylie (2019),

Cambridge Analytica also influenced Nigerian elections aiding Goodluck Jonathan in an ugly manner.

After Donald Trump won the presidential election, Steve Bannon was appointed as his National Security Advisor. He had with him the most powerful weapon, Cambridge Analytica. It has the information on every citizen in the US. Back then, there was no privacy law restricting the collection of data. Christopher Wylie feared that Bannon is nearing to create a deep state. This was the fear of America from the eyes of London whistleblower, not far away from the year 2021, when this book was being prepared. Not just in the American election, but the trend of using advanced tools to dictate electoral outcomes is used worldwide, as well. There are many companies like Cambridge Analytica that also assist governments in carrying out espionage legally and illegally for political ends. Following is an excerpt from Indian print media alleging the Modi government of accessing Pegasus software to snoop over the opposition.

> Modi govt. hunting for a new spyware with a lower profile than that of Pegasus: Cong.
>
> *(The Hindu Bureau, 2023)*

This is the headline in an article published by the Indian print media *The Hindu*. The opposition party accuses that the Directorate of Defense Intelligence has acquired some equipment from an Israeli company, Cognyte, which allegedly develops spyware similar to Pegasus. In another article, *The Wire* accuses Bangladesh of acquiring spyware from Israeli firms. Allegedly, it acquired spyware worth US$12 million during 2019–2022, the latest being the purchase of a 'spy van' from Passitora firm. Spyvan can intercept all communications from electronic devices within a stipulated range of the van. It also includes private messages. Passitora is reported in the research conducted by The Citizen Lab at Munk School of International Affairs, Canada. It is alleged as a mercenary surveillance company. Other company names associated with Passitora are Cytrox, Intellexa, Aliada group, Wispear, and Mirtach Shamir. Not just Bangladesh, but there are numerous government clients for Passitora and its subsidiaries, as well. According to a report released by the Organized Crime and Corruption Reporting Project (OCCRP), clients of a similar spyware company NSO include Azerbaijan, Bahrain, Hungary, India, Indonesia, Kazakhstan, Mexico, Morocco, Rwanda, Saudi Arabia, Togo, and United Arab Emirates. On January 10, 2023, the US Supreme Court allowed WhatsApp to pursue the lawsuit against Pegasus. Earlier, Pegasus filed a petition arguing that it is serving the government. This shows that governments are increasingly using surveillance to uphold their power. All these reports argue that the democratic behavior of the states is slowly vanishing with the heavy usage of digital surveillance.

The concept of mass surveillance and remote control is usually found in dystopian novels like George Orwell's *1984*, Adolf Huxley's *Brave New World*, Ray Bradbury's *Fahrenheit 451*, and Margaret Atwood's *The Handmaid's Tale*. Internet-based digital technologies give enormous capabilities to those who control them. Digital technologies like facial recognition systems and pattern recognition software are increasingly used by the state to capture the granular data on an individual level. Pegasus, a software product developed by an Israeli company, NSO Group, is an example for a software used by the state for surveillance. This software can hack any smartphone or internet-connected device and access its programs without the user's knowledge. It can toggle the camera and microphone, access the files and browsing history, and so forth. There are allegations that the foreign states are using Pegasus to surveil US and other friendly nations. Owing to the latter, the US commerce department has put the NSO group on the blacklist, usually reserved for politically hostile countries. A similar incident has happened in India, and its Supreme Court has ordered an independent committee inquiry into the government usage of Pegasus.

If this is one extant misuse of digital technology and the data, China uses it to make Orwellian policies. Australian Strategic Policy Institute (ASPI) reported that China uses invasive surveillance technologies that infringe Uyghur's dignity of life. Its *predictive policing system* alerts the Xinjiang officials about the possible dissidents when the Uyghurs receive a foreign phone call from an unexpected visitor. It leads to prompt inspections by officials or grassroots informants. There are also reports claiming that China uses facial recognition technology to spot Uyghurs anywhere in the country and alerts the officials regarding the potential threat. The AI technology used in facial recognition helps China to stamp an ethnic group as a threat to the nation. It appears that these technologies strengthen authoritarian governments and undermine democracy. Whatever the output may be, almost all the major powers of the world are vying to have an upper hand in developing advanced digital technologies, especially with AI. It is seen that democracies are increasingly adopting surveillance technologies and moving against democratic norms. Data regarding spyware equipment cannot be attained. However, the digital technology equipment trade can be traced, and it can be correlated with the rising repressive behaviors of the states worldwide.

Way Forward for India

The United Nations had already declared in March 2018 that Facebook was responsible for the mass killings of Rohingya Muslims in Myanmar (Wylie, 2019, p. 226). The military personnel had started online hate propaganda against Rohingya Muslims, and they leveraged the public right-wing sentiment to commit crimes.

> By labeling their architectures as 'services', they are trying to make responsibility lie within customer, through their 'consent'.
>
> *(Wylie, 2019, p. 236)*

Such is the malicious use of data. Without stringent data protection law and other regulations, a country would lose its liberty. While considering the extreme sides of the technologies that use data, and the capabilities of perception control, it would be better for India to take a cautious approach in data regulation. There is an increasing uproar worldwide regarding the protection of data privacy. However, in India, the term 'privacy' has a different understanding. Survey-based research concludes that in India, 'privacy' is understood as private space and home (Kumaraguru et al., 2005). In addition, digital data is generally not considered to be private. It is not possible for an individual to control their digital footprint (Altshuler, 2019). This can be heuristically observed. People easily exchange their phone numbers for the shopping offers they get. An example of such an exchange is giving away phone numbers at billing counters.

Further, numerous applications make data-sharing consent necessary. It is essential to understand that necessary consent cannot be an individual's choice. In such a situation, data privacy does not hold in strict terms. Not just in India, but this is the reality of the digital world, as well. Daniel Solove (2021), professor of law at the George Washington University Law School, asserts that data laws should not focus on privacy but on how information is used, maintained, and transferred. It appears that the Indian government was quick to recognize this aspect and decided to focus on how to streamline the data flow. Accordingly, India launched a trustable data exchange architecture called Data Empowerment and Protection Architecture (DEPA).

DEPA has been launched for the public to easily share their data with various financial organizations to get their services. DEPA empowers people to seamlessly and securely access their data and share it with third-party institutions (NITI Aayog, 2020). Note that it does not provide any framework for the companies detailing which data must be made mandatory and what kind of data security features must be followed. For the latter, a data protection bill has to be passed. DEPA focuses on how an individual can access existing data with a financial institution and share the same with others.

The excerpt from DEPA shows the stand of the Indian government on data sharing. DEPA provides a general framework for all sectors by encouraging the establishment of consent managers liaising between the data providers and the data users.

> *[I]f India's data governance framework focuses solely on increasing protection and at the cost of enabling secure and granular data sharing only with user consent, we will start to entrench further the data silos controlled by large data fiduciary companies, effectively allowing them to use our data in their competitive interests rather than ours.*

However, the document emphasizes one specific segment – financial data streamlining. In this sector, RBI has already rolled out the Account Aggregator (AA) model to decentralize the financial data of Indian residents (not only citizens). It provides an Application Programming Interface (API) that automates the data exchange while blinding the consent managers on the actuality of the data. Importantly, it is mentioned that these APIs are to be updated regularly as per technological advancements and societal requirements. Such language shows that India is aware of the rapid developments happening in digital technology and is ready to launch a flexible framework.

Speaking of financial data streamlining, having a one-stop address for financial data provides micro, small, and medium-scale enterprises (MSME) and individuals loans without credit scores. The DEPA document mentions a 'Credall' start-up that uses AA API and connects lenders and borrowers. Such innovations in providing credit at an affordable interest would help many to start their own business. Leapfrogging on this idea, aAs can also help an interface to connect individuals across the country and allow them to become lenders and borrowers.

DEPA does not create a government body to aggregate all the financial data. It only provides a framework and encourages private businesses to operate. This essentially makes a new business segment pave a new entrepreneurial path. Further, the work of educating new financial information providers, users, and potential aAs about the DEPA architecture and providing technical support for institutions to go live has been given to a non-profit organization – Sahamati. This shows the deviation of government from state-controlled to market-oriented behavior.

The DEPA framework appears to result from best practices borrowed from China and the West. Chinese Communist Party (CPC) provides guidelines and leaves the specifics of implementations to the provincial governments. But it will have strict oversight and decision-making control over all the significant socio-economic aspects. The US provides legal frameworks but does not provide frameworks on how the data should be stored and accessed. The framework leaves those aspects to the market. India's DEPA is a combination of centrally issued guidelines, leaving the execution without strict government control to the private industries.

DEPA is argued to be a facilitator of business. An issue brief published by Observer Research Foundation highlights that the data is reusable, and DEPA provides easy portability of data across platforms. It also argues that DEPA provides user control over the data. However, data portability probably does not come under the data rights for Indian legislators. The ease of data portability and the absence of any mention on the same in DPDP Act 2023 shows that the government is rejecting to consider the privacy and related issues. As mentioned in the introduction, privacy is understood differently by the public and perhaps even by policymakers.

Though it appears that DEPA is an innovative framework crafted specifically for India, it draws heavily from Personal Data Store (PDS) that is being developed in the European Union (EU). This concept has been explained in the book *Data Ethics: The New Competitive Advantage* released in 2016. It is safe to assume that the concept is known to the EU legislators before 2015, and start-ups were also working on it. The DEPA framework has been released in 2020, and only RBI has adopted it. Even while writing this chapter in 2023, no government framework was released. It has been seven years since a similar framework is released by the EU, and still Indian legislators are grappling with the question of how to make a framework.

DEPA helps individuals to access and selectively share their data. However, it does not convey whether the data sharing will be mandatory to provide services by companies. If the data sharing is made necessary, consent becomes meaningless.

The DEPA framework is undoubtedly capable of becoming an alternative to the world's data protection and access systems. However, DEPA has its barriers. Smartphones should become ubiquitous to roll out this API-based framework to all the residents of India. As mentioned in the DEPA discussion paper, every segment has to develop its consent management frameworks. Sectoral development would require multi-disciplinary policy research. Anticipatory Governance approach can be used to conduct ex ante research on the confluence of 'data access to the businesses' and 'socio-economic impact'. Ex ante research includes iterations of risk assessments and public deliberations. After conducting ex ante research, it would be better if sector-specific consent management APIs are tested in different cities. Such testing would bring a competitive spirit among the entrepreneurs accelerating policy innovations.

Smart devices would soon become a general household commodity with the rapid growth of internet-powered devices and 5G communication. In such a situation, the DEPA framework would help use the digital footprint of Indian residents to economic advantage. Accountability and transparency, as a business desideratum, appear to be promising deliverables of this framework.

Conclusion

In conclusion, this chapter has explored the critical intersection of data, technology, and national security, highlighting the potential implications and challenges associated with the ever-increasing data-driven landscape. It has become evident that in the digital age, data is a powerful tool that can be harnessed for both constructive and destructive purposes, and its management, access, and control are crucial for safeguarding democracy and individual rights.

The chapter began by emphasizing the vast amount of granular behavioral data that modern sensors and IoT devices can capture, providing insights into various aspects of individuals' lives. When harnessed and analyzed using advanced AI systems, this data has the potential to shape and manipulate perceptions, presenting a new frontier of non-traditional security threats. The introduction of the DPDP Act 2023 in India underscored the importance of regulating data collection and usage to protect citizen freedoms.

The works of Jamie Susskind and Yuval Noah Harari were invoked to illustrate the profound implications of data-based technologies. Susskind's argument that those who control advanced digital technologies will wield significant power over society aligns with the evolving landscape of data-driven influence. Harari's conceptual exploration of the evolution of intelligence and consciousness through data highlighted the transformative potential of data in creating artificial superintelligence.

The chapter has also delved into real-world examples of data misuse, including the case of Cambridge Analytica, which demonstrated how data analysis could manipulate public opinion and disrupt democratic processes. In addition, it highlighted the global trend of governments and companies using surveillance technologies to enhance control, which poses a challenge to democratic norms.

The way forward for India, as presented in the chapter, suggests a balanced approach. India recognizes the need for data sharing and innovation, as evidenced by DEPA. DEPA's focus on enabling secure and granular data sharing while maintaining user consent aligns with India's aim to balance data protection with economic growth. Furthermore, the government's decision to encourage private businesses and non-profit organizations to operate within the DEPA framework reflects a shift toward a market-oriented approach.

However, it is crucial to note that the understanding of privacy in India may differ from Western perspectives, which may influence the legislative approach. The chapter has highlighted that data portability, a key aspect of data rights, might not align with Indian legislators' priorities.

In summary, the chapter underscores the need for vigilance and thoughtful regulation in the data-driven era to ensure the protection of individual freedoms, democratic processes, and national security. As data continues to play a central role in shaping societies and economies, striking a delicate balance between innovation and safeguarding rights remains a paramount challenge for governments and societies worldwide.

Notes

1 A detailed description of the emerging data-based information technologies brings changes horizontally across all the sectors of society, which has been provided in the author's previous work.
2 Assume that there is no restriction on the computational power.
3 Host country here is the one that is perpetrating the cyber-attacks in order to gain control over public behavior.

References

Altshuler, T. S. (2019, September 27). Privacy in a Digital World. *TechCrunch*. Retrieved from https://techcrunch.com/2019/09/26/privacy-queen-of-human-rights-in-a-digital-world/?guccounter=1&guce_referrer=aHR0cHM6Ly93d3cuZ29vZ2xlLmNvbVS8&guce_referrer_sig=AQAAAKgZ3X5mViKlUXJx69te8c7RPhuaf011 2mxNIyJ0ImeYT8n4nrH_QBcJB_k3kWluLVtxj852FJGwrc_JnSBfBHC2-1

Bridle, J. (2018, July 17). Data Isn't the New Oil – It's the New Nuclear Power. *ideas.ted.com*. Retrieved from https://ideas.ted.com/opinion-data-isnt-the-new-oil-its-the-new-nuclear-power/

Harari, T. N. (2016). *Homo Deus*. London: Vintage.

Hart, J. (1976). Three Approaches to the Measurement of Power in International Relations. *International Organization*, 289–305.

Hrudka, Orysia. (2020). 'Pretending to favour the public': how Facebook's declared democratising ideals are reversed by its practices. AI & SOCIETY. 38. 1-11. 10.1007/s00146-020-01106-8.

Joris Toonders, Y. (2014). Data Is the New Oil of the Digital Economy. *Wired*. Retrieved from www.wired.com/insights/2014/07/data-new-oil-digital-economy/

Kumaraguru, P., Cranor, L. F., and Newton, E. (2005). Privacy Perceptions in India and the United States: An Interview Study. The 33rd Research Conference on Communication, Information, and Internet Policy (TPRC) (pp. 1–13). Retrieved from www.researchgate.net/profile/Ponnurangam-Kumaraguru/publication/265675845_Privacy_Perceptions_in_India_and_US_A_Mental_Model_Study/links/5b7fa7eba6fdcc5f8b6382d7/Privacy-Perceptions-in-India-and-US-A-Mental-Model-Study.pdf

NITI Aayog. (2020, August). Data Empowerment and Protection Architecture. *niti. gov.in*. Retrieved from www.niti.gov.in/sites/default/files/2020-09/DEPA-Book.pdf

O'Hanlon, M. E. (2019). Forecasting Change in Military Technology, 2020–2040. *Brookings*. Retrieved from www.brookings.edu/wp-content/uploads/2018/09/FP_20181218_defense_advances_pt2.pdf

Polcumpally, A. T. (2021). Artificial Intelligence and Global Power Structure: Understanding through Luhmann's Systems Theory. *AI & Society*. https://doi.org/10.1007/s00146-021-01219-8

Solove, D. J. (2021). The Myth of the Privacy Paradox. *George Washington Law Review*, 89, 1.

Srnicek, N. (2017). *Platform Capitalism*. Cambridge: Polity Press.

Susskind, J. (2018). *Future Politics*. Oxford: Oxford University Press.

The Hindu Bureau. (2023, April 11). *Modi Govt. Hunting for a New Spyware with a Lower Profile than that of Pegasus: Cong*. Retrieved from https://www.pressreader.com/india/the-hindu-coimbatore-9WW4/20230411/282733411147521

Wylie, C. (2019). *Mind Fu*k: Inside Cambridge Analytica's Plot to Break the World*. London: Hachette India.

PART II

5

ARTIFICIAL INTELLIGENCE AND ITS PROBABLE MILITARY DISRUPTIONS

Vedant Saigal

Introduction

The importance of data-based technologies has been discussed in the earlier chapter. It is clear that the adoption of those technologies will bring unprecedented change in societies, and the impacts are heuristically seen in the Indian military. These military developments are majorly seen in the 21st century's economic powers – the US and China. Scholarly journals assert that the two technological and economic superpowers – the US and China – are investing heavily in developing Artificial Intelligence (AI)-based military equipment (Allen and Chan, 2017; China Institute for Science and Technology Policy, 2018; Polcumpally, 2021). Recognising the rising investments, this chapter explores the impact of AI on the Indian military. To put the reader into perspective, initially, the author has given a brief about AI and then provides a description of its military implications.

AI, when it achieves its pinnacle, is called superintelligence. If such feat is achieved, Irving Good, a well-known mathematician who worked along with Alan Turing, argued it to be the greatest invention of mankind. It might be the last invention, as some say (Walch, 2020). Stalwarts like Stephen Hawking and Elon Musk also have a similar opinion that making thinking minds would pose a threat to the existence of mankind (Jones, 2014). Following are some quotes from speeches of Elon Musk, who opines regulating AI development is necessary.

AI is far more dangerous than nukes.

(Clifford, 2018)

DOI: 10.4324/9781003482703-8

> The rate of improvement is really dramatic, but we have to figure out some way to ensure that the advent of digital super intelligence is one which is symbiotic with humanity . . . I think that's the single biggest existential crisis that we face, and the most pressing one.
>
> *(Forrest, 2018)*

However, this chapter assumes that AI can be used for the betterment of mankind. AI development cannot be restricted. The world is bound to witness leap-forward advancements in digital technologies. In other words, the evolution of mankind can be timelined alongside AI development. In general, technology has always been a crucial part of living and has been revolutionising over time (Skeen, 2021). On the whole, AI will be a key to global economic development.

Artificial Intelligence

Since the invention of the computers, the performance of the troops at various tasks increased exponentially. To peek deeper inside the modern advancements, let's understand the growth of AI at the first place. The father of AI, John McCarthy, defines the field as "the science and engineering of Making Intelligent machines, especially Intelligent Computer Programs" (Nilsson, 2010). AI has experienced several waves of optimism since it was founded as an academic discipline in 1956.

The continuous development of technologies, mathematical logics, and cybernetics, as well as the improvement of hardware components, laid a sort of theoretical, technical, and ideological foundation for the development of AI research. AI is simply a branch of computer science that alternates human intelligence in performing certain tasks through machines; for instance, problem-solving, logical reasoning, and language understanding. Terms like 'machine learning', 'neural network', 'deep learning', and 'Bayesian network' narrow down the whole concept of AI. The advent of neural networks brought AI to a more mature stage, hence finding its presence in both the domains of civilian and military.

AI has its impacts horizontally across all the sectors. It recognises speech in various languages and even diagnoses the health conditions of patients in a hospital. The usage of AI in transportation industry has given rise to autonomous vehicles like Tesla. The manufacturing industry has given rise to robots that work efficiently and faster than humans without exhaustion. In sports, AI can be used to analyse and determine an athlete's or a team's performance. A wide range of applications that did not exist before are possible now because of AI. AI has made a tremendous impact on the aforementioned industries or sectors and has contributed to their overall productivity. AI does not always have productive impacts. Since AI totally revolves around cyberspace, it might be prone to attacks and hacks from different sources. In order to prevent these hacks or to minimise their potential, the securitisation of the cyberspace becomes necessary.

For instance, there have been several accidents when people were driving the Tesla car. It was observed by the National Highway Traffic Safety Administration that hundreds of car accidents were linked to autopilot technologies and were totally linked to Tesla (Saul, 2022).

Taking a cue from the impacts of AI on numerous sectors, many countries are drafting national AI strategies. With the advancements in digital technology, the world has become cautious about cybersecurity. To mark the regulatory developments in AI, it has now been four years for China since it had established a Next-Generation Artificial Intelligence Development Plan. The document published by the People's Republic of China (PRC) reiterates that it wishes to grab the first-mover advantage in the field of AI, regardless of the technical know-how currently (Ministry of Science and Technology, 2017). Chapter 3 explicitly shows the technology tussle between the US, China, and Russia. Similar to the narrative of China, Russian President Putin has openly said that whoever controls AI will control the world (Vincent, 2017). Such open declarations indicate that countries across the world need to focus on the AI domains to make investments in future for its overall advancement. However, it may not be necessary for countries to follow what China has implemented. The desired developmental goals should be implemented simultaneously by looking at the national requirements.

In 2020, the Indian government unveiled the outlay for the Digital India initiative to boost AI, cybersecurity, and as well as robotics (Online, 2019). Biometric identification, criminal investigation, and traffic and crowd management are some of the great examples in which India is immensely progressing (Shah, 2020). Another relevant example could include the development of Centre for Artificial Intelligence and Robotics (CAIR), which happens to be a laboratory of the Defence Research and Development Organization (DRDO), that has boosted the development of mission-critical products or battlefield communication systems (Topychkanov, 2020). The introduction of these initiatives has helped enhance the traditional techniques that were used to monitor criminal networks and threat data. They help the government to create hypotheses in order to analyse future threats and criminal attacks. These initiatives directly impact India's national security and increase government transparency and public services. It can be simply put into relevance by stating an example of 'one hundred smart cities' – a vision of the Government of India – that essentially aims at calling for a robust cloud computing backend that is intertwined with real-time surveillance and also as techniques of data analytics. Now that the overall relevance and the Indian government's focus on developing AI are established, the subsequent sections will discuss the implementation of AI in the armed forces.

The Role of Artificial Intelligence in the Armed Forces

AI is reported to turn the year 2020 US defence market valued at USD 2335.1 million to USD 16423.09 million in 2026 (Mordor Intelligence, 2019–29). Not just in the US market, AI investments are seen across all developed countries. AI has defined how the combat capabilities of armed forces are getting ready to absorb and equip technology (Maxwell, 2020). It has signified its role in the battlefield both for operational and logistic functions. The application of AI in the modern battlefield can empower weapons that are autonomous and high-speed. In the realm of AI and national security, the US Navy and Army have already made efforts to create virtual reality systems to help soldiers train efficiently and enhance their combat techniques. Looking at the scientific evolutions of the future, many countries have created a sense of priority in using AI in battle-space superiority (Lele, 2011).

Naval Operations

AI and other technological advancements have made their mark on the seas as well. From detecting the hydrostatic pressure to determining the oceanic salinity, unmanned technological advancements make an indispensable asset to the Indian Navy. To explore the uses of AI in the navy, let us take an example. The oceanic topography is often difficult to map. It becomes difficult for researchers and ocean explorers to examine what lies deep inside and to study its properties. The oceans are indeed a whole new world together that is yet to be explored. This is where mechanical innovations and the role of AI come in; it is opined that if one can assess the seabed without going there, it is a significant achievement (Snyder, 2018). AI-based systems help in executing, detecting, calculating, and charting the best actions for vessels, ultimately augmenting existing nautical capabilities (Mukherjee, 2018).

Considering the fact that AI has many potential uses for the Navy, the hype is certain to increase in the coming years. Undoubtedly, if the world witnesses maritime warfare, it is likely that the AI-based battleship will have an advantage. However, the consequences must be kept in mind when deploying AI on the battlefield. If the ship is autonomous, the foremost consequence could be the opposition of the naval officials working on board as the AI model acts as a replacement for their profession. Though this is a fictional case, it emphasises the toggle switch where certain or necessary functions will be switched to manual. Appropriately, the operational paradigms and tactics must be revamped to promote multi-vehicle deployment and, most importantly, man-machine teaming.

Air Force

The discussion will no more be about how AI is to be used in the Air Force, as it has already secured its place in the Air Force. Let's consider an example of the US Air Force equipment powered by AI. It uses the flying boom system, which, with the help of the Boeing-built KC-46 tanker, can refuel any fixed-wing receiver capable aircraft in air itself or when on any mission (Boeing, 2021). In an in-air demonstration in 2007, it was clearly shown by the Defence Advanced Research Projects Agency (DARPA) that high-performance aircraft could easily perform automated refuelling from conventional tankers. It was not fully automated as the pilot had to set the conditions and safety measures during autonomous refuelling operation (Thomas et al., 2014). However, it shows the possibility of having unmanned refuelling aircrafts in the near future.

Another most relevant example is the Skyborg system of the US, which can pilot a robotic wingman. It was indeed a proud moment for the US that the advanced robot brain could fly a Kratos-built Mako drone fighter in the same manner as it was expected to. It is predicted that in no time, this autonomous system will be used alongside human-inhabited planes during several missions (Atherton, 2021).

As far as the Indian Air Force is concerned, Swarm Drones (Smart War-Fighting Array of Reconfigured Modules) have recently outsmarted China (Upadhyay, 2021). However, the claim of outsmarting China can be contentious. India had paraded 75 swarm drones on the occasion of Army Day (National, 2021). These Swarm Drones successfully eliminated various targets (Hambling, 2021). These specific drones are capable of protecting and wreaking havoc deep inside the enemy camps and, at the same time, are also careful of the lives of the civilians. If the number of UAVs increase, it becomes obvious that Swarm Drones content will also increase. It has been noticed that if the number of UAVs increases, it will also lead to an increase in the potential of the Swarm.

In January 2018, Russia's Khmeimim airbase in western Syria was attacked with a collaborative drone strike. It is observed that it was the first time the world saw a swarm drone warfare. It has been reported by the Russian Defence Ministry that the drones used improvised air-dropped munitions during the attacks. They operated autonomously, possessed a range of 30 to 60 miles autonomously, and were possibly launched from the village of Muwazaara (TRIPwire, 2018).

The victory of the Azerbaijan in the six-week long war that broke out with Armenia was indeed successful through the usage of the drones. The war still continues, and it has been observed that Armenia is gaining upper hand in some regions. Unfortunately, for Armenia, it is believed that there is a little alternative, as Azerbaijan dominated the battlefield and annihilated forces opposing them. Much of their success perhaps lied in the effectiveness of their newly acquired drone fleet (Eckel, 2020).

It is interesting to know that the world has witnessed a rapid increase in the number of investments by the countries in such advancing technologies. The US stands at the leading position currently, followed by other countries like Russia, China, and the UK (Ayoub and Payne, 2015).

Army

Lethal Autonomous Weapon Systems (LAWS) do not require any physical human intervention to detect, analyse, and engage the target. It, however, just requires certain algorithms. India should consider adopting Unmanned Combat Aerial Vehicles/Unmanned Ground Vehicles in order to fight in urban areas and combat terrorist threats. This mechanised warfare will generally undergo a paradigm shift in this modus operandi with the development of the Infantry Combat Vehicles (ICVs). A classic example is the termination of the Iranian nuclear scientist Mohsen Fakhrizadeh by a remote-controlled machine gun.

Indian soldiers operate in difficult terrain and harsh weather conditions over long distances. Exoskeleton is an example of such gadgets that are worn as harness by a soldier to augment their strength. India has gone through the most anti-IED operations in which AI robots have been involved. This technology has also been used in the mining and de-mining operations in the conventional scenarios (Jadhav, 2021).

Other Uses of Artificial Intelligence in Armed Forces

Semiotics, simply, is the study of signs, symbols, and their use of interpretation in a given field. There have been several talks about semiotics and AI, and one example is provided next. In his address ('The Birth of a Word') to the audience, Deb Roy talks about how he used the technique of capturing moments of his family members inside his house through video cameras installed, to understand how a child learns. He specifically focused on his infant son's ability to slowly turn from speaking 'gaga' to 'water'. His message suggested to explain if this method could be used in AI functioning, in order for it to enable machines to learn languages on its own and hence becoming able to communicate with humans eventually (Roy, 2011).

From the Deb Roy experiment, it is clear that certain groups will communicate only in certain languages. Similarly, it can be noticed that machines communicate when they are told to in their language. But, how can humans communicate in a language that machines understand? Semiotics is one useful concept in which symbols are used to decrypt or encrypt the language to be used for machine learning.

The concepts of AI and semiotics are sort of intertwined. John Locke, an English philosopher, sort of knotted the advancement of intelligence into a combination of three steps: understanding the nature of things, analysing what must be the steps taken to achieve what is desired, and the ability to spread the message and communicate these things to others (Posner et al., 1993). Semiotics can be reduced to simpler understanding based on John Locke's propositions in the advancement of intelligence. Here is the construct of Semiotic AI for this chapter:

> The technique of understanding the nature, analysing the process of creation of relations, communicate the process to humans, ability to recreate the process for certain outcomes.

Semiotic techniques can be applied in the military to design self-learning machines. However, the war robots or any other weaponry system that acts on the battlefield powered by AI will require human command and monitoring as well. Human supervision is required until foolproof and universally accepted AI ethics are developed. It must be kept in mind of the Indian military officials that human and machine interfaces have to be intertwined and dependable on function properly.

Challenges

The main question that lies is whether the armed forces have enough resources to develop the AI infrastructure. No doubt that these artefacts, which generate a sense of pride, establish a spillover effect providing economic benefits to the public. Though it is believed that this may beautify the heritage of the country, it is not of much importance in the current scenario. The policy makers must realise that the world is now living in a catastrophic situation, in which it becomes increasingly necessary for India to focus on its national security as well as economic development, through (perhaps) foreign direct investments (FDIs). These FDIs should be encouraged in the segment of military AI. India is already moving in this direction. Defence sector is opened up to 90% for Indian private sector participation, with FDI up to 26%, subject to licensing (Ministry of Defence, 2020). With the recent AI stack documents and AI strategy released by the Government of India, the Ministry of Defence should release its white paper on the usage of AI. Without a white paper, it would be difficult for private players or innovators to put efforts on a specific technology.

India's efforts at AI research and development are comparatively nascent. Since China is on a rapid pace of AI development, India must look through the lens of AI advancement for the progress in military. Undeniably, it will be a moiling work for the Indian government to move forward with the AI approach, whether it is the drafting of the policies, creating roadmaps, or even establishing an industrial base for hardware. There must be a prodigious thrust to catch up with the aligned and desired trajectory (Nilsson, 2010).

AI will make it much easier for the military officials to detect and neutralise the target; however, looking at the other side, there might be severe consequences. As a matter of fact, we are taking an example of a terrorist who has an innocent identical twin; his life can be put into danger with the technologies that work with AI.

AI altogether is not at all perfect and, hence, requires a lot of examination and practical testing. Simple challenges might include being able to be fooled by hackers, being brittle on working only in the context trained for and not performing well in the real-time scenarios. It can also happen that AI-capable technology cannot transfer the same knowledge to different tasks or systems. Also, most importantly, working only based on large datasets, it must be continuously monitored. It is necessary that AI must be teamed with the human brain for it to be more efficient and successful in completing its given task. Since there are multiple challenges involved, the evolution of AI and its advancements should be monitored and examined carefully, in order for it to provide the necessary beneficial outcomes. AI, hence, has become a part of our lives and cannot be separated anymore. It can be said that the survival of AI and humans perhaps go hand in hand.

This team can start working on making an AI system right from scratch. As it is already mentioned that semiotics can be used to make the machine learn like a child, AI weapon systems can also learn the processes of military. Ethics, constitutional rights of citizens, global norms, and the like can be taught. It is not difficult to even teach the machine to identify the emotions and lifestyle and segregate the lookalike terrorist and the real terrorist. Having said that, semiotics when combined with AI can bring along fruitful outcomes for the military. For instance, when assessing maps in the military, it may require an understanding of the combination of different symbols that represent various movements, surrounding environments, and as well as types of manoeuvres. These symbols can help the army officials to analyse maps, when provided with a certain system that possesses a full knowledge of those signs and symbols.

Future Prognosis

The world is entering a new era of warfare (Shankar, 2022). The 'new era of warfare', known as the 'modern warfare', is mainly information-driven, AI-enabled, and drone-based system of warfare that encompasses the advancing domains, such as cyberspace and as well as outer space. The modern warfare is influenced through the traditional warfare systems and modified with high levels of intelligence and technologies. Though it can be said that

AI is changing the military, making it faster, smarter, and efficient, it also acts like a dual-sided sword, opening the prospects of danger (Pant, 2018). It is definitely a matter of immediate concern that the political leaders must emphasise. It is assumed that warfare might get started without human decisions and can escalate to disastrous events, in which humans perhaps will not be able to interfere. Although it is highly unlikely that the full spectrum war might take place, there still stands a possibility of a nebulous war that would undoubtedly be technologically driven. For instance, the kinetic war was strengthened when Russia deployed its KUB-BLA drones, which essentially identify targets using AI. There was even a wave of cyberattacks in Russia and the disinformation campaign against Ukraine that together demonstrate the critical role of these technologies in the modern warfare (Scroxton, 2022). It is pivotal for countries to embrace AI within a decade or two as it will play the role of a protagonist in war management.

In this era of nuclear weapons, it becomes crucial to keep up with the pace of the technological developments that are rapidly speeding up in the entire world. Otherwise, there might be a possibility that the Autonomous Weapon System will likely gain dominance and play the role of a protagonist in the warfare of the near future. The connection between AI and nuclear weaponry is not new. The US and the Soviet Union had observed that the AI can play a crucial role in retaliatory capability, that is, the capability to respond to nuclear attacks (Boulanin, 2018). India is represented as one of the leaders in the whole world, be it in economy, agriculture, population, and technological developments. It was noticed that the Defence Minister of India, Shri Rajnath Singh, inaugurated the Artificial Intelligence in Defence (AIDef) symposium to mark the 75th anniversary of India's independence. The inauguration of the Centre of Excellence for Artificial Intelligence at the Air Force Station at Rajokri marks an excellent example of India taking proactive steps to introduce AI-based technologies in its war-fighting processes. This, indeed, is necessary for India to implement and show the world what it is capable of.

Conclusion

With the passage of time, the world has witnessed the evolution of technology. Technology has become an integral part of our lives, with its presence not only in the industries like education, infrastructure, banking, and consumer but also in defence. It is true that AI has not yet entered the combat arena in a serious way; however, one cannot refuse to accept the potential impact it will bring along. The sphere of influence that the adoption of AI in the battlefield creates will include the rate of commercial investments being put in, the race and drive to compete with the international threats or rivals, and, most importantly, what impact it will have on the state of mind of the military personnel.

Unsurprisingly, the importance of AI has increased over time. The United States Department of Defence (US DoD) has increased its investments from some USD 600 million in 2016–2017 to USD 2.5 billion in 2021–2022. China has adopted a Next-Generation Artificial Intelligence Development Plan that essentially aims to make the country a pre-eminent nation by 2030. Therefore, to achieve battlefield dominance, the military forces are continuously seeking greater combat effectiveness, and they can do so by establishing more research and development in the field of AI (Pant, 2018).

This chapter has talked about the importance of AI in the battlefield operations and has given a brief of challenges and future prognosis. It might be necessary for the countries to stimulate certain exercises to foster the growth of the AI-enabled technology on land, air, and sea. It is also clear that the adversary battle networks will probably get on to using AI for different purposes than what this chapter has outlined and accordingly engage with different tactics and fighting techniques.

India is stepping up late in the AI technology implementation and is far behind the countries like the US and China. They are more technologically advanced and possess a definite first-mover advantage. However, it is opined that it will not take much time for India to come closer to becoming competent, considering the pace at which it is developing (Bhattacharya, 2018). The COVID-19 pandemic has caused some restriction in the country's overall AI development. However, it, in fact, increased the deployment of AI. Recently, during the Chennai defence exposition, it was stated by the Prime Minister of India that AI and robotics will be the most necessary determinant for defensive and offensive capabilities of any armed force in the future (Galdorisi and Tangredi, 2021). Finally, this chapter opines that it is naïve for India just to be dependent on the research of the DRDO. It is necessary for India to push funds (direct or indirect) in the development of strategic technologies, not just to the government organisations but also to the private organisations and academia.

References

Allen, G., and Chan, T. (2017, July). Artificial Intelligence and National Security. *Belfer Center*. Retrieved from www.belfercenter.org/publication/artificial-intelligence-and-national-security

Atherton, K. D. (2021, May 14). *An Air Force Artificial Intelligence Program Flew a Drone Fighter for Hours*. Retrieved August 19, 2021, from www.popsci.com/technology/air-force-skyborg-drone-flight/

Ayoub, K., and Payne, K. (2015). Strategy in the Age of Artificial Intelligence. *The Journal of Strategic Studies*, 39(5), 816.

Bhattacharya, A. (2018, February 14). India Hopes to Become an AI Powerhouse by Copying China's Model. Retrieved August 6, 2021, from https://qz.com/india/1198182/modi-government-pushes-for-artificial-intelligence-like-china-but-is-india-ready-for-it/

Boeing. (2021). *KC-46A Tanker*. Retrieved August 19, 2021, from www.military.com/equipment/kc-46a-tanker

Boulanin, V. (2018). AI & Global Governance: AI and Nuclear Weapons – Promise and Perils of AI for Nuclear Stability. *Centre for Policy Research.*

China Institute for Science and Technology Policy. (2018). *China AI Development Report.* Retrieved from www.sppm.tsinghua.edu.cn/eWebEditor/UploadFile/China_AI_development_report_2018.pdf

Clifford, C. (2018, March 13). Elon Musk: "Mark My Words – A.I. Is far More Dangerous Than Nukes". *CNBC.* Retrieved from www.cnbc.com/2018/03/13/elon-musk-at-sxsw-a-i-is-more-dangerous-than-nuclear-weapons.html

Eckel, M. (2020, October 9). *Drone Wars: In Nagorno-Karabakh, the Future of Warfare Is Now.* Retrieved August 14, 2021, from www.rferl.org/a/drone-wars-in-nagorno-karabakh-the-future-of-warfare-is-now/30885007.html

Forrest, C. (2018, March 12). Musk: "AI Is Far More Dangerous Than Nukes," Needs Regulation. *TechCrunch.* Retrieved from www.techrepublic.com/article/musk-ai-is-far-more-dangerous-than-nukes-needs-regulation/

Galdorisi, G., and Tangredi, Dr., S. (2021, April 28). The Importance and Applications of Artificial Intelligence to Naval Operations. *United States.*

Hambling, D. (2021, January 19). *Indian Army Shows Off Drone Swarm of Mass Destruction.* Retrieved August 16, 2021, from www.forbes.com/sites/davidhambling/2021/01/19/indian-army-shows-off-drone-swarm-of-mass-destruction/?sh=ce34a0623840

Jadhav, A. (2021). Leveraging Artificial Intelligence in the Indian Army. Makeshaw Paper (Centre for Land Warfare Studies).

Jones, R. C. (2014, December 2). *Stephen Hawking Warns Artificial Intelligence Could End Mankind.* Retrieved from BBC: https://www.bbc.com/news/technology-30290540

Lele, A. (2011). Virtual Reality and Its Military Utility. *Journal of Ambient Intelligence and Humanized Computing,* 1–10.

Maxwell, P. (2020, April 20). *Artificial Intelligence is the Future of Warfare (Just Not in The Way You Think).* Retrieved from Modern War Institute: https://mwi.westpoint.edu/artificial-intelligence-future-warfare-just-not-way-think/

Ministry of Defense. (2020, September 14). FDI in Defense Sector. *Press Information Bureau.* Retrieved December 9, 2021, from https://pib.gov.in/PressReleasePage.aspx?PRID=1654091

Ministry of Science and Technology. (2017, September 15). *New Generation Artificial Intelligence Development Plan.* Retrieved from http://fi.china-embassy.org/; http://fi.china-embassy.org/eng/kxjs/P020171025789108009001.pdf

Mordor Intelligence. (2019–29). Artificial Intelligence and Analytics in Defense Market Size & Share Analysis – Growth Trends & Forecasts (2024–2029). https://www.mordorintelligence.com/industry-reports/artificial-intelligence-and-analytics-in-defense-market

Mukherjee, T. (2018). Securing the Maritime Commons: The Role of Artificial Intelligence in Naval Operations. *Observer Research Foundation,* 1–24.

National, D. (2021, January 15). *For the First Time Drone Operations Demonstration at Annual Army Day Parade 2021.* Delhi.

Nilsson, N. J. (2010). *The Quest for Artificial Intelligence.* Cambridge: Cambridge University Press.

Online, D. (2019, July 1). *Digital India Initiative: Services Launched So Far under This Programme.* Retrieved August 5, 2021, from www.dqindia.com/digital-india-initiative-services-launched-far-programme/

Pant, A. (2018). Future Warfare and Artificial Intelligence: Visible Path. IDSA Occasional Paper 4–50.

Polcumpally, A. T. (2021, May). What, When, Why of DARPA? *Center for Security Studies.* Retrieved from https://jgu.s3.ap-south-1.amazonaws.com/jsia/Arun+Teja-+DARPA+.pdf

Polcumpally, A. T. (2021, May). What, When, Why of DARPA? *Center for Security Studies*. Retrieved from https://jgu.s3.ap-south-1.amazonaws.com/jsia/Arun+Teja-+DARPA+.pdf

Posner, R., Jorna, R. J., and van Heusden, B. (1993). *Signs, Search and Communication: Semiotic Aspects of Artificial Intelligence*. New York: Walter de Gruyter & Co.

Roy, D. (2011, March). *The Birth of a Word*.

Saul, D. (2022, June 15). Nearly 400 Crashes in Past Year Involved Driver-Assistance Technology – Most from Tesla. *Forbes*. Retrieved from www.forbes.com/sites/dereksaul/2022/06/15/nearly-400-crashes-in-past-year-involved-driver-assistance-technology-most-from-tesla/?sh=71655ecde23e

Scroxton, A. (2022, February 24). New Wave of Cyber Attacks on Ukraine Preceded Russian Invasion. *Computer Weekly*. Retrieved from www.computerweekly.com/news/252513801/New-wave-of-cyber-attacks-on-Ukraine-preceded-Russian-invasion

Shah, J. (2020, March 26). *Biometric Technology: Spreading Its Footprint in India*. Retrieved August 6, 2021, from www.forbes.com/sites/forbesbusinessdevelopmentcouncil/2020/03/26/biometric-technology-spreading-its-footprint-in-india/?sh=3aeb75b765b8

Shankar, R. (2022, July 31). Game of Drones: Unveiling the New Era of War and Conflict. *The Indian Express*. Retrieved from www.newindianexpress.com/magazine/2022/jul/31/game-of-drones-unveiling-the-new-era-of-war-and-conflict-2481707.html

Skeen, G. (2021). Ethics, Technology, and the Fourth Industrial Revolution. *Civil Engineering = Siviele Ingenieurswese*, 29(1), 14–17.

Snyder, A. (2018, February 1). *Using AI to Map the Seafloor*. Retrieved December 9, 2021, from www.axios.com/using-artificial-intelligence-map-seafloor-151751 5616-53ce3985-1064-47be-9319-1ec419ded6c1.html

Thomas, P. R., Bhandari, U., Bullock, S., and Richardson, T. S. (2014). Advances in Air to Air Refuelling. *Progress in Aerospace Sciences*. www.darpa.mil/about-us/timeline/autonomous-highaltitude-refueling

Topychkanov, P. (2020). The Impact of Artificial Intelligence on Strategic Stability and Nuclear Risk. *SIPRI*, 15–88.

TRIPwire. (2018, January 12). *Syria: Drone Swarm Attacks Russian Military Bases*. Retrieved August 3, 2021, from https://tripwire.dhs.gov/news/209478

Upadhyay, L. C. A. (2021, May 12). *Chinese Rocket Systems vs Swarm of Indian Drones*. Retrieved August 8, 2021, from https://timesofindia.indiatimes.com/india/chinese-rocket-systems-vs-swarm-of-indian-drones/articleshow/82276598.cms

Vincent, J. (2017, September 4). Putin Says the Nation That Leads in AI "Will Be the Ruler of the World". *The Verge*. Retrieved from www.theverge.com/2017/9/4/16251226/russia-ai-putin-rule-the-world

Walch, K. (2020, May 26). Is AI Our Final Invention? *Forbes*. Retrieved from www.forbes.com/sites/cognitiveworld/2020/05/26/is-ai-our-final-invention/?sh=5c413e5777b0

6

QUANTUM COMMUNICATIONS IN INDIAN ARMED FORCES

Rushil Khosla

Introduction

In this era of growing digital interconnectedness, the need for robust data security has never been more evident. As societies across the globe become increasingly reliant on electronic communications and data storage, the spectre of mass data espionage casts a long and concerning shadow. Whether it's the realm of e-commerce, the vast landscape of social media, or the very core of democratic institutions, the vulnerability of sensitive information is a stark reality. Recent incidents such as the Cambridge Analytica scandal and the deployment of powerful spyware like the NSO Group's Pegasus software underscore the critical importance of bolstering security measures. In this context, quantum communications emerge as a beacon of hope, not only for protecting military and government communications but also for safeguarding the privacy and data integrity of ordinary citizens. This chapter unveils the immense potential of quantum technologies in addressing the pressing need for data security and protecting the foundations of democratic cultures in an era when information is power and its security is paramount.

Governments worldwide are increasingly wary of data espionage by state and non-state actors. Countering espionage and other cyber-attacks, investment in cybersecurity is increasing. The cybersecurity industry is anticipating a 15 percent year-over-year growth, with defence analysts simulating global cybersecurity budgets to exceed $1.75 trillion in 2025 (Braue, 2021). These investments are spread worldwide, with the US and China being the top destinations and also the investors. The 21st century is no longer unipolar or bipolar. The US is considering protectionist policies against the emerging power China, and the latter wishes to do away with the western world order.

DOI: 10.4324/9781003482703-9

With the emergence of new data legislations, states are inclined towards securing the data within their territories, and a free flow of information is becoming a façade for surveillance. For the states, data security has become an essential pillar in their respective foreign policy development and power aggregation strategy. Data security has already been detailed in the previous chapters. There are many ways in which data is securitised. One way is to use quantum computing power. Accordingly, this chapter focuses on quantum communications technology as it will break all the data processing limits.

Quantum key distribution (QKD) offers a transformative solution, providing an unbreakable shield for securing sensitive military and government communications while simultaneously safeguarding the privacy of everyday citizens. This quantum paradigm promises to protect not only against traditional cyber threats but, crucially, against emerging quantum computing capabilities that threaten to unravel existing encryption methods.

Quantum Technology

Importance and the Current Development

Quantum technologies harness the fundamental aspects of quantum physics to provide numerous advantages over contemporary technological counterparts. The three central theories of quantum technologies – superposition, entanglement and measurement – work in harmony for various purposes, including communication. Although quantum theories have been a fundamental aspect of physics, their adoption for practical, real-world technologies has been expedited. The case for quantum communication technologies arises due to the exponential rise of cyber threats, posed to governments and military alike.

Gordon Moore, the founder of intel, devised a theory that advocates that the computational speeds are going to double year after year. This is generally known as Moore's' law. The trend has been proven right for the past 50 years (chapter is written in 2023), because the elements that make up a computer have become smaller, working faster. The number of electrons in a transistor has reduced year on year, and the processor speeds are doubling. Although such a feat is impressive, there would come a time when such a trend would come to a halt because of physical, material and electrical limitations (Tummala, 2019). Quantum technology might set the next limit to computational power in the post-Moore's law era (Powell, 2008). It is observed that with the development of nanotechnology and its sub-branch Spintronics (Hirohata et al., 2020), the quantum limit can be achieved with electrons being the smallest transistor component (Powell, 2008). It is predicted that with the current trend of technological breakthroughs in nanotechnology, 2036 will be the year when Moore's law will converge with quantum physics (Powell, 2008).

These technical terms might be difficult for a geopolitical analyst or a security studies scholar to understand. In general terms, quantum technology will be capable to increase the speed, efficiency and security of data transmission.

The takeaway from the technical explanation is that with a steady breakthrough in nanotechnology engineering and quantum technology, the speed of digital communications will break all the existing limits. When the industry reaches atomic scales, quantum effects will take precedence and vital importance (if quantum behaviour could be controlled). This claim can be disputed as the industry looks at other ways to counter Moore's law and yet achieve the increased computational speed. Some opine that, by writing a more efficient computer programme and keeping the transistor capacities the same, the speed of the transistor can be increased 47 times (Rotman, 2020). Some argue that reducing chip size is technically possible but economically not (Condliffe, 2016). With these arguments, it is clear that Moore's law, which proposes the reduction of transistor size per two years, is coming to a halt. Controlled quantum behaviour has the potential to not only revise but also revolutionise computation and also communication. The ability to manipulate information through laws of quantum physics will revolutionise the processing ability of any apparatus, especially communication between two parties.

Current Data Encryption Is Breakable Using Quantum Technology

In order to understand the advantages of quantum communication, one must have a good foundational understanding of traditional forms of computation and communication. Most of the communications as of the year 2022 are encrypted end to end by 256-bit encryption. The classical (current) mode of data encryption occurs in the form of bits. The bit is the most basic unit of information in computing. All computers work by receiving and manipulating 1s and 0s. An amalgamation of those bits creates the information we transmit and receive. A bit is representative of either two states or amplitudes. Today, sensitive data is encrypted and sent across fibre-optic cables, along with digital "keys" that are required to access the information. Both the sensitive data and digital "key" are sent in a stream of classical bits representing 1 and 0. This technology is universal, and importantly, it is easy to make or break with the help of quantum computers (Mims, 2019). Whoever possesses the quantum computing power can use brute force to break the encryption. Banking on the traditional encryptions will be vulnerable to espionage and malpractice, since hackers can read and copy these simplistic bits, without leaving any mark/trace that the data's security has been breached.

The laws of quantum physics have allowed researchers to create quantum bits or qubits. Qubits possess much more freedom than their counterparts (classical bits). In order to elucidate their freedom, imagine a sphere consisting of two bits. The classical bits would typically be at opposite poles. A qubit can function anywhere on the sphere. However, the defining feature of the qubit is its ability to be both 1 and 0, simultaneously. This is where the distinction lies between a qubit and a normal bit, and such a development can open up a gamut of probabilities. Classical bits can be either 1 or 0, whereas qubits can be both numbers simultaneously. The qubit's ability to represent multiple combinations of 1 and 0, simultaneously, and being partly "0" and partly "1" is known as superposition state.

There are ways devised by researchers, to physically embody a qubit. Qubits can be reproduced through artificial atoms. This is done in laboratories, by applying high-frequency radio waves (known as microwaves) to the atom. The microwaves (emitted by a microscope's tip) can create a quantum dance, where the artificial atom's north pole spirals, known as "rabi oscillation". The researchers possess the control to point the atom up (being a 0) or down (being 1) or a superposition (Lutz and Yang, 2019). This shows how the qubit can be physically embodied.

The most popular way to synthesise a qubit, arguably, is through manipulating photons of light. Photons interact weakly with their environment, meaning they are relatively protected against de-coherence.[1] Photonic qubits can also be made through simplistic machines such as beam splitter and phase shifters. All in all, super-positions of quantum states can be represented, detected, encrypted and transmitted through photons (NASEM, 2019). Another way of creating qubits is through trapping ions. There are two main types of trapped ion qubits, "optical qubits" and "hyperfine qubits" (NASEM, 2019). Tech giants such as Google, IBM and Intel are investigating and following the latter mentioned methods (Choi, 2021).

The superposition of qubits allows them to store an unsurmountable amount of data. In order to elucidate the potential of qubits, here is a hypothetical example. A bit can only be either 1 or 0. In the case for binary bits, there could only be one possible value between 0 and 7 (decimal numbers). The qubits, however, illustrate a more interesting possibility. Since a qubit can be both 0 and 1 simultaneously, depending on the measurement, the sequence could represent any number between 000 (0) and 111 (7). This provides us with a range of multiplicities and varying values. The qubit, therefore, is far superior to a normal bit, due to its ability of representing innumerable to values. To put into perspective, in classical computing, n bits can store just one number between 0 and 2^n. So, if we choose 3 bits, it could only store one value between 0 and 8. On the contrary, n qubits can store all the numbers between 0 and 2^n. This means that if we choose 3 qubits, the qubit stores all the numbers between 0 and 8. This is a revolutionary advancement in the field of computing. The ability to store all the values (when previously a bit could store only one value) provides us with greater variability. Quantum entanglement of just 10 qubits can, therefore, store 1024 values within them at any time.

The way to gauge the value of any qubit is to measure it. Although a qubit can house all values between 0 and 2^n, when measuring a qubit, the only possible values are 0 and 1. As the person measuring the outcome of the qubit, the measurer can choose the set of possible outcomes by asking it questions. However, the outcomes of a single measurement are random. This is because to preserve a classical bit, the qubit is in a state of superposition and can simultaneously hold the values of 0 and 1 together. One can run exactly the same experiments and expect different answers. A qubit's state of superposition of 0 and 1 gives outcomes 0 and 1 each a 50% chance. Qubits also harbour a quality that makes them suitable for secure communications. Although measurement of a classical bit would not interfere with its coherence, the measurement of a qubit would cause irrevocable damage to the qubit and lead to the de-coherence of its superposition state. A noteworthy con of the aforementioned postulation (fragile state) is that in qubits, the relationship with its environment is incredibly hard to control. Any fluctuations in temperature or vibration can cause the qubit to lose its superposition and quantum state. That means a large thermal instability would cause de-coherence.

To date, researchers have not been able to generate more than 128 standard qubits (Giles, 2019). However, the aforementioned con is dwarfed by the range of opportunities if qubits can be mass produced and maintained. In fact, the qubit's quality of having less de-coherence in a controlled environment is the key pillar for quantum physics' application in communications. The irreversible and unavoidable disturbance of the qubit's quantum state by measurement (to decipher the outcome) can be applied alongside quantum cryptography to provide a level of secure communications inimitable by any contemporary forms of secure communication. If any external entity tries to tamper with the communication line, then the quantum state gets disturbed losing the information.

Alice and Bob Model of Communication Using Qubits

The current model of fibre-optic communications is vulnerable to hacking and stealing key data, without the two communicating parties knowing. However, if the hacker tries to interact with the qubit, the qubit would not be coherent anymore. This disturbance informs the two parties of communication that their line of communication had eavesdroppers. This idea can be elucidated through the BB84 model, more popularly known as the Alice and Bob model (Quantum Cryptography, n.d.). The basis of secure communications revolves around a secure key that leads to access to the encrypted information and decrypts its binary content into messages.

To date, the only known and guaranteed secure communication system is a one-time-pad, also known as OTP. The OTP is a string of random bits, which acts as the secure key. For Alice and Bob to communicate securely, they need to have a common key (in this case being OTP). If Alice and Bob can share the key securely, any interception by the hacker would be useless since Alice and Bob are sharing an encoded message in a unique way. Suppose Alice wants to send a message, she would generate a string of random bits. She would also need the same quantity of bits as the message (randomly generated), which acts as Alice's key. The binary value of the message and the key would be binarily added, to create a cryptogram. This cryptogram is sent to Bob. Bob would now require the exact same key as Alice, and if Bob puts the right key, the message would be communicated securely to Bob. The communication is secured mathematically. However, the communications security is impinged if the key is not shared securely. If the hacker can access the shared key, they can steal vital information. Hackers can do this without leaving any trace of their malicious presence. In such vein, quantum communications can ensure secure key sharing and communication.

In quantum communications, Alice and Bob would send qubits to each other. If any hacker tries to eavesdrop/intercept the key sharing process between Alice and Bob, their presence would be immediately detected. This is due to the qubit's low coherence. If a hacker tries to intercept the qubit, they would have to measure a qubit in order to seek an outcome. However, the measurement of the qubit would lead to its de-coherence. Consequentially, the de-coherence would be clear to Alice and Bob, and they would know that their line of communication is not secure.

The process of sharing keys as qubits is known as QKD. The key is shared through a fibre-optic channel, the same channel since the encrypted communication is done through a public channel as well. Let us examine the qubit encryption case within the same Alice and Bob communication. Alice sends qubits chosen at random. As mentioned earlier, qubit can house superposition of 0 and 1. Therefore, a qubit exhibits two types of outcomes, type-1 and type-H (Quantum Cryptography: Photons and BB84). Alice generates random qubits and sends it to Bob. If the line is secure, Bob receives the randomly generated qubits sent by Alice. However, if there is an eavesdropper attempting to steal information from the quantum channel, the eavesdropper is at a disadvantage. Averse to classical bits, the qubit's superposition state promulgates the hacker to measure the qubit in order to access the outcome of the qubit. The eavesdropper/hacker would inquire whether the qubit is a type-1 0 or type-1 1, or Type-H 0 or Type-H 1. The hacker can only ask any one of these questions, and since the hacker has no knowledge of the true value of the qubit, they would have to ask a question at random. When the hacker asks a wrong question (to inquire upon the state of the qubit), the eavesdropper/hacker is going to randomise the qubits. Therefore, some of the qubits sent by Alice to Bob would be corrupted.

The corruption of the qubits does not hamper communication. Quantum communication does not enable private communication of key/meaningful information; it only enables private communication of random messages. The random messages alongside the key create the meaningful message known as cryptogram. After Bob receives the key via qubits, Alice and Bob communicate to find whether they have a secure key. After Bob records the sequences of 0s and 1s (after measuring it, known as "base sifting"), Alice communicates to Bob which qubits were type-1 and which where Type-H. All communications are done through a public channel. Bob reveals to Alice publicly which questions he asked but not the answers derived. The qubits where Bob's question matched Alice's answers were kept. However, the qubits where Bob's question did not match Alice's answers were discarded. This process leads to the identification of useable qubits. However, both Alice and Bob would also check the veracity of the "useable" qubits. The aforementioned process is known as "key distillation". Due to the fragile nature of qubits, some qubits may become corrupted during the course of communication through the fibre optics.

This would lead to certain errors in measurement between Alice and Bob. However, if the error rate is 25 percent or higher, that means that the eavesdropper is trying to impinge on Alice and Bob's communication. The eavesdropper cannot avoid making his presence felt in quantum communication, due to the fact that measurement of qubits in transit would make them de-coherent. If ¼ of Bob's measurements are not in line with Alice's measurement, both would automatically know that line isn't secure. To verify their beliefs, the process would be repeated again. Alice and Bob would sacrifice a few of their secret bits, sharing them over a public channel. If again ¼ of the measurements don't match between Alice and Bob, they would know for certain that their communication is not secured. Bob and Alice would then ditch the key in question and generate a new key. If the new key does not cross the 25 percent error rate threshold, both Alice and Bob can find and correct the errors. This would typically include reducing the length of their shared string of bits. The last step in the process is known as "Privacy Amplification". All the mentioned processes are automatically done.

Even if the errors are removed, there might be a chance that the eavesdropper has some information regarding their shared string. However, if they reduce the shared string of bits, Alice and Bob can also reduce Eve's knowledge of the shared string to a negligible amount, with great confidence. The error rate of Alice and Bob's measurements influences the number of shared bits cut by Alice and Bob. After all these processes, Alice and Bob can share a secret key that is absolutely secure. The exchanged key could then be used as OTP (Renner, 2015). It is important to note that the secure key is much smaller than the qubits shared. However, the security of the key is guaranteed by quantum physics and mathematics.

Although, theoretically, the model of quantum communication has immense promise, the implementation of the model in reality faces some challenges. The material in fibre-optic cables can absorb photons, which means the qubit will lose its quantum state after a few kilometres. A possible solution to the issue is the creation of "trusted nodes". The nodes would de-crypt the qubits into classical bits and re-encrypt them into their quantum states for the qubit's journey till the next node. However, the supposedly "trusted node" would become a bottleneck for communications, meaning hackers would attempt to breach the nodes' security and could copy the de-crypt (classical bits) and acquire the key. In an ideal world, quantum communication would require quantum repeaters. Similar to the amplifier seen in communication of classical bits, quantum repeaters would ensure the photons quantum structure, amplify them and make the photons travel long distances. This would guarantee safe communication between two parties in reality. Researchers have been able to theoretically build a quantum repeater, and development towards practical adaptations of quantum repeaters has been observed. In April 2021, researchers from Delft University successfully built a multimode quantum network, critically showing entanglement swapping and multipartite entanglement (Pompili et al., 2021). In China, researchers have been able to realise and implement "absorptive" quantum memories. These models reflected a high bandwidth, high fidelity and multiplexity. The research team could achieve this feat because their experiments separated the quantum memory from quantum light sources (Liu et al., 2021). The consulting firm McKinsey & Company has forecasted that quantum repeaters would be ready for commercialisation in the next decade (Batra et al., 2021).

China and Its Quantum Technology

On January 6, 2021, China launched the world's first integrated quantum communications network. The emitter was based in Xinglong (Northeast China) and spanned a total distance of 4600 km till Shanghai. The large-scale quantum communications network encompassed key Chinese cities, such as Beijing, Jinan, Guangzhou, Hefei and Nanjing. The Beijing to Shanghai quantum communication network required 32 "trusted nodes". The project included a network of more than 700 fibre-optic QKD links and two high-speed satellite-to-ground free-space QKD links (Chen et al., 2021). Although the project came to life in 2021, the project to achieve a practical quantum communication network began in 2016. In 2016, China launched the world's first quantum communication satellite known as "Micius". The creation of Micius led Chinese researchers at University of Science and Technology China to achieve QKD with two ground stations, 2600 km apart (Daniel,

2021). In 2017, 2000 km worth of fibre-optic cables were laid between Beijing and China, to achieve QKD. In total, the 4600 km of ground-based fibre network and satellite-to-ground links were integrated to serve 150 industrial users across China (University of Science and Technology of China, 2021). The users included state and local banks, power grids and government websites. The project undertaken by Jian Wei Pan conceptualises the promise that quantum communication networks can hold in reality. The satellite-to-ground QKD connection has a generation rate of 47.8 kilobits per second, 40 times higher than the previous rate. However, the generation rate is still far away from the generation speeds of classical communication. Quantum systems can only muster a generation rate up to a few Mbit/s, which is still ways off from the standard rates of Tbit/s or Pbit/s in classical communication.

The Chinese project also established an alternative model to achieve QKD. As explored through the chapter, the most widely known apparatus for QKD involves fibre-optic cables with trusted nodes. These fibre-optic cables physically transport the photons, from the emitter to the receiver. However, the Chinese model established ground to space QKD sharing, by exploring an ingenious quality of qubits and quantum physics. Unlike other quantum communication projects, the Chinese project took advantage of a principle of quantum mechanics known as entanglement. The laws of quantum mechanics are postulated under three laws. The first is quantum superposition, where qubit can simultaneously hold information about 0 and 1. Second, quantum uncertainty dictates that any measurement of a qubit would provide a random answer, and the measurement of the qubit would cause it to lose its stability. Through the course of the chapter, the two aforementioned postulations have been expounded and analysed upon for quantum communications and the subsequent QKD model. However, the third stipulation of quantum mechanics is entanglement (Giles, 2019). This law postulates that neither pair of entangled qubits has an identity independent of its partner, even if it's far apart. Theoretically, this means there would be quantum teleportation. In order to elucidate the concept, consider the Alice and Bob case. Alice and Bob are at the two opposing poles of the world, and an entangled qubit is generated. If Alice measures the state of her qubit, she would automatically change the measured state of Bob's qubit. Although Bob cannot decipher this development since he has not measured his qubit, Alice would send the results of her measurement. With this information, Bob can realise that the state of the qubit has changed and the quantum data has been teleported.

The Chinese project undertaken by the professors of the University of Science and Technology China uses the laws of quantum entanglement to create a secure QKD system. As mentioned in the chapter, a drawback of fibre-optic communication for qubits is that fibre-optic cables can absorb the photons and break their quantum state. Without the "trusted nodes", the fibre-optic model of quantum communication would create noise, resorting the qubit to only travel for few tens of kilometres. The Chinese project created entangled qubits, which were used to create ultra-secure keys. Therefore, Micius (the satellite for quantum communication) achieved QKD with two ground stations, 2600 km apart. Although the laws of quantum physics ensure secure communications through qubits, practically, there are inefficiencies that limit quantum communications to work smoothly. The satellite-to-ground communication – reportedly – has an error rate of just 4.5 percent. Starting with a low error rate is important so that there is a benchmark, and additional error rates can be pinpointed to eavesdroppers. Also, if the satellites were to be hacked, this would be readily noticed by governments and defence factions. Arthur Ekert – professor at the University of Oxford – believes that entanglement could provide ultimate security (Crane, 2020).

Keeping with the aforementioned thought, professors from Shanghai Jiao Tong University and Jiangxi Normal University have built quantum secure direct communication (QSDC). The model of communication is based on entanglement and can directly transmit confidential information. A key point about QKD was that it only shared the key in a secure manner, not the information along it. The QSDC model promises secure information transmission. Any attack on the QSDC model would only lead to the generation of random numbers. Therefore, no information of meaning can be conferred by hacking this model of communication. The QSDC model was experimented with 15 users and five subnets and over 40 km of fibre-optic communication. The researchers could confer with confidence that the structure of the entangled state of qubits shared by them is greater than 95 percent. The rate of information transmission can be maintained at 1 kbps now. However, information transmission rates could be greater than 100 kbps, in the case of high-performance detectors and high-speed control in modulators (Chinese Academy of Sciences, 2021). This model of global QSDC is a significant step towards satellite-based quantum communication in the future. China has taken the global lead in Artificial Intelligence (AI) and 5G. Their dedication to the level of detail and exploration of practical quantum communication solutions illustrate their Intent to also be the global leader in quantum communications.

Developments in Europe

There have been noteworthy developments regarding quantum communication technology in Europe as well. Toshiba Europe Ltd. has developed the world's first QKD system based on photonic chips. At the advent of classical computing, apparatuses such as semiconductors continued to get smaller and faster as research and development and collaboration garnered steam. A similar trend might also be seen in quantum technologies. The QKD prototype uses a quantum random number generator (QRNG) to prepare and measure the qubits and converted into high-speed modulation patterns for QKD transmitter and receiver, using field programmable gate arrays (FP-GAs). Photonic integration is essential, as it will allow manufacturers to create quantum technologies (including quantum communication devices) in volume and with great consistency. The smaller form factor would lend to faster rollout of QKD into telecommunications and data communication network security (Toshiba Achieves Chip-Based QKD Tech, 2021).

However, the European Union (EU) has devoted more of its time to creating policies and infrastructure to support the development of quantum communications and QKD technology. All 27 EU members have signed up for EuroQCI or European Quantum Communication Infrastructure Initiative. The participant nations would work alongside the European Commission and the European Space Agency (ESA) for this multilateral project. The aim for EuroQCI is to be fully operational by 2027. The model of the project is similar to the Chinese model. The two main components of the EuroQCI are the existing terrestrial fibre-optic communication channels and linked space satellites. The EU's commitment to build GOVSATCOM (Government Satellite Communications) and the EuroQCI would integrate next-generation technologies such as quantum communication, 5G and AI. The commitment to quantum security is also expected to be a central pillar of the EU's cybersecurity strategy for the 2020s (European Commission, 2020). The European members have also drafted steps that need to be taken in the short term for the development of quantum communication technologies. The most important order of business for all European members is defining and articulating stage 1 (2021–2028, Quantum Secured Networks) and stage 2 (2028–2035, Quantum Information Networks). Stage 1 of the EuroQCI would focus on developing and deploying infrastructure to support quantum-enhanced secure communications in Europe by 2028. Although the quantum communication technology is initially being chartered for state use (government offices, embassies, etc.) and vital European infrastructure (electricity grids, hospitals, etc.), the infrastructure is also intended for commercial operations, which would attract private capital down the line. Stage 2 would entail the expansion of the infrastructure established in Stage 1. The development of terrestrial and space-to-ground satellite communication would act as a bedrock towards the goal of stage 2, which is Quantum Information Network. Although secure communications are a top priority (as highlighted by the mammoth efforts entailed in the design of stage 1), there is an offshoot of a greater goal. If everything goes to plan, EuroQCI aims to connect quantum processing centres around the continent, and the transition from academic availability of the technology to its industrial adoption would begin.

In parallel, EuroQCI establishes a strong focus on the education and legislation surrounding quantum communication. Under the programme, universities would be incentivised to educate engineers in the field of quantum technology and would provide them with requisite opportunities to enhance their understanding. European lawmakers would create legislation that would look into the regulation of quantum communications infrastructure. Topics such as rights, use and competition and basic European standardisation are also an important goal to achieve.

European advancement in the field of quantum communications is also upheld by OpenQKD. OpenQKD is a wide-scale cooperation of European academia, industry and start-ups to experiment with large-scale QKD transfer throughout Europe. The project aims to shape the standardisation of QKD model and scale the QKD model to the point where application for the end user becomes seamless. This would include the creation of several QKD testbeds throughout Europe to establish network functionality and develop a cohesive ecosystem for the education and creation for quantum communication technologies in Europe (Objectives What We Are Going for, n.d.).

The US and the Quantum Geopolitics

The development of quantum communication technology and advancement in QKD sharing would perhaps affect the geopolitical ambitions of America the most. Fuelled by their Cold War–type spite with China, China has truly become the gold standard of quantum communication technology. The rift in technological advancement is borne due to varied focus in quantum technologies. China has invested massive capital into quantum communications technology and QKD development, whereas America has highlighted advancements in quantum computing devices. The differences in quantum goals also highlight the geopolitical concerns of each nation. Beijing regards secure communication and networking control as a national priority. Washington, DC's, directive of quantum computing perhaps reflects further integration with private tech firms (Microsoft, Apple, etc.) to develop quantum technologies. It is still early to say whether either country is ahead of the other. Estimates suggest that both countries appear to fund roughly $100 million per year into the field. Although China has more total patents in the field of quantum technology, US companies have a sizable lead in quantum computing patents. For the US, quantum computing is a national security interest, as they believe that the ability to defend their economic and national security interests would be threatened if they fall behind in the field of quantum computing. According to Steve Grobman – senior vice president and chief technology officer for McAfee – the need for quantum computing supremacy is influenced by their past (Grobman, 2018). After all, it was the US leadership in signals intelligence in World War II and the proxy wars of the Cold War that helped the country establish its hegemonic status. It is also important to remember that quantum communications are just one branch of the developing field of quantum technologies.

For quantum communications to sustain and advance, the field would also rely upon the advancement of quantum technologies as a whole. Therefore, the varied goals of US and China may suggest a broad unilateral deal focusing on the transfer of their respective quantum technologies. Their convergence would lead to the creation of a more broad-based quantum information technology base (Stefanick, 2020). However, America has prior history in quantum communication technology giving it a first-mover advantage in the research.

The US has been developing quantum technologies since the beginning of the century, by deploying networks at the Los Alamos National Laboratory (Chip, 2004). In 1999, the Los Alamos Laboratory set a (then) record of 31-mile-long optical fibre QKD. Although the laboratory failed to achieve longer distances (due to absorption of photons in fibre-optic cables), the project successfully connected government offices and bank branches to create the first QKD network (Los Alamos National Security, 2010). In 2003, the first QKD network was established by the Defence Advanced Research Projects Agency (DARPA). The project was operated by BBN Technologies, as a QKD network was established between Harvard University and Boston University Photonics Center, with 10 nodes supporting the key sharing between the two universities. The project also housed the world's first "superconducting nanowire single-photon detector" (Zhu et al., 2019).

Quantum Technology – India

India has also made steps into the vast world of quantum communications. On March 22, ISRO's Space Applications Centre declared that ISRO had achieved quantum communication over a distance of 300 m across ISRO's campus. The project was experimented at night, in order to reduce the interference of rays emitted by sunlight. A notable achievement of the project is that the technologies critical to the project were built by ISRO themselves. NavIC receivers were used for time synchronisation between the transmitter and the receiver modules, and a special gimbal mechanism was also used, instead of a large-aperture telescope, normally used for optical alignment (John, 2021). Although ISRO's development is a step in the right direction, it is far from a technological leap. ISRO was only able to achieve quantum communication between 300 m, whereas global leaders like China have exhibited QKD sharing totalling 4600 km. Although the adoption of the technology makes ISRO's project a practical demonstration, China's rampant development of quantum technologies has meant that QKD sharing has become nationally scalable.

China has laid down roughly 2000 km long fibre optics and has achieved further 2600 km via satellite-to-ground communication. Relatively speaking, India's progress is rather quaint. However, the allocation for the development of quantum technologies would bolster quantum communication technologies development. In such vein, the government has allocated rough 8000 crore rupees for a period of five years to the Department of Science and Technology. The allocation aims to foster a National Mission on Quantum Technologies and Applications (NM-QTA) (Department of Science and Technology, 2020). Supplementary to the monetary commitment to quantum technologies, the Indian government also inaugurated the quantum communications lab of C-DOT. C-DOT is currently the only Indian tech research organisation that offers a complete portfolio of indigenous quantum secure telecom technology. C-DOT is also predicted to be a major global player for private and defence investment. C-DOT is reported to have the capacity to have nearly 100 km of fibre optics, ready for experimentation. C-DOT could thus also become the main hotbed for further quantum communication development in India (Pai, 2021).

The amount of monetary commitment exemplified in India is a serious commitment to be one of the leading players in the sphere of quantum technologies. The grant acts as a long-needed catalyst. The US is pursuing ardent research into quantum computation behind closed doors, with Congress considering allocating roughly \$1.2 billion into quantum computing (Castelvecchi, 2018). The EU is focusing on quantum communication (as highlighted by EuroQCI), and China's rampant research and development in the field has resulted in the country becoming global leaders in quantum communication.

Conclusion

Quantum communications technology and its key mechanism of QKD sharing are absolutely revolutionary. The reason quantum communication is revolutionary is because its security and ergo veracity are ensured by the laws of quantum physics. The qubit is a marvel of theoretical quantum physics, and its properties make the entire apparatus of quantum communication revolutionary. The qubit's state of superposition is miles ahead of the contemporary classical bit. Although a classical bit can only be 1 or 0, the qubit can be both 1 and 0 simultaneously. In addition, a classical bit can only store 1 value between 0 and 2^n; however, a qubit can store all the values between 0 and 2^n. The theoretical conception of qubit and its practical feasibility makes any quantum technology revolutionary for a state's defence purposes. The qubit's key quality of becoming de-coherent under quantum noise makes it especially revolutionary for a state's communication apparatus. Its quality of de-coherence is also advantageous for communication purposes. As mentioned earlier in the chapter, the key issue with the present model of fibre-optic communication is that the communicating parties can't ascertain/know about the presence of a malicious party. The qubits' ability to easily break apart helps in that. If an unintended third party tries to interfere, they would inevitably create quantum noise, which would lead to the de-coherence of the qubit and the communicating parties to know that their line of communication isn't secure.

Quantum communication technologies are borne out of the flaws of fibre-optic-based communication. The targeting of fibre-optic-based communication made the states especially vulnerable to constant cyber threats as hackers can steal vital information without leaving any trace of their eavesdropping. QKD is possible due to the qubit's characteristic of de-coherence. A qubit would break down if there is any disturbance in its vibration field or temperature. Therefore, any intruding eavesdropper would inevitably leave a trace of his malicious presence. The two parties communicating could, therefore, establish a secure key by reducing any uncertainty of an eavesdropper. This is extremely vital for transnational or domestic secure communications, since communication of a state's classified matter can remain truly secure.

The system of communication would not require a complex manned key distribution, which is the current scenario for a nation-state's secure communication. Quantum communication would, therefore, eliminate the prospect of betrayal by an agent. The technology is also future-proof, because there are no future advancements in computational power that can break the model of quantum cryptography established by QKD and the quantum communications network that supports it.

China's huge investment into quantum communications – along with its investment into AI and 5G – highlights Beijing's intention to become the new military vanguard. Its aspirations of economic hegemony are thus envisioned to be supported by hegemony in the defence realm. A nation's victory in future conflicts would be shifting away from its hard power and towards strategising its information-related capabilities. Therefore, a strong and secure communication network is an absolute necessity for India to be considered as a major military power globally and to compete with China for military dominance in Southeast Asia particularly. Quantum communication technologies are not an addition to the existing modes of secure communication. Instead, quantum communications would act upon as the bedrock, upon which new technologies would be built. Quantum communications would revolutionise every aspect of secure and encrypted communications.

The advent of quantum computing would break our current cryptographic models. This would lead to the advent of quantum-safe approach to cryptography. The QKD model is an exemplar of secure communications and is essential for military purposes. If the information is obscured and the control over it is lost, any military mission would become much riskier and the rate of failure would increase. The current model for military-based communication is a model of symmetric encryption. This model of encryption requires keys to both encode and decode data. Yet, it is unrealistic to assume that during warfare or a military mission, the keys would always be distributed between the participant members/stakeholders. QKD ensures that a key is theoretically secure and thus would create ironclad security for military missions.

Suppose a navy ship – such as the INS *Vikramaditya* – is required for a military mission. The ship would also be connected to a military aircraft, submarine and a ground-based station and vehicles (e.g., tanks). It is believed that in such a scenario, QKD can be achieved between any two parties in the aforementioned scenario. Horizontal key change between static points can be achieved by the navy ship with the submarine, the ground stations and an on-ground vehicle. QKD between an airplane and any other aforementioned apparatus is also possible as highlighted in a 2013 experiment focusing on airplane in flight to ground-based receiver and static transmitter to moving receiver. QKD between a static transmitter to moving receiver is also true for links between ship to submarine and ground stations. As the Chinese model of quantum communication and QKD have illustrated, satellite to ground-based secure communication is also possible. A possible military application of quantum communications could also be centred around position-based access to sensitive information. Position-based cryptography dictates that information can only be retrieved at a particular geographical point. Although such an idea is at its nascent stages, QKD-based position cryptography would allow the military greater control over the flow and reception of the information (Krelina, 2021).

The next few decades would be an interesting period in geopolitics and military affairs, since the pillars of modern warfare and missions are changing. Although hard power is quintessential, its importance in military affairs is slowly decreasing and shifting towards an increase in the cyberwarfare infrastructure. In the 21st century, cybersecurity and weaponry would become a quintessential pillar in any nation's defence policies. However, contrary to the correlation between country size and its military power, the advent of cyber-based weapons would make a country's wealth or size a redundant criterion. A nation such as Sri Lanka could become as threatening as China if it adopts cyber-based weaponry. In his paper, titled "India's Path to Power: Strategy in a World Adrift", Shivshankar Menon and his team believed that the integration of foreign policy and cyber power must become a necessity for India's path to become a more potent military power (Aiyar et al., 2021).

In an op-ed published on October 21, 2021, in the *Hindu*, BJP MP and former Union Minister for Law and Justice Mr. Subramanian Swamy outlined a new national security policy, focusing majorly on the integration of cyber technology (Swamy, 2021). The shadow policy dictated that India should be able to anticipate cyber threats posed by any nation and have the power to be demonstrative in its threats. To achieve this objective, the government must focus on critical and emerging technologies, such as quantum technologies, and establish an ecosystem for communication and shared knowledge regarding such technologies. Shivshankar Menon in his book also equivocated similar thoughts as he necessitated the development of a national cyber commission (Menon, 2021). The cyber commission should prioritise integrating cyber operational capabilities into its diplomatic, intelligence and military frameworks.

India is in a critical yet opportunistic position. China continues on its path to establish hegemony, and its investment into quantum communication technology is a testament to that. Countering the geopolitical and military influence of China would be the highest priority for the Indian government. However, India could also become the major player in this new era of cyber operational technology. Amidst the cold relation between China and the US, the tech war between the two nations has become highly contentious. This has promulgated nations around the world to look for alternative routes that are not diplomatically problematic. India is known worldwide for being an outsourcing hub and produces the largest number of engineers. India is a powerhouse in software technologies. If India can provide an inclusive digital infrastructure, as opposed to an exclusive model of the US and China, India could become the cyber power in the 21st century. Also, considering global immigration flows are becoming more restrictive, India could reduce its "Brain Drain" and harness its already great capabilities in the field of technology, to become a cyber-technology powerhouse. Although, in the grand scheme of things, quantum communications is a small slice of the pie, India's investment into this field marks the advent of a new era in military affairs and securitisation.

Note

1 De-coherence is loss of information to the environment.

References

Aiyar, Y., Khilnani, S., Menon, P., Menon, S., Pai, N., Raghavan, S., . . . Saran, S. (2021, September). India's Path to Power – Strategy in a World Adrift. *Takshashila*. Retrieved from https://takshashila.org.in/research-indias-path-to-power-strategy-in-a-world-adrift/

Batra, G., Gschwendtner, M., Ostojic, I., Queirolo, A., Soller, H., and Wester, L. (2021, December 21). Shaping the Long Race in Quantum Communication and Quantum Sensing. *McKinsey & Company*. Retrieved from www.mckinsey.com/industries/industrials-and-electronics/our-insights/shaping-the-long-race-in-quantum-communication-and-quantum-sensing

Braue. (2021). Global Cybersecurity Spending to Exceed $1.75 Trillion from 2021–2025. *https:cybersecurityventures.com*. Retrieved January 22, 2024, from https://cybersecurityventures.com/cybersecurity-spending-2021-2025/

Castelvecchi, D. (2018, October 29). Europe Shows First Cards in €1-Billion Quantum Bet. *Nature*. Retrieved from www.nature.com/articles/d41586-018-07216-0

Chen, Y.-A., Zhang, Q., and Pan, J.-W. (2021). An Integrated Space-to-Ground Quantum Communication Network over 4,600 Kilometres. *Nature*, 214–219.

Chinese Academy of Sciences. (2021, September 23). A 15-User Quantum Secure Direct Communication Network. *Phys.org*. Retrieved from https://phys.org/news/2021-09-user-quantum-network.html

Chip, E. (2004, December 3). The DARPA Quantum Network. *Cornell University*. Retrieved from https://arxiv.org/abs/quant-ph/0412029

Choi, C. Q. (2021, March 5). In the Race to Hundreds of Qubits, Photons May Have "Quantum Advantage" Canadian Startup Xanadu Says Their Quantum Computer Is Cloud-Accessible, Python Programmable, and Ready to Scale. *IEEE Spectrum*. Retrieved from https://spectrum.ieee.org/race-to-hundreds-of-photonic-qubits-xanadu-scalable-photon

Condliffe, J. (2016, October 7). World's Smallest Transistor Is Cool but Won't Save Moore's Law. *MIT Technology Review*. Retrieved from www.technologyreview.com/2016/10/07/157106/worlds-smallest-transistor-is-cool-but-wont-save-moores-law/#:~:text=Size%20doesn't%20matter%20like%20it%20used%20to.&text=Moore's%20Law%20is%20stalling%20in,can%20be%20done%20with%20silicon.&text=Ali%20J

Crane, L. (2020, June 15). China's Quantum Satellite Helps Send Secure Messages over 1200km. *NewScientist*. Retrieved from www.newscientist.com/article/2245885-chinas-quantum-satellite-helps-send-secure-messages-over-1200km/

Daniel, G. (2021, July 15). China Is Pulling Ahead in Global Quantum Race, New Studies Suggest. *Scientific American*. Retrieved from www.scientificamerican.com/article/china-is-pulling-ahead-in-global-quantum-race-new-studies-suggest/

Department of Science and Technology. (2020). Budget 2020 Announces Rs 8000 cr National Mission on Quantum Technologies & Applications | Department of Science & Technology. *dst.gov.in*. Retrieved January 22, 2022, from https://dst.gov.in/budget-2020-announces-rs-8000-cr-national-mission-quantum-technologies-applications

European Commission. (2020). Joint Communication to the European Parliament and the Council: The EU's Cybersecurity Strategy for the Digital Decade. *https:digital-strategy.ec.europa.eu*. Retrieved January 22, 2022, from https://digital-strategy.ec.europa.eu/en/library/eus-cybersecurity-strategy-digital-decade-0

Giles, M. (2019, January 29). Explainer: What Is a Quantum Computer? How It Works, Why It's So Powerful, and Where It's Likely to Be Most Useful First. *MIT Technology Review*. Retrieved from www.technologyreview.com/2019/01/29/66141/what-is-quantum-computing/#whatisdecoherence

Grobman, S. (2018, October 25). Quantum Computing Must Be a National Security Priority. *Scientific American*. Retrieved from https://blogs.scientificamerican.com/observations/quantum-computing-must-be-a-national-security-priority/

Hirohata, A., Yamada, K., Nakatani, Y., Prejbeanu, I.-L., Diény, B., Pirro, P., and Hillebrands, B. (2020). Review on Spintronics: Principles and Device Applications. *Journal of Magnetism and Magnetic Materials*, *509*(1). https://doi.org/10.1016/j.jmmm.2020.166711John, P. (2021, March 29). Ahmedabad: Quantum Leap for Hack-Proof Communication Recorde. *Times of India*. Retrieved from https://timesofindia.indiatimes.com/city/ahmedabad/quantum-leap-for-hack-proof-communication-recorded-by-isro-sac/articleshow/81740670.cms

Krelina, M. (2021, November 2). Quantum Technology for Military Applications. *arxiv.org*. Retrieved from https://arxiv.org/pdf/2103.12548.pdf

Liu, X., Hu, J., Li, Z. F. et al. (2021). Heralded Entanglement Distribution between Two Absorptive Quantum Memories. *Nature*, *594*(41–45). https://doi.org/10.1038/s41586-021-03505-3Los Alamos National Security. (2010). Quantum Cryptography. *lanl*. Retrieved from www.lanl.gov/science/centers/quantum/cryptography.shtml

Lutz, C., and Yang, K. (2019, October 24). Building Single-Atom Qubits under a Microscope. *IBM*. Retrieved from www.ibm.com/blogs/research/2019/10/controlling-individual-atom-qubits/

Menon, S. (2021). *India and Asian Geopolitics: The Past, Present*. Washington, DC: Brookings.Mims, C. (2019, June 4). The Day When Computers Can Break All Encryption Is Coming. *The Wall Street Journal*. Retrieved from www.wsj.com/articles/the-race-to-save-encryption-11559646737

NASEM. (2019). *Quantum Computing: Progress and Prospects*. Washington, DC: The National Academies.Objectives What we are going for. (n.d.). *openqkd*. Retrieved from https://openqkd.eu/objectives/

Pai, S. (2021, October 11). India's C-DoT to Work on 6G, Rolls out Quantum Communication Lab. *developingtelecoms*. Retrieved from https://developingtelecoms.com/telecom-technology/12069-india-s-c-dot-to-work-on-6g-rolls-out-quantum-communication-lab.html

Pompili, M. et al. (2021). Realization of a Multimode Quantum Network of Remote Solid-State Qubits. *Science*, *372*, 259–264. https://doi.org/10.1126/science.abg1919Powell, J. (2008). The Quantum Limit to Moore's Law. Proceedings of the IEEE (pp. 1247–1248). IEEE.

Quantum Cryptography: Photons and BB84. (n.d.). *Web.uvic.ca*. Retrieved from www.web.uvic.ca/~rdesousa/teaching/P280/L13_280.pdf

Renner, R. (2015). *Quantum Information Theory Solutions 13*. Retrieved from https://edu.itp.phys.ethz.ch/hs15/QIT/sol13.pdf

Rotman, D. (2020, February 24). We're Not Prepared for the End of Moore's Law. *MIT Technology Review*. Retrieved from www.technologyreview.com/2020/02/24/905789/were-not-prepared-for-the-end-of-moores-law/

Stefanick, T. (2020, September 18). The State of U.S.-China Quantum Data Security Competition. *Brookings*. Retrieved from www.brookings.edu/techstream/the-state-of-u-s-china-quantum-data-security-competition/

Swamy, S. (2021, October 21). The Outlines of a National Security Policy. *The Hindu*. Retrieved from www.thehindu.com/opinion/op-ed/the-outlines-of-a-national-security-policy/article37098810.ece

Toshiba Achieves Chip-Based QKD Tech. (2021, October 22). *Photonics*. Retrieved from www.photonics.com/Articles/Toshiba_Achieves_Chip-Based_QKD_Tech/a67457

Tummala, R. (2019). Moore's Law for Packaging to Replace Moore's Law for ICS. 2019 Pan Pacific Microelectronics Symposium (Pan Pacific) (pp. 1–6). IEEE.

University of Science and Technology of China. (2021, January 6). The World's First Integrated Quantum Communication Network. *Phys.org*. Retrieved from https://phys.org/news/2021-01-world-quantum-network.html

Zhu, D., Colangelo, M., Korzh, B., and Ramirez, E. (2019). Superconducting Nanowire Single-Photon Detector with Integrated Impedance-Matching Taper. *Applied Physics Letters*.

7

APPLICATION OF BLOCKCHAIN TECHNOLOGY IN MILITARY AFFAIRS

Sonchita Debnath

Introduction

In the digital age, societal systems are becoming increasingly more complex and intertwined. The understanding of these complex systems requires greater use of technologies, which can record, monitor and compute the data. The introduction of sophisticated technologies such as machine learning, Artificial Intelligence, and quantum computing is helping solve complex problems in social and physical sciences. Most of these technologies have their principles in quantum mechanics and thermodynamics, which are adapted and changed to suit the needs of a particular sector or industry. One such technology is blockchain technology.

The recent years have seen variations in adopting blockchain technology in multidisciplinary sectors and industries such as banking and finance (Zhang et al., 2020), medicine and healthcare services (Siyal et al., 2019) and energy (Wang et al., 2021). The distinct features of the technology in providing safe and secure transactions by encrypting the transactions have forced defense organizations across the world to take a note of it (Sealy et al., 2020). The North Atlantic Treaty Organization (NATO), the Defense Advanced Research Projects Agency (DARPA), and the Lebanese Armed Forces (LAF) have been working on leveraging the features of blockchain technology to build robust communications, battlefield operations management, and secured supply chain in defense operations.

The blockchain technology is lucrative for defense because the defense industries are dependent on manual, paper-based documentation to maintain the records of the compliance activities (Wasim Ahmad et al., 2021). When various entities work together in parallel, the manual documentation

DOI: 10.4324/9781003482703-10

is susceptible to human errors such as data entry errors, data duplication and data manipulation. Blockchain provides a single, seamless, synchronized, and immutable data record. It is an economically wise option to eliminate data errors and delegation of authority to oversee transactions. The distinctive feature of smart contracts in blockchain technology maintains trust among participants by being a tamperproof self-executing contract. These smart contracts can be used to verify various machinery components, track supplies on the battlefield, coordinate efforts for rescue operations, create transparency in the supply chain and remove data duplication. This subsequently builds trust among stakeholders in the system.

The following sections will provide a chronological history of the blockchain technology along with its application in defense services. It will give examples of various projects undertaken by governments across the world to include this rapidly growing technology in their militaries.

Background

History of Blockchain

The various elements of current blockchain technology necessitate understanding the origin of the technology. The idea of blockchain technology as a kind of distributed database can be traced back to at least the 1970s (Sherman et al., 2018). A cryptographically secured chain of blocks was introduced by Ralph Merkle (Merkle, 1978). This was further worked on and included in the white paper by cryptographer Haber and Stornetta, which had the feature of time-stamping the records being introduced for the first time (Haber and Stornetta, 1991). In 1992, Merkle tree[1] was added to make the existing design more secure and efficient. And, in 1994, Haber and Stornetta started their company Surety. The concept of time-stamping the documents has become the cornerstone of the current version of blockchain technology.

Technology underwent changes in 1997 when Nick Szabo published a paper introducing the concept of 'smart contract'. He compared smart contracts to vending machines where the vending machine takes in coins and, through simple algorithms, dispenses change and the ordered product in accordance with the price displayed. Through various safety mechanisms, the coins collected in a box are kept secured. In this sense, the vending machine is acting on a contract between the coin bearer and the vendor (Szabo, 1997). In 1998, Szabo came up with the idea for bit gold, which was a secure way of conducting transactions using various elements of cryptography and mining. Although the project was never implemented, his work on using smart contracts for a variety of other purposes that are monitored digitally became a direct predecessor to develop blockchain technology.

Bruce Schneier and John Kelsey's work in 1998 on authenticating and protecting transactions through secured logs on untrusted machines using cryptography proved to be a stepping stone for research on blockchain (Schneier and Kelsey, 1998). In 2000, Stefan Konst published a paper outlining a way to a unified theory to cryptographically protect chains and provided various ways to implement the technology (Konst, 2000). In 2004, computer scientist Hal Finney introduced Reusable Proof of Work (rPoW) as a prototype for digital cash. In addition, blockchain technology solved the problem of double-spending by keeping the ownership of the registered tokens on trusted servers (Finney, n.d.), thus building the foundation for mining, owning and exchanging of cryptocurrencies.

In 2008, Satoshi Nakamoto, who is considered to have changed the way blockchain technology works, provided a comprehensive theory on distributed blockchain. He improved the design to add blocks to the initial chain without being signed by trusted parties. The designs were modified to contain a secured history of data exchanges giving the current blockchain the feature to view all the transactions on the chain (Nakamoto, 2009). It utilizes a peer-to-peer network for time-stamping and verification of each exchange. The system was developed in such a way that it could be managed independently without any overarching central authority. These developments went on to become the backbone of blockchain technology.

The Basic Functioning of Blockchain Technology

Software systems can be designed mainly in two ways: centralized and decentralized/distributed systems (Tanenbaum and Steen, 2006). Both the systems have distinct ways to provide security and integrity. Each system has its own benefits, challenges and specific outcomes on the functional and non-functional facets of the working system. The centralized system has a single central authority, which develops and edits its core code. The authority that is in charge of the code can also impact the working of the software and the way a user views and uses it. The decentralized system has distributed access. This system generates more trust among the users as the status quo is maintained or disrupted by more than one user. Blockchain technology is a distributed software system that ensures trust and security by taking consensus from multiple users or nodes.

The definition of distributed systems is varied in the literature. A distributed ledger can be understood as a distributed system with distributed authority. According to Tanenbaum, 'a distributed system is a collection of independent computers that appears to its users as a single coherent system' (Tanenbaum and Steen, 2006). Jaspreet Bindra defined it as 'a distributed database shared among a network of computers, all of which must approve a transaction before it can be recorded' (Bindra, 2019). The efficiency of the decentralized systems depends on the seamless, transparent, secured communication and cooperation among independent components. In order to record a transaction in the chain, approval from the participants is necessary. This helps in building trust among the platform users.

Further, the benefits of using distributed systems are that they can provide higher computing power, facilitate cost reduction, promote higher reliability by removing a single point of failure and possess a natural ability to grow (Drescher, 2017). The disadvantages of the distributed systems are difficulty in developing coordination among the peers, varying level of dependencies on networks that provide assistance in transfer of information and security issues arising from less restrained access to the ledger.

Blockchain technology works as a tool toward establishing integrity in the implementation layer of the distributed system. It helps in connecting peers in a distributed system where every peer possesses a copy of the global ledger. To authenticate the transactions on the chain, the network employs a consensus algorithm. Without any doubt, blockchain technology changes the way an individual operates their trust. Trust will be anchored to the algorithms and their cryptographic hashing (security encryption).

Types of Blockchain

The blockchain promotes trust by being immutable, transparent, decentralized and highly programmable as per the user's needs (Sun et al., 2020). It is a distributed ledger that documents the transactions in various blocks. Every block on the chain contains a unique hash and a timestamp, which make it tamperproof, collaborative and connected to the previous blocks. The 'nodes', also called 'network users', verify the transactions in regular intervals. Every user can view the transactions that are documented in the block. These transactions are distributed, public and secured through encryption. To change the contents of a single block, one must reconfigure the data at every node, which is computationally a difficult task.

One of the most important characteristics of blockchain technology is its ability to be molded according to the nature of the network's operation. Public blockchain is a type of non-restrictive chain in which anyone can be a part of – as a user, a node, or a community member. A public blockchain is a decentralized, costly, and most secured chain. The public blockchain can be used in sectors to increase transparency, as all the transactions made are visible to every participant. Sectors such as banking systems, elections, public distribution systems (PDS), document archiving and the like can benefit highly from the use of public blockchain.

Systems that plan to operate in a restricted manner and cater to selective people can make use of private blockchain, also known as permission blockchain. Private blockchain provides all the features of a public blockchain, including transparency, immutability and trust, but only to a selected number of users. There is a presence of a central authority that manages the nature of network use and access to the database. Since admission on the network is of selected people, the private blockchain does not allow anonymity. Private blockchains are also easier to maintain and feasible to implement due to lower costs. This type of blockchain can be used by companies or organizations for their own internal use. In private blockchain, alteration of any record is not possible. This will reduce internal bribery to manipulate records, providing greater trust in the system.

The third type of blockchain is consortium blockchain. The chain is open to all, but only a part of the data is visible for public viewing. This chain provides efficiency along with transaction privacy. All the members of the chain are known entities; hence, they can decide who gets to view the transactions and which part. The cost is much lower compared to other types of blockchain. The consensus protocol is managed by pre-selected nodes, where each pre-selected node must verify the validity of the blocks. Consortium blockchain are partly private and are run by a group of varied companies.

Consensus Algorithm

The blockchain technology increases transparency and trust in the system by removing intermediaries by using a distributed verification process known as a consensus algorithm. The commonly known mechanisms are Proof of Work (PoW) and Proof of Stake (PoS). In PoW, authentication of transactions is conducted using a process called 'mining' (Herwejjer et al., 2018). Each block containing data has a unique hash attached to it. The miners are then asked to solve a complex cryptographic puzzle. Once this is solved, the block is mined, and the transaction is verified. The need for users to verify the transactions through the mining process provides higher security to the process, but it requires large computational capacity and speed. One of the criticisms to this process is its consumption of large amount of power. To tackle this, various companies are coming up with innovative technological and business models to make consensus algorithm mechanisms more energy efficient.

The PoS algorithm alleviates the obstacles faced by the PoW consensus mechanism. It simplifies the process of mining by using the users' existing stakes in the currency to validate the changes in the ledger. The validators are chosen at random to authenticate the transactions. To become a validator, the node deposits the network as 'stake'. The correlation between the stake and getting chosen as a validator is positive. Once the transaction is authenticated, the node receives a network or transaction fees. If the node validates a fake transaction, it loses a part of its stake. The PoS does not depend on computational power but instead focuses on economic incentives.

The continuous effort toward innovation to make this system more democratic and less energy-intensive, Delegated Proof of Stake (dPoS) as a consensus mechanism was introduced. dPoS is more technologically democratic where the users of the network elect validators of the next blocks. The chance to get selected as a validator is directly proportional to the number of tokens held by the user. In this mechanism as a participant in the election process, one stakes their tokens in a staking pool. Elected delegates upon successful validation receive the transaction fees, and the users receive rewards based on their stakes in the process. The system works on earning a reputation as a validator over a period of time. A wrongful validation leads to a loss of token as well as reputation. This mechanism promotes trust in the system by incentivizing the delegates' lawful behavior. Trust in the system is achieved through unified agreement, economic incentives, inalterability, storage of history of the transaction and a copy of ledger makes the technology a secure platform. Various other mechanisms have been consequently developed such as Proof of Authority, Proof of Importance and Proof of History (Herwejjer et al., 2018). The organization looking to implement blockchain technology in their systems can choose from numerous algorithms to record the transactions or can develop their own.

Smart Contracts

The main feature of blockchain technology is seen in its capability to remove central authorities and replace intermediaries with the capacity to provide decentralized processes and to facilitate 'smart contracts'. Smart contracts are self-executing programs that run when the predetermined conditions of the contract are met. The code is in the pattern of 'if/when . . . then' command (IBM, n.d.). The 'smart contracts' elicit a response to a pre-set condition, which, when met, initiates the transition. This code controls the execution and transactions. Once the action is complete, it is irreversible and traceable. Smart contacts can be used in maintaining track of the logistics and procurement. They can help in achieving higher levels of automation and efficiency. For example, to facilitate peer-to-peer energy trading between producers and consumers of renewable energy with ease, companies such as Powerledger are using these coded energy supply contracts to carry out the process of producing and exchanging energy without any or negligible interference by the intermediaries. The contracts have the type of energy source, units, where does this energy come from and the like to ensure greater consumer control. Once the criteria selected by the consumers are met, only then money transaction, or token exchange, is completed. This has helped them to automate and encrypt the process. The way the hierarchical structure communicates can be changed with the use of blockchain technology in energy trading. Companies have been using blockchain to ensure the smooth transition from centralized grids to decentralized grids.

Application of Blockchain Technology in Defense

The application of blockchain technology will be greatly beneficial for the defense forces. In the field of defense, as compared to public blockchain, private blockchain would be the most useful. With a private blockchain, access to the chain would be controlled, which is important to protect tactful information. Since private blockchains are characterized by the barriers to entry, with one administration in charge of accepting the participants and defining the rules of the chains (read and write permissions), they are the most suited to defensive uses. The system rules and access will be controlled by one selected entity. To ensure smooth communication among inter-services' governance, a hybrid blockchain would be a better solution.

Cyber Defense

The most important and easily applicable use case of blockchain technology in defense is to optimize cyber security and maintain data integrity. In 2017, the European Commission stated that there were more than 4,000 ransomware attacks per day, and as high as 80% of European companies experienced at least one cyber security incident (European Commission, 2017). The economic impact of these cyberattacks has risen five-fold during 2013–2017 (European Commission, 2017).

Cyber security depends on secrets and trust to be secure. Blockchain helps in preserving trust in two ways. The malware attacks against a system are attacks on the integrity and the configuration of the system. This technology promotes perimeter security by hashing, continuous monitoring and making it physically and computationally impossible to alter the data. Thus, instead of trying to hold up the perimeter walls, it monitors the wall and everything inside the wall. The implementation of the technology is low in cost and can provide high returns on investment.

Military Supply Chain Management

The present military supply chain and logistics have multiple contributing parts from various government/public and private actors. The relationship between the suppliers and the consumers is getting increasingly complex due to the association with developers, industry players and start-ups. With so many participants being part of the delivery system, miscommunication or failure points become unavoidable. The resolution of these miscommunications leads to increased costs and inaccuracies. The blockchain with its high delivery pace, security and traceability at a lesser cost has the potential to become a part of the solution. Since the traceability of the materials and parts is crucial in the defense industry, blockchain technology can help the industry register the origin of the machinery from production to delivery. This can also help to decrease the number of counterfeits.

Each part of the machinery is manufactured by manufacturers from all over the world, who source raw materials too from different parts of the globe. Thus, to procure one single machine involves numerous actors. The capability of blockchain to monitor every single step of the manufacturing process, including designing blueprint, prototyping, conducting tests and finally production of the machinery, can help build a secured chain. The scanning of goods and entry of the data at each step will also provide an overview to the logistics team and help maintain product paths. In case a part is found to be dysfunctional, the origin of the part and its path can be easily traced because of this technology. The absence of such tracking and visibility leads to miscommunication, confusion, and lack of trust among the network peers. Private blockchain, in which a private key is used by the node to make changes in the network, will help identify the partner. Information of varying degrees of sensitivity can be encrypted and made visible only to the allowed participants.

Increasingly, defense systems are using commercial off-the-shelf components for the installed software systems. This has given rise to suspicion about the deliberate vulnerabilities that these components might have, which can be exploited by an adversary as and when it wants. The blockchain can provide the origin of every component from 'cradle to cockpit' with greater auditability and identification of responsibility in real time.

Blockchain technology can also provide near real-time overview of products such as food and pharmaceuticals. This can make food-related outbreaks and the matter of healthcare on the battlefield a much more assured and transparent process.

Resilient Communication

Resilient communication is very useful in the Army especially during operations. In a high-end conflict, securing channels of communication takes utmost importance. These conflicts give the adversary a chance to attack on the electromagnetic spectrum, specifically on the systems such as satellites, undersea and on land cables and the strategic datalinks that form an important part of communications channels. These adversaries will also make an attempt to take control of the data that can be used to complete the kill chain. To tackle this threat, the data needs to be generated, stored and shared across the network in a secure manner. Along with this, communication systems would also need to be highly secure. In 2016, DARPA of the US Department of Defense had called for proposals from companies that can build a robust and secure messaging platform that the military can use to communicate, receive and send intelligence and store procurement contracts by using a decentralized system. Taking a note from other powers and understanding the need to tackle the fragility of India's cyber security (Krishnan, 2022; Yadav, 2017), the Indian Armed Forces have also stepped up its cyber security by launching 75 AI products during Artificial Intelligence in Defence (AIDef) symposium in 2022 (PIB, 2022a). The Indian Air Force (IAF) also inaugurated the Centre of Excellence for Artificial Intelligence in New Delhi (PIB, 2022b).

The blockchain technology secures every piece of information with cryptographic encryption. This provides personal data confidentiality, which can be useful to create combatant trackers. These distributed trackers can be provided to all participants, which would make the tracking of the soldier possible in real time. The tracking team can make use of this technology in tandem with other digital technologies, such as AI and quantum communications, in pursuit of the target. Unmanned aerial systems and various space-based sensors collect information that is sensitive. Blockchain technology can help in storing the data that would be impossible to falsify. The application of blockchain technology with specialist skills and attitudes of the century-long development of human skills and canine training will give a higher edge to the militaries (Berrill, 2020).

Blockchain through its smart contract feature can also help in managing funds among multiple transacting partners. It can help to automatically commit funds toward mutually agreed projects, such as supranational infrastructures. Increasingly, 3D printing is also used to manufacture a range of simple to complex parts, such as the small drones for surveillance, components of jet engine and submarine hulls (Klöckner et al., 2020). The use of technology in making defense services more efficient with less human loss will save a country's resources, which can be utilized for other development purposes.

Application of Blockchain Technology in Military Affairs

The use of blockchain technology in military affairs can be seen in various militaries around the world like Russia, the USA, China, France, Japan and South Korea. The use of traditional warfare techniques clubbed with modern technologies can be seen in the recent Ukraine-Russia war. The use of tanks and guns and the use of Unmanned Aerial Vehicles (UAV), AI and even social media has changed the nature of war.

European Union

The European Commission has funded various blockchain projects since 2013. It firmly believes that blockchain technology can impact various sectors across the European Union (EU) and can become an integral part of the foundation building for digital EU. The Digital Single Market initiative of the

EU is to convert national digital markets into a single market place for EU citizens and businesses. To increase the speed of innovation and assimilation, it has built an independent unit as the Communication and Technology Directorate-General (DG-CONNECT). The commission has set up a separate unit to develop blockchain technology under DG-CONNECT to assimilate the technology in the ongoing digitalization. The European Commission has commenced multiple initiatives to enable a chain of cooperation, governance and investments in developing and implementing blockchain-related solutions (European Commission, n.d.).

The European Blockchain Partnership (EBP) between the EU member states and some members of the European Economic Area (Norway and Liechtenstein) establishes a political collaboration to recognize the potential of blockchain technology (Verbeek and Lundqvist, 2021). The partnership was formed in 2018 to deliver several cross-border public services to the citizens to help the society and the economy transition into a secured digital age. The European Blockchain Services Infrastructure (EBSI) is the core aim of the partnership between the European Commission and EBP. The blockchain infrastructure's objective is to create a network of distributed nodes that can help public administrations and their ecosystems a foolproof method to verify information and build trustworthy public services (Verbeek and Lundqvist, 2021). Various initiatives that will fund start-ups, small and medium enterprises (SMEs) and eligible companies working on developing blockchain-based solutions have been taken up by the commission. Its upcoming support mechanism called Horizon Europe will support projects that will have dual use, that is, civilian-military blockchain systems, in Europe (European Commission, 2017).

The European Defense Agency (EDA) is exploring the potential that blockchain technology has in providing data authentication, information security, data integrity and resilience, communication and cyber security (Sanchez, 2017). In 2019, France's Minister of Defense signed a cyber security pact with eight defense industrial groups to enhance cyber defense capabilities.

The focus of the EU to become a strong security and defense force is a result of various factors such as Brexit, growing tensions within the European defense industries amidst budget cuts and increased technological competition at the global level (Csernatoni, 2021). The ability of EU to establish greater presence of the blockchain technology in defense services was further facilitated by the various partnerships among multiple stakeholders taking the central position in policymaking.

United States

Since the 1990s, the US has included advanced technologies to improve their military capabilities. Today, battlefield soldiers use digitally controlled tools, connected to devices for airstrikes, spy drones, communication and streaming videos of battlegrounds. This has amounted to an increasing influx of data that consists of sensitive information. The current communication system of the US Armed Forces is proving inadequate in the face of rising cyber-attacks. In 2018, the Pentagon confirmed a cyber-breach of the Defense Department, which compromised the personal information and credit card data of US military and civilian personnel (Baldor, 2018). As many as 30,000 workers were estimated to have been affected. In its Information Resource Management Strategic Plan FY 2019–2023, it prioritizes cybersecurity, AI, cloud computing and the three Cs: command, control and communications (DoD, 2019). The report outlines that DARPA will experiment with blockchain technology to create robust communication channel and develop a secured platform using cryptography that will allow to process transactions that can be tracked down through multiple channels of a decentralized ledger (DoD, 2019).

In 2021, a cyber security firm, Galois, received $15.3 million to design a system that will aim to secure data confidentiality (Zimmerman and Archer, 2021). Bespoke Asynchronous Silicon-Accelerated LWE Intrinsics through Software/Hardware Codesign (BASALISC) is a part of DARPA's Data Protection in Virtual Environments (DPRIVE). DPRIVE aims in designing and implementing systems that can perform difficult tasks such as Fully Homomorphic Encryption (FHE) computations (DARPA, 2020).

It is also working on bringing blockchain as a part of solution for issues like tackling supply chain attacks, managing military logistics and creating secured communication channels from the battlefield. Lockheed Martin is the first US defense contractor to have used blockchain technology to secure its development processes (Guardtime, 2022). The firm has also worked on creation of detection and communication solutions for the US National Security market. Since 2015, Lockheed Martin and Guardtime Federal have led various pilots of data integrity technologies to solve the threat of manipulation in a network (Guardtime, 2022).

The US Navy has signed a $1.5 million contract with Consensus Networks to develop a logistics system named HealthNet using a blockchain-enabled system. The network aims to dispense logistics for sailors and marines with real-time monitoring via the HealthNet platform (Nelson, 2021). In 2020, SIMBA chain, a blockchain firm, received a $9.5 million contract to develop and deploy a blockchain-based messaging and transaction platform for the Naval Air Warfare Center (Bhardwaj, n.d.). It also offers a cloud-based smart contract to be used by the Naval Information Warfare Systems Command (NAVWAR). The urgency to adopt blockchain technology is brought in by private companies in the US. These companies are forcing the government to take note of the technology and is part of growing blockchain advocacy groups with leading tech companies such as IBM, Deloitte and Accenture; global law firm Norton Rose Fulbright; and security and aerospace company

Lockheed Martin along with foundations such as Value Technology Foundation are spearheading the race. There is a growing recognition of the need of this technology among the policymakers and government heads, which is making this technology more mainstream in defense services.

Russia

Russia in an official statement by Voentelecom mentioned that they see the use of blockchain technology in private and state agencies in the near future including Russian Defense Ministry (TASS, 2017). The Russian DoD has also launched a blockchain technology lab, under the nation's military technology accelerator known as ERA, to identify cyber-attacks and secure critical infrastructure (Shen, 2018). Often, online intruders after accessing the logs on the devices clear the traces to hide the routes. The distributed nature of the blockchain technology minimizes this risk.

Unlike the US where the need for the technology is brought to the forefront by private companies, Russia's advancement in technology is coming from its government. The blockchain lab is the proof that Russian government is looking to use this technology to help make their defense services efficient and better and to find real-life uses. This may also seem as Russia's attempt to regain its prowess in military warfare.

China

China has been very supportive and active in adopting blockchain technology to transform its industries. In 2019, President Xi Jinping urged his country's tech community to help in accelerating the development of blockchain technology (Kharpal, 2019b). China has registered for the greatest number of 3.0 web patents that use a decentralized model of internet (Cliffe et al., 2020). It has also created a favorable environment for innovative firms working on this technology by providing access to funds and infrastructure. The Chinese government has spent an estimated sum of $300 million in FY19 and $1 billion in FY20 on initiatives related to blockchain (Cliffe et al., 2020).

The development of blockchain technology in China is seen as an opportunity to make not only defense but also other sectors such as finance, logistics, manufacturing and healthcare more efficient. The Chinese government has registered more than 500 blockchain projects under the Cyber Administration of China (Kharpal, 2019a). It is leveraging the technology to make the financial settlements transparent and free from a single country's control. The People's Liberation Army (PLA) plans on using the blockchain technology for managing the distribution of funds for intelligence operations, protecting data on personnel and weapons' life cycle, maintaining military logistics and making operations safer (Cliffe et al., 2020). PLA is also planning to use the technology to give the soldiers non-financial incentives based on the data on their career path, missions undertaken and performance reports (Zhen, 2019).

China is investing heavily in modern technologies. These technologies such as AI, quantum computing and blockchain technology are becoming a major part of the country's defense services. By entering the blockchain tech market at a nascent stage, China is attempting to better its stakes at becoming a global superpower. China's policy of experimenting with blockchain technology but no to bitcoin also says that it will look at various other industries where blockchain technology can be used. China's success in implementation and integration of blockchain technology in multiple industries can determine the course of development in the technology as well as China's goals of becoming a world leader.

Conclusion

The advent of the blockchain technology created a race to develop and implement the technology to the existing operations. Blockchain technology is seen as a panacea for all the issues and difficulties that are currently being faced by the systems. However, the technology is not without challenges. The adoption of permissioned blockchain networks in military will be different than the existing hierarchical system. The implementation of the technology has to be done carefully and seamlessly without disrupting the DoD operations, which demands quick response to the dynamic conditions on the field. The adoption of permission-less blockchain raises concern over privacy and data protection while transmitting sensitive information on the chain. This has to be mitigated using specific controls and proper access keys to the chain. Most of the attributes of the blockchain technology are applicable to the transactions included in a published block. Transactions outside are still susceptible to various kinds of on-chain and off-chain breaches. On-chain breaches such as Sybil attack, 51% attack and man-in-the-middle attack can hamper the working of the chain. Off-chain breaches like Oracle problem, which arises when the technology has to interact with the real world, showcase the lack of maturity of the technology (Yaga et al., 2019).

In conclusion, while the technology promises some solutions for our existing gaps in maintaining robust communication channels or cyber security, it also poses some new challenges in terms of control and command operations. As Yaga puts it, the question that developers must ask is, "How could the block-chain technology potentially benefit us?" rather than retrofitting our problems into the blockchain technology paradigm (Yaga et al., 2019). The technology is still undergoing a lot of changes based on continuous efforts to make it more energy-efficient, secure and affordable that will make it more applicable. However, the newness of the technology also raises novel social, ethical, financial and even political issues. The policymakers must be more mindful of the greater implications of this technology rather than looking at it from a narrow lens. To identify the probable issue and to ensure its scalability and interoperability, the technology must be piloted using various regulatory sandboxes.

Note

1 Merkle tree is a hash-based data structure that helps in verifying large data especially in distributed systems. This is useful as it allows the users to download a specific transaction and not the whole chain. It derives its efficiency by summarizing the transactions that have taken place in a block and produces a unique digital fingerprint.

References

Baldor, L. (2018). Pentagon Reveals Cyber Breach of Travel Records | AP News. *AP News*. Retrieved from https://apnews.com/article/7f6f4db35b0041bdbc5467848225e67d

Berrill, D. (2020, September 24). The Emergence of Combined Technologies: Establishment of a Combat Tracking Unit. *The Cove*. Retrieved from https://cove.army.gov.au/article/emergence-combined-technologies-establishment-combat-tracking-unit

Bhardwaj, S. (n.d.). US Air Force taps SIMBA Chain for Budgeting and Accounting System. *Forbes India*. Retrieved September 21, 2022, from www.forbesindia.com/article/crypto-made-easy/us-airforce-taps-simba-chain-for-budgeting-and-accounting-system/77389/1

Bindra, J. (2019*On Digital Transformation and the Technologies that Enable It*. Gurgaon, Haryana; New Delhi: Penguin Random House India Private Limited.

Cliffe, A., Eyre, P., and Gitlitz, M. (2020). *Potential Uses of Blockchain by the U.S. Department of Defence*. Retrieved from www.crowell.com/NewsEvents/Publications/Articles/Potential-Uses-of-Blockchain-by-the-US-Department-of-Defense

Csernatoni, R. (2021). The EU's defence ambitions: Understanding the emergence of a European Defence Technological and Industrial Complex. Retrieved from https://carnegieendowment.org/files/Csernatoni_EU_Defense_v2.pdf

DARPA (2020). *Data Protection in Virtual Environments (DPRIVE)*. Retrieved from https://www.darpa.mil/program/data-protection-in-virtual-environments(Accessed: 21 January 2024).

DoD (2019). *DoD Digital Modernization Strategy Information Resource Management Strategic Plan FY2019–FY2023*. Retrieved from https://media.defense.gov/2019/Jul/12/2002156622/-1/-1/1/DOD-DIGITAL-MODERNIZATION-STRATEGY-2019.PDF (Accessed: 21 January 2024)

Drescher, D. (2017). *Blockchain Basics: A Non-Technical Introduction in 25 Steps*. Frankfurt: Apress.

European Commission. (n.d.). What We Do- Communications Networks, Content and Technology. *European Commission*. Retrieved September 20, 2022, from https://ec.europa.eu/info/departments/communications-networks-content-and-technology/what-we-do-communications-networks-content-and-technology_en

European Commission. (2017). *Dual Use Technology in the EU, Publications Office of the EU*. Retrieved from https://op.europa.eu/en/publication-detail/-/publication/e501f0c4-cb49-11e7-a5d5-01aa75ed71a1 (Accessed: 19 January 2024).

Finney, H. (n.d.). Reusable Proofs of Work. *Satoshi Nakamoto Institute*. Retrieved September 23, 2022, from https://nakamotoinstitute.org/finney/rpow/index.html

Guardtime. (2022, April 27). Lockheed Martin Contracts Guardtime Federal for Innovative Cyber Technology. *Guardtime.* Retrieved from https://guardtime.com/blog/lockheed-martin-contracts-guardtime-for-innovative-cyber-technology

Haber, S. and Stornetta, W. S. (1991). How to Time-Stamp a Digital Document. *Journal of Cryptology, 3*(2), 99–111. https://doi.org/10.1007/bf00196791.

Herwejjer, C., Waughray, D., and Warren, S. (2018). *Building Block(Chain)s for a Better Planet.* Retrieved from www3.weforum.org/docs/WEF_Building-Block chains.pdf

IBM. (n.d.). What Are Smart Contracts on Blockchain? *IBM.* Retrieved September 23, 2022, from www.ibm.com/sa-en/topics/smart-contracts

Kharpal, A. (2019a, December). With Xi's Backing, China Looks to Become a World Leader in Blockchain as US Policy is Absent. *CNBC.* Retrieved from www.cnbc.com/2019/12/16/china-looks-to-become-blockchain-world-leader-with-xi-jinping-backing.html

Kharpal, A. (2019b, December 15). With Xi's Backing, China Looks to Become a World Leader in Blockchain as US Policy is Absent. *CNBC.* Retrieved from www.cnbc.com/2019/12/16/china-looks-to-become-blockchain-world-leader-with-xi-jinping-backing.html

Klöckner, M., Kurpjuweit, S., Velu, C., and Wagner, S. M. (2020). Does Blockchain for 3D Printing Offer Opportunities for Business Model Innovation? *Research-Technology Management, 63*(4), 18–27. https://doi.org/10.1080/08956308.2020.1762444

Konst, S. (2000). *Secure Log Files Based on Cryptographically Concatenated Entries.* Retrieved from www.konst.de/stefan/seclog.pdf

Krishnan, A. (2022, February 24). U.S. Group Hacked Top Research Institutes in India, Russia and China, Says Beijing Cyber Firm. *The Hindu.* Retrieved from - www.thehindu.com/news/international/us-group-hacked-top-research-institutes-in-india-russia-and-china-says-beijing-cyber-firm/article65079559.ece

Merkle, R. C. (1978). Secure Communications Over Insecure Channels. *Communications of the ACM, 21*(4), 294–299. https://doi.org/10.1145/359460.359473

Nakamoto, S. (2009). Bitcoin: A Peer-to-Peer Electronic Cash System. *Cryptography Mailing List at Https://Metzdowd.Co m.*

Nelson, D. (2021, May 20). US Navy Launches Blockchain Research in Mission to Improve Tracking System. *CoinDesk.* Retrieved from www.coindesk.com/markets/2020/05/20/us-military-is-falling-behind-china-russia-in-blockchain-arms-race-ibm-accenture/

PIB. (2022a). Raksha Mantri Launches 75 Artificial Intelligence Products/Technologies During First-Ever "AI in Defence" Symposium & Exhibition in New Delhi; Terms AI as a Revolutionary Step in the Development of Humanity. In *Press Bureau Information.* Press Information Bureau (PIB). Retrieved from www.pib.gov.in/PressReleasePage.aspx?PRID=1840740

PIB. (2022b). Artificial Intelligence (AI) Centre of Excellence (Coe) launched by IAF. In *Press Bureau Information.* Press Information Bureau. Retrieved from www.pib.gov.in/PressReleasePage.aspx?PRID=1840695

Sanchez, S. (2017). Blockchain Technology in Defence. *European Defence Agency,* 17.

Schneier, B., and Kelsey, J. (1998). Cryptographic Support for Secure Logs on Untrusted Machines. USENIX Security Symposium. Proceedings of the 7th USENIX Security Symposium San Antonio, Texas, January 26–29, 1998

Sealy, R., Gray, C., Brady, G., Thompson, S., Denosky, M., and Lemasson, M. (2020). *How Blockchain Can Transform Defence Assets and Give Armed Forces an Advantage on the Battlefield?* Retrieved from www.pwc.com/blockchain-defence

Shen, M. (2018, July 2). The Russian Military is Building a Blockchain Research Lab. *CoinDesk*. Retrieved from www.coindesk.com/markets/2018/07/02/the-russian-military-is-building-a-blockchain-research-lab/

Sherman, A. T., Javani, F., Zhang, H., and Golaszewski, E. (2018). On the Origins and Variations of Blockchain Technologies. *IEEE Security & Privacy*, 17(1), 72–-77. https://doi.org/10.1109/msec.2019.2893730.

Siyal, A. A., Junejo, A. Z., Zawish, M., Ahmed, K., Khalil, A., and Soursou, G. (2019). Applications of Blockchain Technology in Medicine and Healthcare: Challenges and Future Perspectives. *Cryptography*, 3(1), 3. https://doi.org/10.3390/cryptography3010003

Sun, R.-T., Garimella, A., Han, W., Chang, H.-L., and Shaw, M. J. (2020). Transformation of the Transaction Cost and the Agency Cost in an Organization and the Applicability of Blockchain – A Case Study of Peer-to-Peer Insurance. *Frontiers in Blockchain*, 3, 24. https://doi.org/10.3389/FBLOC.2020.00024

Szabo, N. (1997). Formalizing and Securing Relationships on Public Networks. *First Monday*, 2(9). https://doi.org/10.5210/fm.v2i9.548

Tanenbaum, A. S, and Steen, M. Van (2006). *Distributed Systems: Principles and Paradigms* (2nd ed.). Harlow: Pearson, Prentice Hall.

TASS. (2017, August 22). Blockchain Technology May be Introduced in Russia's Armed Forces. *TASS*. Retrieved from https://tass.com/defense/961423

Verbeek, A., and Lundqvist, M. (2021). *Artificial Intelligence, Blockchain and the Future of Europe: How Disruptive Technologies Create Opportunities for a Green and Digital Economy*. Luxembourg: European Investment Bank.

Wang, Q., Li, R., and Zhan, L. (2021). Blockchain Technology in the Energy Sector: From Basic Research to Real World Applications. *Computer Science Review*, 39, 100362. https://doi.org/10.1016/j.cosrev.2021.100362

Wasim Ahmad R., Hasan, H., Yaqoob, I., Salah, K., Jayaraman, R., and Omar, M. (2021). Blockchain for Aerospace and Defence: Opportunities and Open Research Challenges. *Computers & Industrial Engineering*, 151, 106982. https://doi.org/10.1016/j.cie.2020.106982

Yadav, Y. (2017). Hackers from China Break Into Secret Indian Government Video Chat. *The New Indian Express*. Retrieved from www.newindianexpress.com/nation/2017/nov/19/hackers-from-china-break-into-secret-indian-government-video-chat-1705010.html

Yaga, D., Mell, P., Roby, N., and Scarfone, K. (2019). *Blockchain Technology Overview*. https://doi.org/10.6028/NIST.IR.8202

Zhang, L., Xie, Y., Zheng, Y., Xue, W., Zheng, X., and Xu, X. (2020). The Challenges and Countermeasures of Blockchain in Finance and Economics. *Systems Research and Behavioural Science*, 37(4), 691–698. https://doi.org/10.1002/sres.2710

Zhen, L. (2019, November 13). Reward Chinese Soldiers in Cryptocurrency, Military Mouthpiece Says. *South China Morning Post*. Retrieved from www.scmp.com/news/china/military/article/3037592/reward-chinese-soldiers-cryptocurrency-military-mouthpiece-says

Zimmerman, D., and Archer, D. (2021). Galois's BASALISC Project Wins $15.3M DARPA Contract and Aims to Finish "The Last Mile" of Data Confidentiality – Galois, Inc. *Galois*. Retrieved from https://galois.com/blog/2021/03/galois-basalisc-project-wins-15-3m-darpa-contract/

8

CYBER SECURITY STRUCTURE IN INDIA

Vedant Saigal and Arun Teja Polcumpally

Introduction

The earlier chapters on data, Artificial Intelligence (AI), quantum communications, and blockchain revealed the intensity of the digitization of society and its impact on the Indian military. It is time to understand the cyber security structure of India and assess whether it can handle the technologies like AI, blockchain, and quantum communications effectively. The mere existence of these technologies will not prompt a state to re-organize its priorities and accommodate the new technologies into its security structure. Reorganization of security structure because of digital technology requires securitization of digital technology. Heuristically proceeding, all technologies will be considered essential to national security when they are deemed to be essential and inevitable. It is because security is not only about military issues but also continuously revolves around safeguarding the vital, political, economic, and strategic interests of the nation.

From the perspective of the English school of thought on security studies, these technologies have to be securitized. Only then would the state take necessary steps to adopt these technologies to strengthen national security. This chapter premises that the securitization concept will provide a better framework to understand how and when the state assigns priorities to the technology and reorganizes its security structures.

Barry Buzan, Ole Weaver, Japp Wilde, and others at the Copenhagen school developed the concept of securitization (Stritzel, 2014). According to the Copenhagen school of thought, securitization is the mantle of the state (Kaunert and Yakubov, 2017). The state can categorize some aspects to be exceptions to protect them holistically. It includes state, population, economy,

DOI: 10.4324/9781003482703-11

identity, national culture, and so forth. These aspects are mentioned to have objective reality because, within the securitization concept, there are no subjective definitions of these terms. In the context of technologies and national security, when the usage of these technologies impacts the existence of any of these aspects, the state shall categorize them as exceptions. By doing so, the state takes measures by rising above the existing constraints (political, bureaucratic, and legislative).

Kaunert and Yakubov (2017) assert that securitization is a mix of social constructivism and realism. That means certain entities are socially constructed to be important to national security. With the latter as a premise, the securitization of emerging digital technologies can happen in various ways. A sudden crisis can elevate their importance, and an emergency panel can be constituted to look into these technologies. Alternatively, if the existing structures already consider cyberspace as a platform to realize a state's social contract, these technologies will be given priority on the national level. The outcome of such prioritization again depends on the perceived uses of the technology. On the whole, with securitization, the state deems a particular event or a technology to have national importance. With the emergence of national AI policies and increased budgets for the science and technology departments worldwide, it is safe to assert that digital technologies have been securitized.

India must urgently overhaul its cybersecurity framework to confront the evolving landscape shaped by emerging technologies such as AI, quantum computing, and blockchain. While India has made strides in recognizing the importance of cybersecurity with initiatives like the National Cyber Security Policy and Digital Personal Data Protection Act 2023, the cyberspace dynamics are quickly changing. India has a cyber security framework established in 2013 (Ministry of Electronics and Information Technology, 2013). However, it is opined that this framework is outdated and poorly implemented (Bhattacharjee, 2022). Realizing the changing dynamics of digital technologies and their rapid advancements, India has released National Cyber Security Policy draft in 2021 (Chandrasekhar, 2022). The actions taken on evolving digital technologies must be situated within the draft cyber security framework. If the framework does not fit, it has to be updated to fit the new technologies.

Before moving ahead, think about the question – *Is it necessary to securitize digital technologies?*

The Need for Cyber Security

There are ample examples that show that unprepared cyber security can cripple the country's economy and integrity. For example, private companies often do not implement strict cyber security protocols. Because of this, incidents like a customer data breach and hacking of critical infrastructure become prevalent. Other types of cyber-attacks are distributed denial of service (DDoS), false data injection, and injecting malicious code into the algorithm (Kumar and Prince, 2019). Not just the private companies or public sector companies, there are incidents of attacks on institutes of national importance. In 1998, Pakistani hacker groups targeted the website of Bhabha Atomic Research Centre (BARC). Since that incident, attacks on Indian scientific and military establishments have been a routine (Subramanian, 2020). The high cost of implementing the security protocols into its design is the major reason for the partial implementation of security protocols (Kumar et al., 2014). Because of this, cyber security has become voluntary in nature. Another example of not implementing strict IT security protocols is the situation of 'State Electricity Boards.' Due to their dire financial situation, they do not tend to implement high-level data security (Kumar et al., 2014, p. 131).

India ranks second in terms of the highest number of internet users in the world (Johnson, 2022). Considering that it is the most populated country, it is not really surprising. However, taking into consideration the levels of poverty the country has, being in such a position is commendable. This shows that the poor can also easily avail the internet services. High internet usage with low security paves the path for frequent cyber-attacks. As per the report published by Symantec Corp, India ranks among the top five countries to be affected by cybercrime (The Economic Times, 2018). The economic interests and national security face direct threats from professional cyber criminals from around the globe. Since India possesses a huge digital landscape, it also becomes vulnerable to cyber-attacks that threaten government initiatives like Smart India, E-Governance, and Digital India. With great power comes great responsibility.

Since the onset of the coronavirus pandemic in 2019, India witnessed an increase in cloud adoption, because most people shifted to working from home instead of being physically present in their respective offices (Sharma, 2021). This has simply led to magnifying the cyber security challenges. From this data, it is clear that there is a need to secure India's existing infrastructures. Further, elaborating on the above problem regarding the need to secure the information systems, the US President George W. Bush passed an executive order on 16 October 2001 that summarized the key issue after the 9/11 attack on the trade tower in the US:

> The information technology revolution has changed how business is transacted, government operates, and national defence is conducted. Those three functions now depend on an interdependent network of critical information infrastructures. The protection program authorized by this order shall consist of continuous efforts to secure information systems for critical infrastructure, including emergency preparedness communications, and

the physical assets that support such systems. Protection of these systems is essential to the telecommunications, energy, financial services, manufacturing, water, transportation, health care, and emergency services sectors.

(Bush, 2002)

The US, having realized the cyber threats in 2001, quickly developed significant cyber security apparatus. It developed systems to survey domestic and international information flows (Snowden, 2019). For the US, most of the security projects are directly funded by the Defence Advanced Research Projects Agency (DARPA). As of 2021, DARPA has active projects venturing into quantum-level precision of subatomic particles, human-machine interface, interpretation and prediction of world events, and so forth (Polcumpally, 2021). This is a quick peek into the US cyber security readiness.

Undoubtedly, the impact of digital technologies can be seen on the international arena. The wars that were fought before are not the same as those fought today. The earlier discussed digital transformations made military policies less attractive and favoured soft power over hard power. The security paradigm shifted from traditional to non-traditional. With the collapse of the Soviet Union in 1991, realism, as a school of thought, experienced a state of shock and brought along new concepts of security, such as human security, food security, cyber security, as well as environmental and social security (Snyder, 2005).

Cyber security entails using methods and technologies that protect computer software and hardware, networks, and data from any unauthorized access that is primarily supplied through the means of the internet, essentially by terrorist groups, cyber criminals, or hackers (REDDY, 2014). The internet has become the battlefield for cyber war. It is primarily a labyrinth as it is so interconnected, and it becomes impossible to define boundaries, especially when its commercialization aspect is looked at. It has truly become a medium for cybercrimes. As all the essential communications, including basic social interactions, are digital, cyber security should be securitized and given national security importance.

In the year 2020, during the Independence Day speech, Prime Minister Narendra Modi asserted that cyber threats would badly impact Indian society. To secure India holistically, he announced that the country would soon get a national cyber security policy (Indian Express, 2020). During an event organized by the Public Affairs Forum of India (PAFI) in July 2021, National Cybersecurity Coordinator at the Prime Minister's Office (PMO), Rajesh Pant, said that a new national cyber security policy is going to be released in that year (Zeebiz, 2021). In the year 2022, while addressing a webinar on 'Atmanirbhar Bharat in Defence-Call to Action,' Prime Minister Modi again reiterated that cyber security is of national importance. The following excerpt shows that Prime minister Modi considers IT to be a significant power enhancer to the military.

> India's IT sector is our great strength. The more we use this power in our defence sector, the more confident we will be in our security. For example, cyber security is no longer limited to the digital world only. It has become a matter of national security.
>
> *(Economic Times, 2022)*

Securitization should be followed by drafting a national framework for cyber security and protecting critical information infrastructure. There have been workshops conducted on cyber security frameworks and the protection of critical infrastructure that have highlighted the need to establish national frameworks (Bansal, 2018). However, India is yet to have a national cyber security policy. An attempt has been made to investigate the role of India as a developing nation state to secure cyberspace by building up cyber deterrence capabilities in the form of plausible deniability and retaliation capability. Further, operationalizing these capabilities through a comprehensive policy framework takes into account factors peculiar to India; the existing digital divide between developed and developing nations; the coexistence of multiple socio-economic categories in the country; and the interdependence of cyberspace-related resources among nation-states, political will and vision on the information age.

Cyber Security in the Indian Context

In order to understand the cyber security structure of India, it is advised first to understand how the Indian economy transited to e-economy. The story of India's growth continues even in the backdrop of a global economic slow-down triggered by the COVID-19 pandemic (Kugler and Sinha, 2020). The use of information technology (IT) has witnessed a continuous increasing thrust. The Government of India is seen by the world as a huge consumer of IT services. India is using IT not only to create new age channels for public services but also to manage its critical infrastructure (Telecom Regulatory Authority of India, 2020).

One example to showcase the IT-assisted economic development is e-commerce. According to the report by the Indian e-commerce industry, the e-commerce market is expected to grow from USD 46.2 billion in 2020 to USD 111.40 billion by the year 2025 (IBEF, 2021). The rationale behind such a predicted improvement is the increase in the usage of the internet and smartphones. Figure 8.1 is a representation of the quick increase in the internet penetration in India.

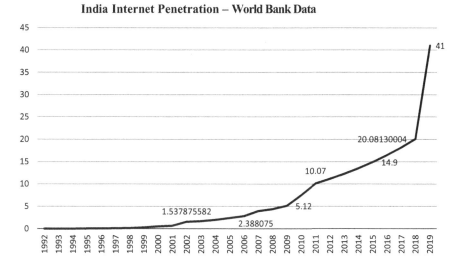

India Internet Penetration – World Bank Data

FIGURE 8.1   Internet Penetration Graph of India (World Bank, 2022)

The penetration percentage values are shown to represent the rapid increase in the usage of the internet. Internet penetration skyrocketed from the year 2018. It was 20% in 2018, and by the next year, it went to 41%. India's internet penetration as of January 2022 is 47% (Kemp, 2022).

Thanks to the government initiatives such as Digital India, Make-In India, Start-up India, Skill India, and Innovation Fund, which contributed to making the citizens aware of the country's cyber potential, though there are many other initiatives launched by the Government of India. The following paragraph discusses on one particular initiative called Digital India, as it has direct relevance to the cyberspace of the country (Borah, 2020).

Digital India is a platform that integrates government departments and the people of India. It aims to ensure that the services that the government provides for its citizens are available to them electronically. This not only reduces the use of paper and saves trees but also reduces the time and effort for an individual to travel to nearby government offices to collect the documents. The creation of this digital infrastructure not only encourages digital literacy but also provides a platform to voice out public opinion and demand. It shall be the duty of all the stakeholders to support such an initiative, for the country's growth. However, the initiative has been criticized by some scholars, as they noticed a lack of a legal framework, absence of privacy and data protection, insecurity of Indian cyberspace, lack of parliamentary oversight for e-surveillance in India, and also the lack of intelligence-related reforms (Erkut, 2020).

Policymaking in the area of cyber security is very sluggish. Perhaps it is not a stretch to say that policymakers in India have paid relatively less attention to cybersecurity, to such a point where the government is unable to address the country's growing need for a robust cybersecurity apparatus. There are advanced malwares such as Stunt, Flame, and Black Shades present in the cyberspace, which India perhaps have less potential to tackle with. Flame, for example, is a highly advanced piece of malware that attacks, gathers information systems, and leaks important or probably confidential files. It was named after one of the modules of Russian Security firm Kaspersky Labs. Stuxnet, however, targeted industrial programme logistics controllers (PLCs) and their related software as well as hardware.

There have been many projects that had been listed out, but they have only been seen on paper. For instance, India's National Critical Information Infrastructure Protection Centre (NCIIPC) stands as an organization under the Government of India under Section 70A of the IT Act 2000 through a gazette notification (Nickolov, 2005). NCIIPC simply takes care of the measures that facilitate the protection of the Critical Information Infrastructure and ensures that it stays protected from unauthorized use, malware, as well as modification and disruption. India witnessed a failure of National Cyber Security Policy in the year 2013, as its implementation lacked on the grounds of privacy violations and civil liberties intrusions in general. Though it is acknowledged by the Government of India that cybercrimes have shown an increasing graph recently, India appears to have taken less actions to protect its critical infrastructure (Rai, 2020).

There was a small empirical research conducted during the management development program consisting of 75 public service officers of India (Srinivas and Vivek, 2015). The research concluded that only 10.7% of respondents were affirmative on providing user awareness of cyber risks. This shows that the government does not consider educating its employees or the end users about the cyber risks involved. Removable media are one of the major sources of malware, and approximately 65% of the respondents say they do not have or follow any stringent policy on external devices. Scanning for malware also stands at 32% only. Another significant result is that 80% government officers replied that they do not check for new technical vulnerabilities and do not filter content.

As soon as the introduction of the United Nations Commission on International Trade Law (UNICITRAL) model law on e-commerce in 1996, there were many countries that adopted this law to regulate e-governance (Basu, 2004). The Information Technology Act of India in 2000 stands as a relevant example to support the penology related to cyber security. Eventually, the act saw a back step in its progress when it was heavily criticized for its failure to achieve its targets, when it came to protection of data including sensitive personal data, crimes that particularly targeted women and children, and cyber terrorism. The attack on 26/11 in Mumbai at Taj Hotel was an awakening call for the government officials to realize that the IT Act was not working at its full potential. Hence, it was later revamped in the year 2008 (Asawat, 2010).

The concept of world politics is essentially a struggle for power between nation-states. Influenced by the school of thought dealing with the political realism, George Kennan and Hans Morgenthau emphasized the importance of military strength as an index of state power. Eventually, the historians delved into the journey to study how the nation state was increasingly finding itself challenged for the events that originated beyond its borders and whose impact transcended national boundaries.

To understand the impact of IT on the contemporary societies, it is first important to understand what the reality is. The reality of today is that the transnational architecture of global information network has made transnational borders less significant. The application of IT to both the military and the civilian realms relevantly blurs the boundaries between the political, military, and the civilian spheres. It can be rightly said that the information domain has moved to a centre stage in combat operation.

Challenges of Cyber Security Within India

An incident took place in the year 2013, wherein a video image of a couple in a compromised position was captured inside a Delhi Metro station, and the video was allegedly recorded on a smartphone to feed on websites containing adult sexual content. Though Delhi Metro Railway Corporation lodged a complaint against the unidentified couple for obscenity in a public place, the case raised questions regarding the loopholes present in cyber security and privacy. It is the authority's duty under the Government of India to install surveillance cameras in public places and maintain the confidentiality and integrity of those persons recorded on cameras. However, in this case, Delhi Metro looked only at one side of its responsibility.

More than 11 lakh cases of cyber-attacks were tracked and reported to Computer Emergency Response Team in 2021. Power companies, oil and gas majors, and telecom vendors have been continuously reporting cybercrimes and ransomware attacks. The ransomware attacks in India have now crossed a 100% mark and are increasing annually.

It is only after the bourgeoned cyber-attacks and national security failure that the Government of India aimed at strengthening the rules and policies for ensuring security for government infrastructure and databases. For instance, after the Mumbai attack on 26/11, several reforms were within the Indian Information Technology Act 2000, and the main focus was put on cyber terrorism, henceforth providing stringent punishments for the crime committed (Halder, 2011). The punishments depending on the crime extended to life imprisonment as well. Even though the government has pulled up the socks in curbing cybercrime and increasing cyber security, the execution of the laws remains poor. This is simply because of the reason that several stake-holders, including government bureaucrats perhaps, are not aware of the measures regarding cyber security that need to be strictly and immediately implemented to protect confidential data and maintain privacy (Janssen and de Bruijn, 2017).

Another reason for the dismal functioning of the current cyber security structure is not having a clearly defined structure of a cyber security system. India has 35 separate organizations to deal with cyber security (Ali and Sukhkirandeep, 2021). This shows the bureaucratic un-understanding of the issue. The priority is given to uphold the control of the separate departments over the issues cropping up in their sector. No priority is given to address-ing the cyber issues. Why can't there be a central agency taking up all the cybercrime reports and have a machine learning (ML) algorithm to distribute the registered cases to respective wings/departments using the Natural Lan-guage Processing (NLP) techniques? Companies use the Application Tracking System (ATS) to track the applications and filter them based on text from résumés. That means the technology is already in practice. Why doesn't the government take it into account and deploy it? It appears that cyber security policymakers are unaware of the technology itself. This is one of the major challenges that the Government of India faces regarding cyber security.

Cyber Security in Indian Military

India has an extensive industrial base and maintains the third-largest armed forces in the world. India has been majorly linking its defence sector with the new technologies, be it in terms of surveillance, anti-drone defence systems, advanced missiles, and more. It is in the process of opening up to a set of ever-evolving threats due to a dependence on these particular set of advanced technologies. There was an incident that took place in the year 2012, wherein a cyber-attack was launched by hackers against the Indian Navy's eastern command computer systems (Patil, 2016). The computer system was particu-larly used for monitoring the activities in the South China Sea, concerning ballistic missile submarines. The virus that had affected the computer system secretly and undoubtedly illegally collected confidential documents, eventu-ally delivering them to the Chinese IP addresses (Patil, 2016).

It was not only the Indian Navy that was affected by cybercrime; it was also the National Security Agency and the Air Force that fell into that trap. It was two years before the attack on the Navy that the hackers were some-how able to open small numerous windows in the computer mainframes of the Air Force and were able to steal classified files. The main challenge that lies here is that India needs to be careful when merging its defence sector with the private sector operating the emerging technologies. There needs to be a cyber-defence environment to have a smooth functioning of the public sector and the private sector in the military. Like environmental assessments, technology compatibility, impact assessments, and ex ante threat assessments should be frequently conducted.

Another challenge that hinders the cyber security structure of India is the lack of awareness among not only the citizens but also the government officials. There have been cases where people were found to have kept passwords and username credentials saved in their mobile devices and encrypted in different websites (Jančis, 2022). By doing this, many individuals throw themselves to certain risks and enter the world of hackers, where they end up losing their data and privacy. Some people also share personal information on websites that involve certain transactions from the consumer end, which ultimately are declared fraud, and they end up empty pocketed.

The Stuxnet is a well-known incident among the security analysts that signifies the nuclear power plants being vulnerable to cyber-attacks. Taking an example of India, the malware attack at the Kudankulam Power Plant in Tamil Nadu took place in the year 2019. The malware named Dtrack attacked financial institutions in India and was built by Lazarus Group, a North Korea-linked company (Jay, 2019). As a consequence, it lessened the already-limited confidence in the nuclear power within the public, and hence, the Computer and Information Security Advisory Group ended up with strengthening measures like hardening of internet and blocking of certain websites that reckoned malicious activities (Selvaraj, 2019).

It was the domestic and international pressures that made the Government of India release the National Cyber Security Policy in the year 2013. This policy specifically outlined the strategies required to establish a secure and resilient cyberspace for citizens and businesses. It was two years before the US and India signed a Memorandum of Understanding (MoU) that aimed at promoting cyber security and easy exchange of information. It has been a pressing concern for the businesses in the US to conduct proper orientation of the Indian businesses in the field of cyber security, also because it happens to be an offshoring destination for back offices as such (Kshetri, 2016a, 2016b).

With regard to India's policies towards China in terms of cyberspace, India views Chinese firms with suspicion and hence generates a widespread fear that its national security might be a stake. There was an incident that took place around 2014, wherein Xiaomi Redmi Note, a cell phone model manufactured by the Chinese firm Xiaomi, was being used to secretly send the data of the Indian users to China-based servers. It was at right time that the Indian military was warned of the incident, and the transfers that were supposed to happen in the future were stopped (BBC, 2014).

In an article published by the *Indian Express*, it is expressed that India is without an end-to-end cyber security system for its government, including one for the PMO (Bhattacharjee, 2014). Regarding the proceedings of the G-20 Summit, the experts rightly pointed out India's weak potential in the cyber security architecture and regarded that as a primary problem. Moreover, the Prime Minister of India, Shri Narendra Modi, also expressed his concerns on tightening the cyber security standards of the country in the summit itself (Bhattacharjee, 2014).

A report titled 'Cyber Capabilities and National Power' was released by the International Institute of Strategic Studies. It is an influential think tank, specifically assessed the cyber capabilities of 15 countries inclusive of India. The capabilities were assessed on the governance, command and control, core cyber-intelligence capability, and global leadership in cyberspace affairs. Three countries were divided into three tiers of cyber power; the first one consisting of just the US as per its world-leading strength across all categories, the second one containing the strengths in some categories, and the third one containing potential strengths in some of the categories but significant weaknesses in others. India lies in the third tier. According to the report, India must harness its great digital-industrial potential and adopt a whole-of-society approach in order to step up in the second tier (IISS, 2021).

It was assessed in the report that India's thinking on cyber policy, in particular, for the civil sector has shown a stagnant graph. There were, however, some halts due to the onset of the COVID-19 pandemic. India still continued to proactively reframe each and every aspect of cyber security policies (Gurjar, 2021).

It is noted by scholars that though India deals with its own domestic threats daily, its cyber intelligence capabilities are much more focused on the neighbouring countries such as Pakistan and China. This is the primary reason for India's inability to expand its cyber intelligence reach and thus rely only on partnerships with successfully developed countries like the US, UK and France as such (Gurjar, 2021). India majorly depends on the private sectors in order to boost its technological advancements. The Minister of Defence has also urged the private defence manufacturers to invest in research and development, with special focus on the cyberspace altogether. India must take on further initiatives to curb down problems at the root levels, looking at not only cyber security as a main factor but also the ones that are associated with it such as corruption, information technology, lack of awareness, and unlimited access to internet. While protecting the cyberspace, the state itself should not assume the role of paternal despot. There are incidents with the Indian government where it takes an undue advantage of the communication lines to meet certain political goals. During the emergency period, Indira Gandhi ruthlessly controlled press (Subramanian, 2020). Even under Prime Minister Modi, there have been many accusations of internet control and abuse of human rights (Pearson, 2021). A proper cyber security should also consider state as a potential abuser of the cyberspace.

Future Prognosis

India has witnessed an increasing trend in cyber-attack reporting every day. For instance, if one looks at the increase in the ransomware attacks, India witnessed a 120% increase in 2021. There were almost 80% of the companies that possess a digital presence that experienced at least one ransomware attack. It was seen on the other side that 49% of the companies experienced multiple attacks (Murthy, 2022). These trends have formed a pattern and have transformed gradually. Moreover, it is likely that these trends will continue despite heavy investments in increasing cyber security. Table 8.1 depicts a trend that shows the transformation of cyber security in the country.

Perhaps, there is a need to realize that the complexities of cyber security framework are increasingly intricate.

It is righteously said that in no time, the world will experience the wars fought in cyberspace between the network of countries (Gartzke, 2013). India must be able to cope up with the benchmarks set by other countries in cyber security for it to deem fit in the battle and precisely be victorious. It is suggested that there needs to be a reform of the cyber security policy of 2013, in order to ensure that there are no ambiguities present (Rai, 2020). It is vital for India to maintain public-private partnerships domestically to contribute to its overall performance in curbing the cybercrimes. The coordination between the two will solve the problem of funds. Looking at the triple helix model of innovation, which essentially deals with capturing the interplay

TABLE 8.1 Transformation of Cyber Security

Mainframes	Client/Server	Internet	E-Commerce	Digital
1970s	1980s	1990s	2000	Recent Times
Natural hazards Physical response measures in place, such as evacuation and first aid	Dependence on a few new technologies Elementary disaster response to system failures Virus protection developed	Enterprise-wide risk management introduced common regulatory compliance policy Business continuity focus	Innovation in information Shift to online outsourcing, third party, like cloud-connected devices	Global shocks (terrorist, climate, political) Business resilience Internet of Things (IoT) Critical infrastructure State-sponsored cyber-attack Cyber war

Source: Ernst and Young (2017)

between the government, industry, and academia, one can relate it to cyber security policies. If the cyber security policies build up using the framework provided by this model, it could definitely turn out to be high-yielding not only for the industry leaders but also for the government itself. India must take inspiration from the propositions of the triple helix model to build more advancements in cyberspace itself (Hohmann, 2016).

It shall not be ethical and trustworthy for India to involve too much of international collaboration, when it comes to its data protection and cyber security. This simply is a micro-macro paradox, which explains why international collaboration could be essential, on one hand, and dangerous, on the other, and the same is the case with the domestic level. Broadening reliance on collaboration might lead to more information transfers and increase the chance of cyber frauds and cyber-attacks. Taking Google and Meta as examples, they are efficient service providers to the country but can also be accountable to steal confidential data. However, when it comes to operating at the domestic level, it can be said that the state might not have sufficient funding and resources to initiate cyber security mechanisms.

There is a need to promote cyber security campaigns through the help of social media, radio, newspaper, news channels, and other means of communication. People today lack awareness of the crimes that take place online, and they end up suffering for a lifetime; hence, this step is essential to be safe from online frauds and thefts. In order for the military to protect its information and operation details, and its increasing dependency on information technology, it regularly keeps conducting cyber security awareness campaigns. India must also create counter-terrorism cyber cells in each state so as to make the complexities of cyber-attacks easy to solve. In addition, there derives a need to monitor the cyber security cells or centres regularly, in order to analyse accountability and proper functioning (Hajoary and Akhilesh, 2020). India has five separate cyber security departments that do not coordinate with one another. The cyber security cells that are proposed here perhaps shall not be controlled by the central government but by the state governments. There shall arise many complexities while monitoring the cyber cells within the state and would require intellectuals in the fields of cyberspace to regularly monitor them.

Concluding Remarks

Cyber security is understood to be operated in two segments. On paraphrasing Samir Saran and introducing two new terms, it can be categorized as securitization by business and securitization by the state (Saran, 2017). Private firms come under the first category. They are already taking enough steps to implement cyber security structures to protect their lifeline – business. Those companies that do not hold data segregation and processing as their core business will straight away outsource the security handling. Security is provided for the storage of data and to have secure network connectivity. There is more or less good improvement in this category. As India does not have strong legislation, private companies still involve in data porting. Stringent legislation should include legal logics to be encoded within the design of the algorithms. This is called 'regulation by design.'

The second category that Samir Saran mentioned is the lack of efficient cyber security by the state. This is mainly because securitization is different for private companies and the state. For the private players, protecting the valuable assets that bring profit is only the agenda. In the line of securing those assets, they can also sideline data privacy, conduct data portability, and many more. For the state, securing the digital world should be aligned with the fundamental rights and legal provisions promised to its citizens. The constitution and legislation have been written in an age that has not witnessed the digital transformation of society. For better governance, the state has to revisit its fundamentals of governance and reshape them as per the changing dynamics.

Cyber security is not just a matter of internal security. It is an international security issue. One loose securitization and the country might compromise the entire global data flow. Having strong domestic data regulation and weak international data regulation will result in data portability from the strong state to the weak state. Data processing will be done in the weak state, and also the data can be ported to any other place from the weak state. This makes the country's critical data vulnerable.

Observing the cybercrime becoming more pervasive in our daily lives, it is clear that the problem is critical but less examined in social science research. Given the rise of cybercrimes, especially in India, there is a need to develop an ecosystem that is capable of understanding new age complexities and offers a swift mechanism to flourish the overall growth of the economy.

This chapter has emphasized on the cyber security structure in India and discussed how the country responded to cyber security and data protection challenges. The development of an ecosystem that is underway in recent years has been discussed. The chapter has highlighted the challenges that are faced by India about the cyber world.

According to many security analysts, the security incidents touched the skies in the year 2019. The upward trend of phishing, ransomware, and dark web continuously grew till 2020. With the help of the coronavirus pandemic, cyber criminals were able to manage the exploitation of the growing dependency of individuals and corporations working on online platforms (Kshetri, 2016a, 2016b).

Recent developments like Unique Identification Authority of India (UIDAI) are a big achievement for India to curb down cyber terrorism and promote e-governance. It is, however, due to the practices like corruption and weak law enforcement that the country's cyber security structure gets affected altogether. What India also lacks is the human resource participation in this field. It would be highly recommended for the Government of India to take up initiatives that encourage new talent to participate in the domains to learn about data protection and security. By doing this and training the youth appropriately, India can immensely progress resisting cyber-attacks. It can be understood that the Government of India puts poverty and underdevelopment as priority sectors, but it must not forget that it may put national security at risk if this sector is ignored or put behind. These important sectors must be analysed and looked at the same level and should be taken care of simultaneously.

References

Ali, Md, I., and Sukhkirandeep, K. (2021). The Impact of India's Cyber Security Law and Cyber Forensic On Building Techno-Centric Smartcity IoT Environment. *International Conference on Computing, Communication, and Intelligent Systems (ICCCIS)* (pp. 751–759). IEEE Xplore.

Asawat, V. (2010). Information Technology (Amendment) Act, 2008: A New Vision through a New Change. *SSRN*, 1–9. Retrieved from https://economictimes.india times.com/tech/ites/meity-seeks-ideas-on-it-act-revamp/articleshow/75017401.cms?from=mdr

Bansal, M. (2018). An Overview of Cyber Security in India. *Journal of Emerging Technologies and Innovative Research (JETIR)*, 108–113.

Basu, S. (2004). E-Government and Developing Countries: An Overview. *International Review of Law Computers & Technology*, 109–132.

BBC. (2014, October 27). *Xiaomi to Open India Data Centre to Allay Privacy Fears.* Retrieved March 1, 2022, from www.bbc.com/news/technology-29786324

Bhattacharjee, S. (2014, November 17). *In the Fight Against Black Money, Cyber Security Remains a Weak Link.* Retrieved February 18, 2022, from https://indianexpress.com/article/business/business-others/in-the-fight-against-black-money-cyber-security-remains-a-weak-link/#sthash.HimI9Nxs.dpuf

Borah, B. (2020). Digital India: Challenges & Prospects. *European Journal of Molecular & Clinical Medicine*, 525–530.

Bush, G. W. (2002). Executive Order on Critical Infrastructure Protection. Proceedings of the 12th Annual Conference on Computers, Freedom and Privacy. San Francisco: Association for Computing Machinery. Retrieved March 08, 2022, from https://georgewbush-whitehouse.archives.gov/news/releases/2001/10/text/20011016-12.html

Chandrasekhar, R. (2022, April 01). National Cyber Security Strategy 2021 Draft Formulated By NSCS: Rajeev Chandrasekhar. *Outlook.com*. Retrieved from www.outlookindia.com/national/national-cyber-security-strategy-2021-draft-formulated-by-nscs-rajeev-chandrasekhar-news-189571

The Economic Times. (2018, April 4). *India Ranks 3rd among Nations Facing Most Cyber Threats: Symantec.* Retrieved February 25, 2022, from https://economictimes.indiatimes.com/tech/internet/india-ranks-3rd-among-nations-facing-most-cyber-threats-symantec/articleshow/63616106.cms

Economic Times. (2022, February 25). *Cyber Security is a Matter of National Security: PM Modi.* Retrieved March 20, 2022, from https://government.economictimes.

indiatimes.com/news/governance/cyber-security-is-a-matter-of-national-security-pm-modi/89826376

Erkut, B. (2020). From Digital Government to Digital Governance: Are We There Yet? *Sustainability*, 1–13.

Gartzke, E. (2013). The Myth of Cyberwar: Bringing War in Cyberspace Back Down to Earth. *International Security*, 41–73.

Gurjar, Dr. S. (2021). India's Cyber Security: A Look at the Approach and the Preparedness. *Indian Council of World Affairs*.

Hajoary, P. K., and Akhilesh, K. B. (2020). Role of Government in Tackling Cyber Security Threat. In K. B. Akhilesh and Dietmar P. F. Möller (Eds.), *Smart Technologies Scope and Applications* (pp. 79–97). Singapore: Springer Nature Singapore Pte Ltd.

Halder, D. (2011). Information Technology Act and Cyber Terrorism: A Critical Review. *SSRN Electronic Journal*, 75–89.

Hohmann, L. (2016). *To What Extent Is the Triple Helix Model of Etzkowitz & Leydesdorff of Use for the Implementation of Smart Governance – An Analysis Referring on Implemented Triple Helix Constellations.* Retrieved March 2, 2022, from www.glocality.eu/articles/10.5334/glo.7/print/

IBEF. (2021). *Indian E-commerce Industry Analysis.* New Delhi: India Brand Equity Foundation.

IISS. (2021). *Cyber Capabilities and National Power: A Net Assessment.* Washington, DC: The International Institute for Strategic Studies.

Indian Express. (2020, August 15). *PM Modi: India Will Soon Have a New Cyber Security Policy.* Retrieved March 20, 2022, from https://indianexpress.com/article/technology/tech-news-technology/pm-modi-india-will-have-a-new-cybersecurity-policy-soon-6555565/

Jančis, M. (2022, August 18). How Do Password Managers Work? *cybernews.* Retrieved from https://cybernews.com/best-password-managers/how-do-password-managers-work/

Janssen, M., and de Bruijn, H. (2017). Building Cybersecurity Awareness: The Need for Evidence-Based Framing Strategies. *Government Information Quarterly*, 1–7.

Jay, J. (2019, October 31). *Lazarus Group's dTrack Malware Infects Indian Nuclear Power Plant.* Retrieved March 13, 2022, from www.teiss.co.uk/news/lazarus-groups-dtrack-malware-infects-indian-nuclear-power-plant-7513

Johnson, J. (2022, March 24). Countries with the Highest Number of Internet Users as of February 2022. *Statista.* Retrieved March 25, 2022, from www.statista.com/statistics/262966/number-of-internet-users-in-selected-countries/

Kaunert, C., and Yakubov, I. (2017). Securitizatio: Turning an Approach Into a Framework for Research on EU Justice and Home Affairs. In A. R. Servent and F. Trauner (Eds.), *The Routledge Handbook of Justice and Home Affairs.* Routledge. Retrieved from www.routledgehandbooks.com/doi/10.4324/9781315645629-3

Kemp, S. (2022, February 15). *Digital 2022: India.* Retrieved March 21, 2022, from https://datareportal.com/reports/digital-2022-india#:~:text=Internet%20use%20in%20India%20in,at%20the%20start%20of%202022

Kshetri, N. (2016a). Cybersecurity in India. In *The Quest to Cyber Superiority* (pp. 145–157). Switzerland: Springer International Publishing.

Kshetri, N. (2016b). Cybercrime and Cybersecurity in India: Causes Consequences and Implications for the Future. *Crime, Law and Social Change*, (Springer) 66(3), 313–338.

Kugler, M., and Sinha, S. (2020, July 13). The Impact of COVID-19 and the Policy Response in India. *brookings.edu.* Retrieved from www.brookings.edu/blog/future-development/2020/07/13/the-impact-of-covid-19-and-the-policy-response-in-india/

Kumar, V., Ananda, K., Pandey, K., and Kumar, P. D. (2014). Cyber Security Threats in the Power Sector: Need for a Domain Specific Regulatory Framework in India. *Energy Policy*, 126–133. http://dx.doi.org/10.1016/j.enpol.2013.10.025

Kumar, V., and Prince, I. (2019). Overview on Cyber Security Threats Involved in the Implementation of Smart Grid in Countries like India. *Proceeding of the International Conference on Computer Networks, Big Data and IoT (ICCBI – 2018)* (pp. 678–684). Springer. https://doi.org/10.1007/978-3-030-24643-3_81

Ministry of Electronics and Information Technology. (2013). National Cyber Security Policy-2013. *www.meity.gov.in/*. Retrieved from www.meity.gov.in/sites/upload_files/dit/files/National%20Cyber%20Security%20Policy%20%281%29.pdf

Murthy, R. (2022, March 24). Cybersecurity Trends in 2022. *Times of India*. Retrieved from https://timesofindia.indiatimes.com/blogs/voices/cybersecurity-trends-in-2022/

Nickolov, E. C. (2005). Critical Information Infrastructure Protection: Analysis, Evaluation and Expectations. *An International Journal*, 105–119.

Patil, S. (2016, March 17). *Countering Military Cyber Espionage*. Retrieved March 14, 2022, from www.gatewayhouse.in/countering-military-cyber-espionage/

Pearson, E. (2021, November 15). The Abuse of Technology Modi Won't be Talking About. *Human Rights Watch*. Retrieved March 21, 2022, from www.hrw.org/news/2021/11/16/abuse-technology-modi-wont-be-talking-about

Polcumpally, A. T. (2021, May). What, When, Why of DARPA? *Center for Security Studies*. Retrieved from https://jgu.s3.ap-south-1.amazonaws.com/jsia/Arun+Teja-+DARPA+.pdf

Rai, G. (2020, June 20). India Needs to Review its 2013 Cyber Security Policy. *Times of India*. Retrieved from https://timesofindia.indiatimes.com/india/india-needs-to-review-its-2013-cyber-security-policy/articleshow/76502600.cms

Reddy, G. N. (2014). A Study Of Cyber Security Challenges and Its Emerging Trends on Latest Technologies. *arxiv.org*. Retrieved February 16, 2022, from https://arxiv.org/ftp/arxiv/papers/1402/1402.1842.pdf

Saran, S. (2017). Strategic Motivations for India's Cyber-Security. In S. Kumar (Ed.), *India's National Security*. Routledge. https://doi.org/10.4324/9781351240819

Selvaraj, S. A. K. (2019, November 28). Cyber Attack on Kudankulam Nuclear Power Plant. *dae.gov.in*. Retrieved March 13, 2022, from https://dae.gov.in/writereaddata/rssq109.pdf

Sharma, S. (2021, June 29). *India Breaks Into top 10 Countries on UN's Index Measuring Commitment to Cybersecurity*. Retrieved February 6, 2022, from https://economictimes.indiatimes.com/news/defense/india-breaks-into-top-10-countries-on-uns-index-measuring-commitment-to-cybersecurity/articleshow/83962167.cms

Snowden, E. (2019). *The Permanent Record*. London: Macmillan.

Snyder, R. S. (2005). Bridging the Realist/Constructivist Divide: The Case of the Counter Revolution in Soviet Foreign Policy at the End of the Cold War. *Foreign Policy Analysis*, 55–71.

Srinivas, T. R., and Vivek, G. (2015). Cyber Security: The State of the Practice in Public Sector Companies in India. *International Conference on Computing and Communication Technologies*. IEEE Explore. doi: 10.1109/ICCCT2.2014.7066700

Stritzel, H. (2014). Securitization Theory and the Copenhagen School. *In: Security in Translation: New Security Challenges Series*, 11–37.

Subramanian, R. (2020). Historical Consciousness of Cyber Security in India. *IEEE Annals of the History of Computing*, 42(4), 71–93. doi: https://doi.org/10.1109/MAHC.2020.3001215

Telecom Regulatory Authority of India. (2020, September 22). Smart Cities in India: Framework for ICT Infrastructure. *dsci.in*. Retrieved from www.trai.gov.in/sites/default/files/White_Paper_22092020pdf.pdf

World Bank. (2022, February 15). *Individuals using the Internet (% of population) – India*. Retrieved March 21, 2022, from https://data.worldbank.org/indicator/ IT.NET.USER.ZS?locations=IN

Zeebiz. (2021, March 20). *Modi Government to Release New Cyber Security Strategy- All You Need to Know*. Retrieved March 20, 2022, from www.zeebiz.com/technology/ news-modi-government-to-release-new-cyber-security-strategy-all-you-need-to- know-159929

9

IS INDIA READY WITH THE DIGITAL ARMY?

Arun Teja Polcumpally

Introduction

India, from its inception as an independent state, tried to take advantage of the major powers to kick-start its own economy and military. During the cold war, it exploited both the US and Russian technological superiority. David Engerman (2018) has made a detailed analysis of the cold war politics in India with two conclusions. One is the major powers tried to use the cold war as an opportunity to sell their technology to India in addition to their ideological politics. The other is that the Indian political elite is also divided across the bipolar cold war era in advancing their ideological and political objectives. Indian military imports and developments also were strangled into these two facets during the cold war. After 75 years of India's independence, one more superpower has been added to global politics – *China*. These three technologically superior countries, along with other states like Israel, occupy the top positions in weapons research and development. Most of the superior technologies are developed either by these countries or in collaboration with other developing/developed countries. This assertion is made by considering the overall geopolitical influence these three countries have but not on per capita statistics (Cordesman, 2022). With this premise, this chapter infers that current geopolitics laden with advanced digital technologies will revolve around the decisions of these three powers, and India's policymaking should consider moving parallel to the technological developments of these major powers. It also argues that India's major competitor in the 21st century is China. If the Indian military has to compete with China, it has to surpass the Chinese *Informatization* of its military.

DOI: 10.4324/9781003482703-12

India's Quest to Be a Significant Military Power on the Continent

After independence, India started off with only just one hostile military state – Pakistan. The website of the Indian Army well documented its history (Indianarmy, n.d.). From the documentation, it is observed that India's military capacities acquired from the colonial British were sufficient to tackle one belligerent state. With the acquired capabilities, India's strategic thinking was based on four pillars (Ganguly, 2015):

1 Maintain conventional military superiority over Pakistan
2 Maintain friendly relations with China
3 Stay away from the cold war politics
4 Promote solidarity and cooperation among the developing countries

These four strategic pillars quickly changed when Pakistan behaved opportunistically. When Pakistan started receiving military assistance from the US in the 1950s, India started expanding its ties with Russia to strengthen its own military. In this manner, it anchored to the cold war politics to modernize its military. With time, the quest for modernizing the military pushed India to import technology from the best deal providers. As of the year 2021, India is the largest importer of arms. Its total imports stand at USD 4.4 billion, while the second position is taken by Qatar with USD 1.7 billion. There is a vast difference between first- and second-largest arms importers. This shows the importance given by India in upholding its defence capabilities to dynamic standards. The data provided by SIPRI shows the upward trend in the import of military technology by India (Figure 9.1). The figure shows that India

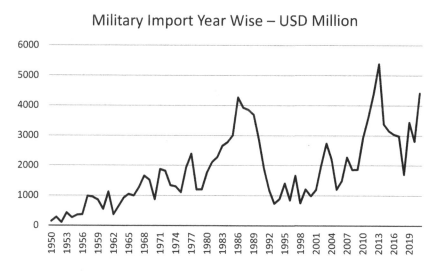

FIGURE 9.1   Military Imports of India From 1950 to 2019

spends a considerable amount of its budget on importing the required arms (SIPRI, 2022).

The growth of Indian economy and scientific and technological expertise show the capacity of India to be a regional leader. The current geopolitical scenario includes the rise of China, change in the geopolitical stance of the US, and aggressive foreign policies of Russia. In these changing geopolitical conditions, India is opined to substantially contribute to shaping a new global order (Mohan, 2022). India's security concerns today are much beyond the four pillars of strategic thinking during the early 1950s.

India competes with the major militaries to keep up with technological advancements. The military is no longer re-configured to handle two northern fronts – Pakistan and China – but to be a regional superpower with groupings like the Bay of Bengal Initiative for Multi-Sectoral Technical and Economic Cooperation (BIMSTEC), South Asian Association for Regional Cooperation (SAARC), and Indian Ocean Region (IOR). The advancements of digital technologies like Artificial Intelligence (AI), blockchain, and quantum communications have forced militaries across the world to adopt the informatization of their operations. As asserted by the US Department of Defense (DoD) official, India has to upgrade its military and organizational structure with information technologies at the core.

India Needs Digitized Military, But It Lags Behind the Global Competition

Having to defend the long borders actively, India should routinely upgrade its military systems. Add to this routine the advancements of information systems integration into the Chinese military that increases their weapon precision and joint command coordination using AI (Bommakanti, 2020). Informatization might change the way the military conducts itself. Some scholars actuated the Revolution in Military Affairs (RMA) to informatization of the military (Sahgal and Vinod, 2007). However, the era of informationalization of the military should not be the desired change for India. The benchmark has already been pushed further ahead. Today, it is about making the military autonomous and intelligent (Bommakanti, 2020). It is intelligentization of the military.

Many papers have been written regarding how China is aiming to informatize and intellegentize its military (Fravel, 2020; Elsa, 2021; Wei, 2022). But there are few works emphasizing the importance of the digitized military for India. In-depth research is not required to show that the Indian military requires modernization in terms of information technologies. Heuristic observations show that the advancement in digital technologies will leap forward military efficiency and also disrupt the existing organizational structures within the military.

Keeping aside the informatization and intelligentization of the Indian military, the previous upgrades provided by Indian defense establishments are delayed frequently. It is opined that Indian defense establishments like Defense Research and Development Organization (DRDO) have not delivered any substantial upgrades to the Indian military in decades (Raghavan, 2018). Military upgrades like the development of the Main Battle Tank (Arjun Mk – II) have been delayed for decades due to the tussle between the Army and DRDO. The Light Combat Aircraft (LCA) commissioned in 1985 was deployed only in 2015. These delays are probably because of the incoherent operation between the Air Force and Aeronautical Development Agency (ADA). If the usual upgrades and the development of existing technology take decades, perhaps adopting new technology and making breakthroughs in AI and quantum communications would be too much to ask from India.

Modernizing the military to the level of advancing digital technology is no longer a luxury, but it is a necessity. Thus, even though it is difficult to adopt informatization and intelligentization of the military quickly, India should break its limits to do that. To reach such milestones, Observer Research Foundation (ORF) published a paper that advises the Indian military to cultivate scientists, in-house research institutions, and multi-stakeholder collaborations in developing military technologies (Gopal, 2021). These recommendations, though appear to be generic and commonsensical, will lay the foundation for the rapid advancements in the military.

Is India Prepared for the Digital Revolution in Military Affairs?

India imports most of its military equipment. In comparison to its imports, exports are just 2.17% of the total imports.[1] In developing indigenous AI and quantum technologies, India is a few decades behind. One example substantiating the latter statement is India's huge number of military imports. The essential components for developing AI and quantum communication systems are sensors, and they are imported (Table 9.1). India's capacity to remain self-reliant on these critical technologies and its raw materials is necessary to become a regional leader upholding peace.

Let's consider one technology – AI – that impacts horizontally across societies. Advances in AI potentially increase the scope and intensity of biological and psychological weapons. Advancements in biotechnology that are capable to modify genes and other fundamental bio-functionaries are increasing pace (Brockmann et al., 2019). These advancements are easy to invent new pathogens and viruses. The world, as of 2022, is already gripped with the dangerous coronavirus and has already lost many lives. What if such a virus is weaponized?

AI technology combined with robotics aids the development of autonomous weapon systems with little human intervention (Polcumpally, 2020;

TABLE 9.1 Total Imports to India According to Weapon Category From 2015 to 2020 (Millions USD)

Category	2015	2016	2017	2018	2019	2020	Total
Aircraft	2057	1546	1133	704	1839	1559	8838
Air defense systems	90	360	360				810
Armored vehicles	80	120	213	171	16	15	615
Artillery			2	30	203	226	461
Engines	285	318	322	288	292	316	1820
Missiles	382	565	558	274	333	609	2721
Naval weapons	41	29	12			10	91
Sensors	181	66	11	18	93	65	433
Ships			299		299		598
Total	3117	3003	2909	1485	3075	2799	16,388

Source: SIPRI Database

Boulanin et al., 2020). There are many reports recommending varied controls for autonomous systems, but none have been implemented. Not only autonomous weapons systems but AI is also used in developing deepfakes and releasing false information to the public. Robert Downey Jr's TV show *The Age of AI*, aired on YouTube, explains the rapid developments in deepfakes and other AI-related advancements. These developments create a trust deficit among the public. It might also increase the existing vagaries and vicissitudes within society. This is the crux of psychological warfare.

Similar is the case with the quantum communications technology that increases the computational speeds assisting in a wide range of other technical possibilities. Blockchain advancements and its implementation have the capacity to reduce information tapping and hacking by adversaries. The challenge is that these are dual-use technologies and they are easy to be obtained by any other country, be it rich/poor, technologically advanced or not (Malik, 2021). For India, it becomes increasingly necessary to have its hands on emerging technologies to gain an advantage over its adversaries. The conventional understanding of states being adversaries is no longer the case. The enemy of the country can be extremist organizations within and outside the country, or it can also be a highly skilled individual who is capable of releasing a dangerous pathogen into the public. India could not wait for a crisis to make a policy on innovating technologies for the military. It has to pre-emptively act.

Accordingly, in the coming sections, readiness of India will be assessed from its official reports and other commentaries.

It is interesting that the impact of sensors, which make up most of the fundamental parts of any AI system, is decreasing. India is ranked 17th in the global AI index published by Tortoise media. The Stanford AI index of 2022 placed India in third position in the global vibrancy rankings (Stanford

AI Index, 2022). It shows that India's capacity to develop its own AI systems for its defense is increased. However, the breakthroughs in the field of AI are not coming from India. One example of that would be the computer vision deep learning algorithms. Table 9.2 shows all the deep learning algorithms with maximum efficiency. India's contribution to this is zero, while China has contributed two algorithms.

Table 9.2 shows that the techniques to make use of the data are not being efficiently developed by India. In addition, engines and missiles are being imported at an increasing pace (Table 9.1). Indian military has improved tremendously since 1947.

Indian Navy has shown some noteworthy development. In the year 2016, India exported 26 ships, and after four years, in the year 2020, it exported 145 ships (see Table 9.3). In addition to ships, there is no data to show any improvement in other technologies. Of course, the development of supersonic missiles, BrahMos, is a commendable joint development with Russia.

However, military development is always relational. When geopolitics is considered, there is no absolute measurement. What matters is how developed is Indian military in comparison to its competitors and adversaries. And the struggle for military excellence is never-ending. In this context, India has a long road ahead in informatizing and intelligentizing the military.

The Current Upgrades of Indian Military

The latest technology upgrades include the induction of new nuclear-powered submarine INS *Arihant* and other Kaveri Class Submarines. The Air Force increased its strength with Rafale jets, Apache helicopters, and Chinook vertical troop carriers. The Army enhanced its strength with the induction of new lightweight howitzers and the proud BrahMos supersonic cruise missile. However, India couldn't develop and deploy its own small arms rifle. The developed Indian Small Arms Systems (INSAS rifle) is being replaced with a Russian-made AK-203 rifle (First Post, 2021).

Now that the recent upgrades are known (Table 9.4), let's move to the requirements specified by the Army Design Bureau in 2015 and see whether these requirements are fulfilled by the above upgrades (Table 9.5).

The upgrades made to the military equipment as per the 2019 Army Design Bureau report appear not to bridge the requirement gap mentioned in the 2015 report. None of the problem statements mentioned in all the compendium reports of Army Design Bureau are solved and implemented. Problems referred in one volume reappear either in the next volume or in the trial stage. It has been six years after the launch of this compendium of problem statement reports by Army Design Bureau, but the improvement appears insignificant. There are projects that require existing engineering technology and systems that are already in use in the US and Israel. Throughout the report, it was mentioned that

TABLE 9.2 Global Computer Vision AI Algorithm Performances

Sl No	Method	Top-1 Accuracy	Source	Year	Type	Agency
0	AlexNet	0.633	ImageNet Classification with Deep Convolutional Neural Networks	2012	Without Extra Training Data	Google
1	Five Base + Five HiRes	0.663	EfficientNet: Rethinking Model Scaling for Convolutional Neural Networks	2013	Without Extra Training Data	Google
2	VGG-19	0.745	EfficientNet: Rethinking Model Scaling for Convolutional Neural Networks	2014	Without Extra Training Data	Google
3	Inception V3	0.788	EfficientNet: Rethinking Model Scaling for Convolutional Neural Networks	2015	Without Extra Training Data	Google
4	ResNeXt-101 64x4 + multi-scale dense testing	0.823	Billion-scale Semi-supervised Learning for Image Classification	2016	Without Extra Training Data	Facebook
5	PNASNet-5	0.829	Dual Path Networks	2017	Without Extra Training Data	China
6	GPIPE	0.844	Densely Connected Convolutional Networks	2018	Without Extra Training Data	China
7	AdvProp (EfficientNet-B8)	0.855	Adversarial Examples Improve Image Recognition	2019	Without Extra Training Data	Google
8	Fix-EfficientNet-B8 (MaxUp + CutMix)	0.858	Fixing the Train-test Resolution Discrepancy: FixEfficientNet	2020	Without Extra Training Data	Facebook
9	MAE (ViT-H, 448)	0.878	Masked Autoencoders Are Scalable Vision Learners	2021	Without Extra Training Data	Facebook

10	AlexNet – 7CNNs + ImageNet 2011 pretrain	0.633	Self-training with Noisy Student Improves ImageNet Classification	2012	With Extra Training Data	Google
11	VGG-19	0.745	EfficientNet: Rethinking Model Scaling for Convolutional Neural Networks	2014	With Extra Training Data	Google
12	Inception V3	0.788	EfficientNet: Rethinking Model Scaling for Convolutional Neural Networks	2015	With Extra Training Data	Google
13	JFT-300M Fine-tuning	0.792	EfficientNet: Rethinking Model Scaling for Convolutional Neural Networks	2017	With Extra Training Data	Google
14	ResNeXt-101 32x48d	0.854	Xception: Deep Learning with Depth-wise Separable Convolutions	2018	With Extra Training Data	Google
15	BiT-L (ResNet)	0.8754	Big Transfer (BiT): General Visual Representation Learning	2019	With Extra Training Data	Google
16	EfficientNet-L2–475 (SAM)	0.8861	Sharpness-Aware Minimization for Efficiently Improving Generalization	2020	With Extra Training Data	Google
17	CoAtNet-7	0.9088	CoAtNet: Marrying Convolution and Attention for All Data Sizes	2021	With Extra Training Data	Google

Source: Stanford University Human Centered Artificial Iintelligence (2022).

TABLE 9.3 Total Indian Military Exports From 2015 to 2020 (Millions USD)

Category	2015	2016	2017	2018	2019	2020	Total
Aircraft	15	8	–	4	–	3	30
Missiles	–	–	–	–	3	3	6
Sensors	27	12	–	3	–	–	42
Ships	–	26	56	37	15	145	279
Total	42	46	56	44	18	151	356

Source: SIPRI Database

TABLE 9.4 A Short List of the New Upgrades to the Indian Military

Latest Technology	Origin Country	Category of the Technology	Status of Induction
Agni V	India	Inter-continental Ballistic Missile	In development
VC11184 (INS *Dhruv*)	India	Missile Tracking Ship	Yet to commission
INS *Arihant*	India	Nuclear-Powered Submarine	Commissioned
INS *Khanderi* and INS *Karanj*		Kaveri Class Submarines	Commissioned
Rafale Fighter Planes	France	MMRC	Inducted and squadrons are being increased
Apache AH-64 E	US	Attack Helicopter	22 attack helicopters with the Indian Air Force (IAF), and the Indian Army has signed agreement with Boeing for 6
Chinook CH-47F (I)	US	Vertical Airlift Troop Carrier	15 inducted in IAF
M777 and K9 Vajra		Howitzers	Inducted
AK-203	Russia	Standard Issue Rifles	Signing the deal
BrahMos Supersonic Cruise missile	India and Russia	Supersonic Cruise Missile	Under development

Source: Philip (2019), Aryan (2021), Center for Strategic and International Studies (2021), India News (2021), and Boeing (n.d.).

there was no local innovation to solve the problems, and even if there were any solutions, it was found in the other country's military equipment. Another noteworthy point from the Army compendium report is that the upgrades are in the form of complete products. There is no knowledge transfer happening. There might be some technical skill transfer, but India needs more than that.

TABLE 9.5 Improvements in Existing Military Machines

Probable Required Improvements in the Indian Military	What Are the Required Improvements
Armored Vehicles	Speed, strength, fuel efficiency, central command unit, data transfer, g radar, acoustic and electro-optical systems, temperature camouflage, improved fire power
Night Vision Technology	Image intensification, thermal imaging, improved range, compactness
Engine Improvements	Absence of rotor shafts with an electric power alternative
Smart soldier	Advanced digital equipment
Artillery	Light artillery with advanced metallurgy
Surveillance Systems	UAV, micro and nano UAV, AI-based systems
Missile Technology	Improved precision
Dynamic Camouflage	Battle suits, asset covers, paints, spectral camouflage equipment
Water Supply	Mobile de-salination plants, lightweight water pumps
Directed Energy weapons	Electromagnetic research needed
Electronic Warfare Helicopters	Jammers and radars equipped
Sensors	Mine detections, ariel surveillance, foliage cut through surveillance

Source: Army Design Bureau (2016, 2017, 2019, 2020).

The requirement table (Table 9.5) mentions AI-based surveillance, image intensification, strong and lightweight materials, spectral camouflage, and directed energy weapons. These include fundamental research in STEM sciences and in the engineering field. However, there was no mention of nanotechnology, 3D printing, or genomic research, which are currently being considered on priority bases by DARPA (Polcumpally, 2021). Just by referring to the two tables, it can be partially concluded that India has not taken cognizance of the rising advancements in the digital sphere.

There are a separate set of requirements that specifically require breakthrough research in the digital technologies. Table 9.6 is the list of the digital technologies and their uses mentioned. This table is not directly taken from the Army Design Bureau reports but is developed from a close understanding of the technology required and problem statements mentioned in the reports.

Table 9.6 provides a list of digital technologies that mostly include quantum communications, AI, and blockchain technology. Substantiating the same, 'The Army Make Projects' list is provided by the Federation of Indian Chambers of Commerce & Industry (FICCI) report of 2020 (Federation of

TABLE 9.6 Required Digital Technologies for the Indian Military

Probable Required Improvements in the Indian Military	What Are the Required Improvements
Radios	Long battery, easy access to spectrum
Smartphones	Military-based build quality, military-based applications
Optical Fiber	Replace the copper wired network
Digital Device Integrations	Cross-platform integration (data flows through different protocols)
Social Media Analytics	Sentiment analysis, content analysis of civilian world
Semiconductor Manufacturing	Indigenous semiconductor manufacturing
Cloud Computing and Big Data Analysis	Military server, private access protocols
Quantum Communications	Far and secure communications, and cryptography
Communications Media	5G, Laser-based wireless communication
Artificial Intelligence	Autonomous systems, VR, sensor-based automatic detection systems, inventory management
Man Machine Interface	Autonomous systems
Simulators Using Virtual Reality (VR) Technology	Training, Battlefield readiness
Blockchain Technology	Human resource management
Geoinformatics	Software-based geography mapping and dynamic updating

Source: Army Design Bureau (2016, 2020, 2019, 2017).

Indian Chambers of Commerce and Industry, 2020). All the advanced systems that have the application of AI, nanotechnology, blockchain, and quantum communication technology are listed. These projects should definitely employ these advanced technologies for an efficient outcome. Some of the projects are infantry training simulators, augmented displays mounted on the soldier's helmet, field cipher equipment, robotic surveillance systems, and so forth. These defense reports vividly represent the importance of advanced digital technologies, and the analysis of the reports shows the increasing delay in the research.

With the current upgrades and military equipment, though India appears to be capable enough to take on the two adversaries to its north, it is fallible. A research report from Al Jazeera says that the Indian Army, though appears strong, it is just on paper (Gatopoulos, 2021). It should also be concluded that the recent crash developments undertaken by the military are an ad-hoc reaction to the China factor. More importantly, there is no white paper that puts a trajectory to the research and development on all the defense equipment.

Digitization of Indian Military and the Issues Faced

A 2013 technology perspective and capability road map drafted by the Indian Army shows the need for digital technologies in the field of battlefield transparency, command control architecture, smart communication systems, and more (Ministry of Defence, 2013). Table 9.7 shows the areas where digital technologies and Indian military's progress in the implementation of informatization are required. The categories are borrowed from the technology perspective and capability roadmap (2013) document. Commander Ashok Menon asserted that from the information available in the public, it will be difficult to judge the cyber capabilities of the Indian military (Menon, 2021). However, efforts have been made to assess the readiness of the Indian military regarding the technologies mentioned in Table 9.7. The status of each technology is shown in terms of Not Implemented/Implemented/In process/Under consideration.

A basic model that clarifies a state's readiness for an RMA is given by RAND researcher Dr. Hundley in 1999 (Hundley, 1999) The same is used to assess whether India is ready for the upcoming digital RMA. Following is the paraphrased model of the analysis:

1 Keep an open eye on the probable RMAs.
2 Conduct an early assessment to decide on which RMA the state has to focus.
3 Be responsive for the potential RMAs.

TABLE 9.7 Digital Technologies and Military Readiness

Technology Area	Readiness
Smart Communication Systems	In Process (ET Government, 2024)
Electronic Warfare	Not Implemented (Indian Defence Research Wing, 2024)
Nanotechnology	In Progress (Tomar, 2015)
AI and Robotics	In Progress (Department of Defence Production, 2022)
Chemical, Biological, Radioactive Defense	In Progress (DRDO, n.d.)
Miniaturization	Under Consideration (Hindustan Times, 2022)
Unmanned Systems	In Progress (Karunakaran, 2022)
EMP	Not Implemented (Pant, 2017)
Weapon Guidance	InProgress (Standing Committee on Defence, 2023)
Space-based Radars	Implemented (Banerji, 2023)
Stealth	In Progress (Standing Committee on Defence, 2023)
Sensors	Under Consideration (Standing Committee on Defence, 2023)

Source: Misra (2022) and Chowdhury (2021).

In India, IT-related RMA has been discussed for decades. In an article published by Manohar Parrikar Institute of Defence Studies & Analysis in 2008, the technologies like precision-guided missiles, stealth technology, battle space awareness, and command and control architecture were discussed to be the key technologies that India should look into (Kapoor, 2008). These are broad areas, and any new technology will invariantly impact at least one of these areas. However, the article's overall thought process agrees with the RAND model. It espouses that technology advancements, doctrinal changes, and organizational changes are required to witness an RMA.

These changes are fundamental requirements to witness a visible shift from traditional military operations to digitized operations. However, there is an opinion that the existing military structures are unwilling to adopt the digital change. Lt. General D. S. Hooda, a former northern army commander, in a newspaper article, says that the Indian military is reluctant to accept the RMA incorporating the technological and structural changes (Hooda, 2020). He also affirmed that there is an urgent need for RMA aided by digital technologies. In order to achieve it, he opined that focusing on government research institutes would be futile and that taking aid of the expertise from academia and civilian sectors is advised.

Another hurdle that keeps the Indian military establishment from quickly achieving the digitization is its slow-paced institutional changes. From the existing history of institutional changes in the defense sector, it is clear that they happen due to a crisis. New agencies are created as a response to a crisis in India (Sood, 2016). Aviation Research Center was set up as a result of 1962 war with China. After the 1965 war with Pakistan, the need for a dedicated external intelligence wing was understood. Later in 1968, Research and Analysis Wing (R&AW) was established. Defense Intelligence Agency (DIA) was set up post Kargil skirmish in 1999. The 26/11 attacks led to the establishment of National Investigative Agency (NIA). There is no ex ante research on the requirement of institutional changes based on the upgradation of the technology. If the advanced digital platforms are to be used, crisis should not be awaited. If the crisis looms once, there will not be going back, and redesigning the structures will become an impossible task.

Note

1 This percentage is calculated as a cumulative for the 2015–2020 SIPRI data.

References

Army Design Bureau. (2016, December 5). Compendium of Future Core Technologies and Problem Statements. *Confederation of Indian Industry*. Retrieved from www.cii.in/PublicationDetail.aspx?enc=FxSSH2eg93iekTkQqV2qzs6mdT3rqij5i 2UbLV2x6dDr/4obBGZWq3w2iuX7OH9trVBiOA8x+9yNmfnfSXzheSCoLyY4 hRIwDrY42d+FmLn7LNUcbTyhBBAHWbmo10hnRk7CRJ7jFNQBKFvo3tCW+ kVu8zOf2revxFTWUI5I36NLOlcTRcI6QN5uoQJRXH2a

Army Design Bureau. (2017). Compendium of Problem Statements Vol II. *Directorate of Perspective Planning*. Retrieved from https://indianarmy.nic.in/makeinindia/PDS%2023%20Mar%202017%20FINAL.pdf

Army Design Bureau. (2019). Compenium of Problem Statements. *Directorate of Perspective Planning*. Retrieved from https://indianarmy.nic.in/makeinindia/CPDS%20Vol%20IV%202019.pdf

Army Design Bureau. (2020). Compendium Problem Definition Statements. *Directorate General of Perspective Planning*. Retrieved from https://indianarmy.nic.in/makeinindia/CPDS_2020_ADB.pdf

Aryan, J. (2021, February 26). India's Quest for a New Assault Rifle Is Almost Over. *Observer Research Foundation*. Retrieved from www.orfonline.org/expert-speak/india-quest-new-assault-rifle-almost-over/

Banerji, A. (2023, September 30). The Slow Militarization of India's Space Sector. *The Diplomat*. Retrieved from https://thediplomat.com/2023/09/the-slow-militarization-of-indias-space-sector/

Boeing. (n.d.). CH-47F (I) Chinook. *Boeing.co.in*. Retrieved from www.boeing.co.in/products-and-services/defense-space-and-security/boeing-defense-space-and-security-in-india/ch-47-chinook.page

Bommakanti, K. (2020). A.I. in the Chinese Military: Current Initiatives and the Implications for India. *Observer Research Foundation: Occassional Paper*. Retrieved from www.orfonline.org/wp-content/uploads/2020/02/ORF_Occasional-Paper_234_AI-ChineseMilitary.pdf

Boulanin, V., Moa, P. C., Netta, G., and Davison, N. (2020). *Limits on Autonomy in Weapon Systems: Identifying Practical Elements of Human Control*. Stockholm: SIPRI. Retrieved from www.sipri.org/publications/2020/other-publications/limits-autonomy-weapon-systems-identifying-practical-elements-human-control-0

Brockmann, K., Sibylle, B., and Vincent, B. (2019). *BIO PLUS X Arms Control and the Convergence of Biology and Emerging Technologies*. Stockholm: SIPRI. Retrieved from www.sipri.org/sites/default/files/2019-03/sipri2019_bioplusx_0.pdf

Center for Strategic and International Studies. (2021, November 21). Agni V. *missilethreat.csis.org*. Retrieved from https://missilethreat.csis.org/missile/agni-5/

Chowdhury, M. (2021). Emerging Dynamics of Warfare – Role of Artificial Intelligence (AI) and Robotics and How India Can Exploit It. *Journal of the United Service Institution of India*. Retrieved from https://usiofindia.org/publication/usi-journal/emerging-dynamics-of-warfare-role-of-artificial-intelligence-ai-and-robotics-and-how-india-can-exploit-it/?_sf_s=digit

Cordesman, A. H. (2022, May 16). Ranking the World's Major Powers: A Graphic Comparison of the United States, Russia, China, and Other Selected Countries. *CSIS*. Retrieved from https://csis-website-prod.s3.amazonaws.com/s3fs-public/publication/220427_Ranking_Major_Powers.pdf?FVCpij.NHeBefpwCDCt9WDdzWNGlV19E

Department of Defence Production. (2022). AIDef: Artificial Intelligence in Defence. *www.ddpmod.gov.in*. Retrieved January 18, 2024, from https://www.ddpmod.gov.in/sites/default/files/ai.pdf

DRDO. (n.d.). *CBRN Defence | Defence Research and Development Organisation– DRDO, Ministry of Defence, Government of India*. Retrieved January 18, 2024, from https://drdo.gov.in/cbrn-defence-0

Elsa, B. K. (2021). Artificial Intelligence in China's Revolution in Military Affairs. *Journal of Strategic Studies*, 515–542. https://doi.org/10.1080/01402390.2021.1894136

Engerman, C. D. (2018). *The Price of Aid*. New Delhi: Harvard University Press.

ET Government. (2024, January 13). SAMBHAV: Indian Army Indigenously Develops End-to-end Secure Mobile Ecosystem. *ETGovernment.com*. Retrieved

January 18, 2024, from https://government.economictimes.indiatimes.com/news/defence/sambhav-indian-army-indigenously-develops-end-to-end-secure-mobile-ecosystem/106799061

Federation of Indian Chambers of Commerce and Industry. (2020). Webinar on 17 August 2020 Army Make Projects-2020. *Federation of Indian Chambers of Commerce & Industry*. Retrieved from https://ficci.in/ArmyMakeProjects2020_Booklet.pdf

First Post. (2021, November 24). India Clears AK-203 Rifle Deal with Russia: Why New Firearm Is Freedom from INSAS Gun's Shortcomings. *fIrstPOst*. Retrieved from www.firstpost.com/india/india-clears-ak-203-rifle-deal-with-russia-why-new-firearm-is-freedom-from-insas-guns-shortcomings-10160201.html

Fravel, T. M. (2020). China's "World-Class Military" Ambitions: Origins and Implications. *The Washington Quarterly*, 85–99. https://doi.org/10.1080/01636 60X.2020.1735850

Ganguly, R. (2015). India's Military: Evolution, Modernisation and Transformation. *India Qarterly*, 71(3), 187–205. Retrieved from www.jstor.org/stable/45072753

Gatopoulos, A. (2021, February 11). Project Force: Is India a Military Superpower or a Paper Tiger? *Al Jazeera*. Retrieved from www.aljazeera.com/features/2021/2/11/india-military-superpower-or-paper-tiger

Gopal, V. (2021). The Case for Nurturing Military Scientists in the Indian Army. Observer Research Foundation, Occasional Paper 320.

Hindustan Times. (2022, February 26). *Miniaturisation and Electric Are Future of Defence Design: Army Chief*. Retrieved January 18, 2024, from https://www.hindustantimes.com/india-news/miniaturisation-and-electric-are-future-of-defence-design-army-chief-101645898843665.html

Hooda, D. S. (2020, November 28). Sharpen Tech Focus to Boost Defence Prowess. *The Tribune*. Retrieved from www.tribuneindia.com/news/comment/sharpen-tech-focus-to-boost-defence-prowess-176926

Hundley, R. O. (1999). *Past Revolutions, Future Transformations: What Can the History of Revolutions in Military Affairs Tell Us about Transforming the U.S. Military?* Santa Monica, CA: RAND Corporation.

Indianarmy. (n.d.). Know Your Army. *indianarmy.nic.in*. Retrieved from https://indianarmy.nic.in/Site/FormTemplete/frmTempSimple.aspx?MnId=Rq+n8BtjbIi6 4LAhL4VwCA==&ParentID=6NkJ1lk2/Fr6Xo+7d8Zirw==&flag=8CKP966uzg 96kLov0aWdfQ==

India News. (2021, March 16). INS Dhruv That Can Track Satellites, Strategic Missiles, to Join Navy Soon. *Hindustan Times*. Retrieved from www.hindustantimes.com/india-news/ballistic-missile-tracking-ins-dhruv-to-join-india-s-strategic-assets-in-2021–101615886801327.html

Indian Defence Research Wing. (2024, January). DRDO's Dharashakti EW System Successfully Completes Field Trials, Boosting India's Electronic Warfare Capabilities. *Indian Defence Research Wing*. Retrieved January 18, 2024, from https://idrw.org/drdos-dharashakti-ew-system-successfully-completes-field-trials-boosting-indias-electronic-warfare-capabilities

Kapoor, V. K. (2008). RMA and India's Military Transformation. *Journal of Defense Studies*, 125–142.

Karunakaran, A. (2022, January 27). *Unmanned Aircraft System and Indian Industries*. Retrieved from Manohar Parrikar Institute for Defence Studies and Analyses: https://www.idsa.in/idsacomments/unmanned-aircraft-system-and-industries-akarunakaran-270122

Malik, A. (2021). *Technology and Security in the 21st Century: A Demand-Side Perspective*. Stockholm: SIPRI. Retrieved from www.sipri.org/sites/default/files/files/RR/SIPRIRR20.pdf

Menon, A. K. (2021). Cyber Defence – India's Critical Infrastructure. *The United Service Institution of India*. Retrieved from https://usiofindia.org/publication/usi-journal/cyber-defence-indias-critical-infrastructure/?_sf_s=digit

Ministry of Defence. (2013). *Technology Perspective and Capability Roadmap*. Retrieved January 18, 2024, from https://www.mod.gov.in/sites/default/files/TPCR13.pdf

Misra, P. (2022). Trends in New Generation Warfare: Lessons for India. *Journal of the United Service Institution of India*. Retrieved from https://usiofindia.org/publication/usi-journal/trends-in-new-generation-warfare-lessons-for-india/?_sf_s=digit

Mohan, R. C. (2022, January 26). India and the Post Pandemic Geopolitics. *Oberver Research Foundation*. Retrieved from www.orfonline.org/expert-speak/india-and-the-post-pandemic-geopolitics/

Pant, A. (2017). *EMP Weapons and the New Equation of War | Manohar Parrikar Institute for Defence Studies and Analyses*. Retrieved January 18, 2024, from https://www.idsa.in/idsacomments/emp-weapons-new-equation-of-war_apant_131017

Philip, S. A. (2019, January 1). The 10 Big Defence Inductions by Indian Military in 2019. *Theprint*. Retrieved from https://theprint.in/defence/the-10-big-defence-inductions-by-indian-military-in-2019/171303/

Polcumpally, A. T. (2020, September 1). Autonomous Weapon Systems: Understanding and Operationalizing Human Control. *Modern Diplomacy*. Retrieved from http://dspace.jgu.edu.in:8080/xmlui/handle/10739/4456

Polcumpally, A. T. (2021, February). AI and the Disruptive Impact on the Society. *Defense Security Alert*, 36–40.

Raghavan, S. (2018). Military Technological Innovation in India: A Tale of Three Projects. *India Review*, *17*(1), 22–141. https://doi.org/10.1080/14736489.2018.1415286

Sahgal, A., and Vinod, A. (2007). Revolution in Military Affairs and Jointness. *Journal of Defense Studies*, *1*(1). Retrieved from www.idsa.in/system/files/jds_1_1_asahgal_vanand.pdf

SIPRI. (2022). *TIV of Arms Exports to All, 1950–2021*. Stockholm: Stockholm Institute of International Peace Research Institute. Retrieved from https://armstrade.sipri.org/armstrade/page/values.php

Sood, V. (2016). The Future of Intelligence. In G. Kunwal (Ed.), *The New Arthashastra* (pp. 108–126). New Delhi: Harper Collins publisher India.

Standing Committee on Defence. (2023). A Review of Working of the Defence Research and Development Organisation. *Ministry of Defence*. Retrieved January 18, 2024, from https://sansad.in/getFile/lsscommittee/Defence/17_Defence_42.pdf?source=loksabhadocs

Stanford AI Index. (2022). 2021 Global Vibrancy Ranking. *Global AI Vibrancy Tool*. Retrieved from https://aiindex.stanford.edu/vibrancy/

Stanford University Human Centered Artificial Iintelligence. (2022). *Stanford AI Index*. Retrieved from https://drive.google.com/drive/folders/1LLHYjtZabHQHGrVpHOh9Ak-2rkP6d5Wj

Tomar, S. (2015). *Nanotechnology: The Emerging Field for Future Military Applications|Manohar Parrikar Institute for Defence Studies and Analyses*. Retrieved January 18, 2024, from https://www.idsa.in/monograph/nanotechnology-emerging-field-for-future-military-applications

Wei, I. S. (2022, April 22). China's "World-Class" Military Modernisation. *e-ir*. Retrieved from www.e-ir.info/2022/04/22/chinas-world-class-military-modernisation/

CONCLUSION

Pankaj K Jha

The United States is seen as the beacon of democracy. It is the oldest democracy standing tall for its individualism and free market economy. These two facets are considered to be the torchbearers of democracy. Given the stature of the United States in world politics, it would be logical to assume its achievements and progress as the benchmark for other democracies. The book has extensively discussed on the impact of Artificial Intelligence (AI), blockchain, quantum communications, and cyber security. To gauge the extent of the importance given to these digital technologies in maintaining national security, a reference to the US government would again be logical.

If one looks into the list, which has been updated by the US Executive Office in its report presented by the subcommittee on critical and emerging technologies, an emphasis was found on a need for enabling capabilities for securing data, developing a modernised and capable cyber workforce, and working on a time-bound basis for developing necessary support infrastructure for the emerging technologies (Fast Track Action Subcommittee on Critical and Emerging Technologies, 2022). The list highlights the need for work on core areas such as advanced engineering materials, supersonic delivery systems, human-machine interface, directed energy instruments, communication and networking technologies, semiconductors and microelectronics, AI, biotechnology, autonomous systems, and robotics, along with many others. The list, which comprises 19 core focus areas, highlights the need for a futuristic approach, particularly focusing on sensors, sensor processing and data fusion, AI, sensory perception and recognition, next-generation 5G and 6G networks, particle beams, augmented reality, materials, quantum computing, quantum networking, and similar such areas. The basic argument made in this report is that for future preparedness in areas relevant to national

DOI: 10.4324/9781003482703-13

security, the whole ecosystem should take note of the technological requirements for the future and work cohesively so that better coordination and
plan management can be done at the highest levels.

Within India, there has been an awareness of tapping into various technological domains to achieve a military advantage. In this regard, the Ministry
of External Affairs instituted a division known as New Emerging Strategic
Technologies (NEST) in 2020 (Ministry of External Affairs, 2020). It looks
into those technologies that can provide an extra edge in civilian and military
activities. This division also works with possible joint ventures and scouts
for those pioneering efforts made by countries across the world, which can
be the reference point for Indian institutions and their scientific community
for collaboration and joint research. In India, several institutions, such as the
Indian Institutes of Technology (IITs), Indian Institute of Science (IISc), and
other such institutions under the Ministry of Defence, work to bring about
synergies in these fields. However, in the context of bringing synergies between private and public partnerships, there exists hesitancy because of the
confidentiality and trust deficit in carrying out highly confidential research
and developing cutting-edge technologies.

Though there is a lack of trust between various entities, India is slowly
preparing to adapt to a Revolution in Military Affairs (RMA) with structural
and functional changes. Generally, RMA has been characterised by changes
in terms of precision, improvised command control and intelligence, highly
sophisticated information warfare, and improved non-lethal weapons. RMA
anchored to the precision and guided missile systems were globally visible
during the Gulf War of 1991 (Operation Desert Storm). It highlighted the
effective use of technology both in terms of precision strikes and lowering
the mortality rate of the soldiers on the ground. There are opinions that this
revolutionary technology would bring about a tectonic change in standoff
strikes and disruptive warfare. A decade earlier, retired Indian Air Marshal
Inamdar asserted that there are three RMAs in military history. One is mech-
anisation, the second is the introduction of nuclear weapons, and the third is
the introduction of cybernetics and Information Technology (IT) (Inamdar,
2008). The third RMA, which Air Marshal Inamdar referred, brings more
deterrence along with first-strike capabilities. Therefore, it is fair to conclude
that the revolution in military affairs (strike capabilities) should be halted to
bring about parity and push the revolution in a non-lethal direction, primarily working in the deterrence domain.

The best choice is to redefine the military revolution concept and direct
the discourse about the RMA regarding building peace and managing long-
drawn wars. As per the assessments, it has been stated that the closest allies
of the United States would be highly capable of absorbing the new kinds of
technologies, which are coming up on the horizon, and the second tier of
technology absorbers will be China, Taiwan, and Singapore. The developing

countries that might not have the capacities would be less likely to absorb the revolution in military affairs faster. The examples cited could be India, Pakistan, a few Asian countries, and many other developing countries because of their dependence on arms' imports and licensed production.

Necessary Focus Areas for RMA

One of the essential aspects of RMA by digital technologies is integrating systems and the likelihood of developing a network of networks that can be self-sustaining and working autonomously. New technologies and revolutionary changes are found in intelligence gathering through surveillance and reconnaissance areas. These revolutions have been facilitated by new types of encryption software, pattern recognition, and network technologies, which enhanced C4ISR. Not only in intelligence gathering, but there is also a plethora of digital military devices that are changing military operations.

A good work is noted on tactical internet, sensors, cloud storage development, space networks, jointness, and data fusion. Combining all the mentioned IT frontier technologies with military requirements would enable futuristic command centres, enabling the network of networks. They enable the coordination of various fleets, contingents, and sorties to actualise a single agenda. India already has a tri-forces command, and it is worth extensively to invest in the latter mentioned integrated command centre with advanced communication systems with quantum encrypted signals and AI-assisted decision-making.

The precision munition and more reactive platforms have brought about new changes and the development of stealth technologies with hypersonic speed, reducing the response time drastically. New force structures with smaller armed forces, equipped with better digital communication, handheld devices, and unmanned aerial vehicles, can sustain themselves in a more extensive network system. As has already been discussed, countries such as India and many others in the mid-rung of the technology ladder will find it challenging to adapt to new systems because of variance and faster changes in technologies. Therefore, there is a need for a new kind of adaptation that can bring about further development in military research and associated technologies. These technologies can have both positive and negative effects, but they can also multiply the capabilities in terms of destruction.

The concern is increasing over innovations in the civilian domain, particularly in autonomous systems, robotics, AI, the Internet of Things, nanotechnology, material sciences, 3D printing, and quantum computing. The significant challenges are to understand the newer dimensions that these technologies bring and include them in securitising the new social segments of a nation. This reiterates the importance of building revolutionary digital technologies to enhance deterrence capabilities rather than first-strike capabilities. Therefore, monitoring the developments in the advanced digital field is instrumental for a better comprehensive understanding of future warfare and adjusting to the new global realities.

In India, the ecosystem that has supported innovation in military technology was in the case of missile delivery systems, which befitted from rocket launching capacities of ISRO. India needs to reinvent the same ecosystem to harness the benefits of big data, AI, and quantum computing. The investment in the private sector for long-term R&D is still meagre. However, the civil defence research ecosystems have synergised efforts and look for trickle-down effects. Within the United States, there is increasing investment under the Department of Defence in advanced capability enablers, which would facilitate high-end cyber warfare capacities. The US Department of Defence investments have been in hypersonics, autonomy, microelectronics, and related fields. In India, long-term research provisions through outcome budgeting and project financing are still in the elementary stages.

Defence and AI

One of the areas that have again been highlighted and discussed in the book is related to AI and how it is critical for developing systems that can provide defensive means to a nation through highly developed precise and autonomous weapons, equipment, and platforms, which can synergise the data and use it for better efficiency and reducing error. From Chapter 6, it is observed that AI can be a leader in new kinds of military operations and hybrid warfare. Recent AI developments through machine learning and integration of big data with artificial neural networks help humans make better decisions in operational and functional spaces. The induction of new areas, such as space and cyber warfare, has also directly put the onus on building encrypted networks, which can counter these attacks and incursions into the cyber networks of a nation. The human-machine interface, which is critical for the success of AI, reduces human error to such an extent that the operation's success is completely decided. AI is considered to be the new changing face of defence technologies. The data generated through various defence platforms, ships, aircraft, and other military equipment can be integrated with data generated from war games, tabletop exercises, training, and simulation acts. The AI can also look into how behavioural aspects influence the person's mind in a war-like situation. This perfectly aligns with what RMA in digital technologies would bring. Earlier mentioned RMA in deterrence and non-lethal weaponry is possible by the advanced AI systems.

The handheld devices that monitor the metabolical and biological parameters of a human body can also help to understand how a person will react in a particular situation. The big data generated from military operations and other sources such as audio, video, social media, open-source information, and other intelligence inputs seamlessly connects and correlates the data from sensors and satellites and can work on defining possible outcomes. Even in terms of detecting mines, protecting personnel, and acting on AI-filtered information can protect military assets as well as the lives of the personnel. Within the defence domain, there is increasing talk of military robots, performance-enhancing exoskeletons, and uncrewed vehicles such as drones, autonomous land systems, and ships. AI and machine learning can also help unmanned aerial vehicles take off and return safely, even without human intervention. For a nation where cyber security is critical, even AI can be synchronised with antivirus tools, firewall systems, encryption of data, and data vault systems.

Not only AI but blockchain technology (BCT) is also found to be equally important in changing military affairs. Though it might not revolutionise the current operations, it will streamline them. BCT is useful in maintaining transparency in defence deals and trace the manufacturer of each and every part of defence equipment. All the supply chain management would be hassle-free and securely automated with the combination of AI and blockchain.

Quantum communications are observed to provide unprecedented encryption to military communications. While RMA hinged on digital technological innovations emphasises non-lethal weaponry, cyber forces with quantum technology will create an undisputed defence system for all the country's critical infrastructure.

Challenges of the New Technologies

Disruptive technologies have created a new foundation for fighting new kinds of war and incorporating hybrid warfare in the larger scheme of things. Several developments, particularly in the context of emerging technologies such as the Internet of Things, human-machine interface, biotech, and the evolution of warfare in space and cyber, stress quicker adaptation and seamless transition to new platforms. National defence edifice and platforms have been shifting from traditional military hardware and looking for technical superiority through integrating new technologies. In fact, in the military domain, 3D printing is also likely to transform the horizons, which will also be assisted with better advances in bioinformatics, leading to a better-augmented soldier. Handheld devices, regular monitoring of body parameters, an integrated soldier with the larger ecosystem of network-centric warfare, and the evolution of new kinds of weapon systems, including biochemical weapons, have also brought new challenges in addressing the global future battle space. It has been stated that with the increasing digital disruption, it will be difficult to adjust to new technologies in a shorter period. Therefore, armed forces worldwide would be working on smaller projects, looking for the shelf life of those new technologies. It has also been stated in Chapter 8 that quantum sensing and related research might transform the strategic space and leave reduced error percentages in cyber security, better accurate GPS positioning systems, and threat assessment through security sense. The development of new nanobots and mini-drones also completely transformed how wars will be fought in the future.

One of the areas that can provide a glimpse of how military across the world would adapt to this change is the fusion between civil and defence purposes. This collaboration is beneficial because it enables better data mining and citizen profiling to understand behavioural aspects. Citizen profiling should not be understood in a pessimistic way. Maintaining a profile of citizens is an old practice. However, in-depth profiling should follow certain safeguards and citizen rights. The revolution in technology that will permeate into a revolution in military affairs also brings new challenges in terms of ethics and behavioural aspects. This is where a significant investment in social science research on impact assessments and risk evaluation should be encouraged. Sadly, this aspect is the most neglected one in India.

The RMA has brought a vast increase in military capability because of enhanced systems, operational methods, and new command structures within military organisations. It has been stated that an RMA was brought because of a reduction in munition usage; improvised command, control, and intelligence; use of information warfare; and reducing collateral damage through better-guided ammunition. RMA is at a crossroads as the technical revolution is bringing it in different directions. Therefore, the choice is between new technologies and old conventional forms of fighting a war.

The new digital innovations can completely obliterate the moral issue concerning wars. In developing countries, the challenge of systems integration and honing the skills for adopting those new technologies along with new kinds of innovation and ideas would be a key challenge for harmonisation and improving the core foundation of supplanting these technologies through educational support. Training and capacity building would also be critical as the requirements for the recruits would be based more on their scientific skills and acumen.

In intelligence, surveillance, and reconnaissance, there is an increased reliance on military-grade software encryption and sharing confidential information through dedicated channels among friendly countries. Prolonged encryption will require further enhancement in command, control, and communication with the development of tactical internet. In terms of collaborated control and military data fusion, there is always the requirement for sensors, storage platforms, data repositories, and integration with new kinds of space networks and airborne early warning and control systems. To store that kind of data and for easy access, it is critical to develop data vaults and better individual recognition technology and preserve these data in deep sea beds where the temperatures are at sub-zero levels, which can help sustain the efficiency of the machines. In terms of avoiding geospatial location tracking and stealth technologies, there is also a demand for new critical materials that can reduce acoustic and materials signatures and help better delivery systems. Quantum computing would open new doors for GIS-independent location tracking submarines and ships. This would avert any sabotage undertaken by enemy countries by intruding into space-based systems.

Many countries across the world are also trying to reduce their forces to bring important soldiers who can undertake multiple tasks with the assistance of technology. It has also been discussed in this book how AI autonomous systems, robotics, 3D printing, nanotechnology, material science, and quantum computing can bring about an unprecedented change in both civilian and defence domains. However, these technologies with multifaceted applications might also completely revolutionise military and security reliance on systems.

Big data can also revolutionise integrated logistics, which will help in reducing inventories and provide time-based support to military establishments. However, in many of the countries in Asia where the investment in research and development has been minuscule, except for countries such as Korea, Japan, Israel, and Singapore, the problem has been in developing a fertile research ecosystem, which can help in the development of dual technologies and thereby support innovation and research for the future.

In many developing countries such as India, given the paucity of funds and lack of scenario building, which can envision the future requirements for the civil society and the defence forces, it becomes difficult to work for the future while allocating regular funds for futuristic technologies. This is not to deny that India is not in sync with the global trends, as there is already a lot of research that has been going on in terms of 3D printing, strategic materials, and composite alloys, which can revolutionise the new systems and their utility in defence. The Ordnance Factory Board (OFB), which is now fragmented into separate units dealing with ballistics, explosives, materials, and military hardware, has been working on pilot projects related to 3D printing, and also there have been efforts in the Navy in the shipbuilding sector where there is a talk about big data and also BCTs, which can help in reducing the time gap between supply and demand. The scheduling of maintenance, reducing turnaround time for ships and submarines, quality controls, and time-bound delivery of navy platforms can all be enhanced through BCTs. The F-35 fighter aircraft programme is one such example.

Military Advantages of Big Data

China and the United States have been working on collecting a large amount of data that can be utilised for actionable intelligence, and these zettabytes of data can be analysed to change the digital warfare space. In terms of big data and its utility in the military, there are multiple operational security aspects. Inducing ultra-high reliability through these data can help maintain autonomy and protection of grounds assets. As new kinds of data emerge, it will continuously outpace utilisation across industries, including the military sector. This will induce innovation, which will be compelled rather than automatic progression. The challenge of big data has been primarily in terms of speed, value, variety, volume, and veracity, which can induce changes in periods and infuse efficiency in practical applications. One of the aspects that have been talked about is related to observing Orient Decide Act Loop (ODA), which means the AI will have to make precise predictions while diving into quadrillions of datasets and provide better-informed decisions. Big data has also been held as a critical component in surveillance, reconnaissance, and intelligence gathering. Facial recognition and better mapping of facial features would also help in targeted operations. Tactical intelligence, which can provide actionable directions to the soldier, will be critical in a new age war.

Big data, which might be mined from various sources such as messages, emails, classified documents, and audio and video files, would be a difficult task for human intelligence. If necessary, algorithms can be charted to filter large volumes of data and bring about better context and directions. In the military domain, there might be other sources that include signals and communications intercepts, interrogation reports, and even log files of military assets. However, there might be errors in the data if there is human intervention or conditional spoofing, which can refract the actual output. These errors can be reduced by introducing automated data collection.

Cyber Security Strategy of India Awaited

India has worked on its cyber security architecture, but it is not enough. India is yet to release its cyber security strategy, which has been in preparation for a long period of time. A robust cyber security strategy requires a comprehensive future blueprint that can look into the synergies between the civil and the defence sectors for better support for the systems and preparedness against large-scale cyber-attacks launched by state-sponsored groups. These cyber-attacks have been seen in India, particularly in the context of attacks on the electricity grid and other associated systems. Even though in the civilian domain, the computer emergency response team (CERT-IN) has been effective, but in terms of workforce, it is still limited. Two significant aspects need to be addressed from cyber security in the context of India, which includes training and compulsory education of the kids in terms of coding and cyber security. India also started very late with regard to cyberspace command and has deputed few technically savvy personnel for the cyber command. However, given the magnitude of operations and use of networks within the established frameworks, it has become essential to build adequate cloud storage and encryption protocols. Even in terms of software development, increasing reliance on Microsoft instead of Linux systems is one of the challenges in addressing trojans and bots. A comprehensive plan of action for developing synergies between the defence sector and academic institutes like the Indian Institute of Technology is required. There should be a revolving door where defence personnel can gain critical information about the new developments in this field.

Within India's defence sector, a few pilot projects have been commissioned in select military establishments, such as in Mhow, with necessary financial and innovation support. However, these are just face-saving efforts. The requirement is to work on critical technologies that can address gaps in defence preparedness and create effective deterrence systems. India has the required talent and education systems that can support long-term planning. For India, the civilian sector has to take the lead in IT research and development, which might trickle down to the military sector. The new disruptive technologies require project-based funding and a blueprint for the future. In this regard, there are five recommendations that need to be undertaken in right earnest. This includes forming a committee on new technologies, creating a task force on long-term planning, upgrading infrastructure, and taking technical experts on board. Lastly, look into training and capacity building with collaboration with international agencies and like-minded countries. The shape of technology and its role in defining new battle space are still unknown. However, to prepare for uncertain battlespaces, it would be prudent to understand requirements and plan capabilities accordingly. India needs a capability plan in 2050 for AI, big data, and BCTs.

References

Fast Track Action Subcommittee on Critical and Emerging Technologies. (2022, February). Critical and Emerging Technology List Update. *whitehouse.gov*. Retrieved from www.whitehouse.gov/wp-content/uploads/2022/02/02-2022-Critical-and-Emerging-Technologies-List-Update.pdf

Inamdar, S. (2008). "Revolutions in Military Affairs" and "RMA". *Journal of Defence Studies*, 2(2). Retrieved from www.idsa.in/jds/2_2_2008_RMAASelectiveMonographicOverview_SGInamdar

Ministry of External Affairs. (2020, May 2). Question no 552: New and Emerging Strategic Technologies Division. *mea.gov.in*. Retrieved from https://mea.gov.in/lok-sabha.htm?dtl/32359/question_no552_new_and_emerging_strategic_technologies_division

INDEX

Note: Page numbers in **bold** indicate a table on the corresponding page.

Printed in the United States
by Baker & Taylor Publisher Services